Kingsthorpe

-4 DEC 2010

WITNESS TO
WORLD
WAR II

WITNESS TO WORLD WAR II

Karen Farrington

ABBEYDALE PRESS

This paperback edition published in 2005 by
Abbeydale Press
An imprint of Bookmart Ltd
Registered Number 2372865
Blaby Road, Wigston,
Leicestershire, LE18 4SE
United Kingdom

3 5 7 9 10 8 6 4 2

ISBN 1-86147-164-5

PICTURE CREDITS

The publisher would like to thank the following organisations for supplying
photographs for use in this book.
Every effort has been made to contact the copyright holders for the pictures.
In some cases they have been untraceable, for which we offer our apologies.

Imperial War Museum; Musee d'Histoire Contemporaine; US Marine Corp;
US Coast Guard; US Library of Congress; US National Archives; US Army
Photo Services; USAF Photo; US Navy Photo Section; Smithsonian Institute;
J Baker Collection; Ford Motor Co; Robert Hunt Library; Bundersarchiv;
Bibliothek fur Zeitgeschichte; Public Records Office of Hong Kong; Kyodo
News Services; Australian High Commission, London; BFI; British Airways;
The Scout Association; The Morning Star via The Marx Memorial Library,
London; Oxfam; Novosti; National Archives of Singapore; Daimler-Benz;
RCA; London Transport Museum; National Museum of Labour History; The
Truman Library; VSEL Vickers; Ufficio Storico Fototeca; National Maritime
Museum; Biggin Hill Archives; Stato Maggiore Aeronautica; RAF Museum;
The Boeing Co. Archives; Renault; Vickers; Los Almos Scientific Lab; Polish
Underground Movement; Manx Museum; Red Cross Archives; Far East War
Collection/ Vic Brown.

THE AUTHOR

Karen Farrington is a writer and former Fleet Street journalist who has
specialised in the study of conflict throughout the 20th Century. In
compiling Witness to World War II she has personally interviewed scores of
veterans from around the world, obtaining a unique insight into the war
through the eyes of the men on the front line. Among her previous books is
'Fated Destiny', an historical pot pourri of the curious, shocking and
mysterious which includes accounts of some of the greatest military
blunders in recent history. Karen Farrington is married with three children
and lives in Exmoor, Devon.

Printed in Singapore

CONTENTS

WITNESS TO WORLD WAR II

World War II was the most immense conflict mankind has ever known. WITNESS TO WORLD WAR II shows exactly how it took shape, from its beginnings in the confused politics of the 1920s and 1930s to its apocalyptic end in the ruined and shattered cities of Germany and Japan in 1945.

Not only was this the largest conflict ever seen; it was also the most militarily complex, with events at sea and in the air having a defining effect on warfare on land. In order to unravel these complexities, WITNESS TO WORLD WAR II treats war in the skies, on (and under) the oceans and on land separately so that all the details can be fully examined. But the approach is far from being coldly technical: hundreds of separate eyewitness accounts throughout the work illustrate clearly what the war meant to the individuals involved, while the horrors of war – from casual atrocities to the mass-produced death of the concentration camps – are unflinchingly examined.

WITNESS TO WORLD WAR II shows how and why the war was fought and what happened to the ordinary men and women caught up in it. For some it brought out reserves of courage and endurance that they never knew they possessed, but for others it became a terrifying inferno that led mankind to the depths of hell.

The Soldier's War

BLITZKRIEG!

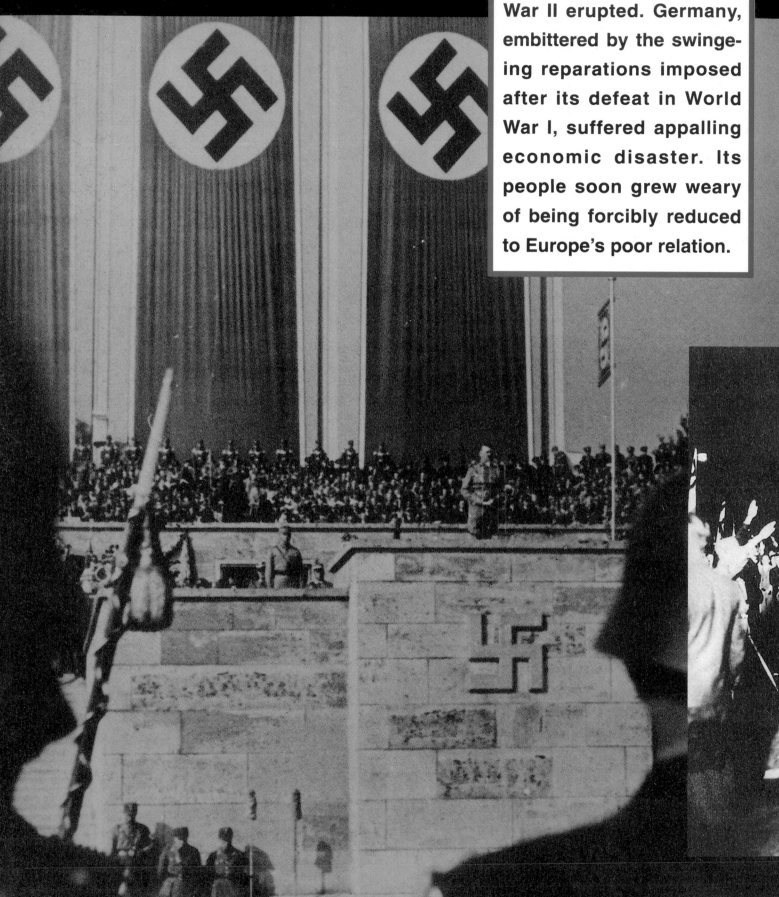

With hindsight, it is easy to see how and why World War II erupted. Germany, embittered by the swingeing reparations imposed after its defeat in World War I, suffered appalling economic disaster. Its people soon grew weary of being forcibly reduced to Europe's poor relation.

The time became ripe for a charismatic leader to sweep into power on the promise of returning Germany to its former glory. Unfortunately for the rest of Europe, those pledges for prosperity at home went hand in hand with an aggressive foreign policy. Nevertheless, Hitler offered the Germans an irresistible chance of stability, vitality and solidarity.

The only difficulty with which to wrestle is just how Britain and France missed the warning signs – and were catapulted into a war in September 1939 for which they were ill-prepared and poorly armed.

Both countries were weary of war, still reeling from the enormous loss of manpower and struggling following a deep world recession to remain on an even keel. At home they were far too preoccupied with domestic problems to heed the warnings of the few who witnessed what was really happening in Hitler's Germany. Violent anti-semitism was put down to the work of a few extremists. Many in power had a sneaking admiration for Hitler who achieved so much by cutting unemployment and building prestigious new 'autobahns'. His admirers conveniently overlooked the fact that Germany had concentration camps, no free press and no free parliament. And few outside the Reich had any idea of the military strength and firepower that the Führer was amassing.

When Hitler marched into the demilitarised Rhineland in 1936, many considered he was only taking back what rightfully belonged to Germany. The annexation of Austria in 1938 was looked upon virtually as an internal matter. Only with Hitler's demands for land from Czechoslovakia later that same year did Britain and France begin to sense the threat.

Hitler relished the chance to 'free' fellow Germans from 'Polish barbarism'

Their chosen path was appeasement, a negotiated agreement with Hitler designed to end his expansionism. When Hitler marched into Prague in the face of that agreement, Britain and France finally realised the folly of their actions.

All thoughts turned to Danzig, the free city in a Polish-held corridor which split Germany from East Prussia. It had long been a thorn in Hitler's side as he believed it was part of Germany. Hitler relished the chance to 'free' fellow Germans who he claimed were being subjected to Polish barbarism. There was considerably more trepidation in the minds of the Allies.

■ CARDBOARD TANKS ■

Much of Germany's rearmament had gone on covertly. Even when war broke out many British people were convinced that their former enemy, hampered by the treaty which ended the previous conflict, had tanks made of cardboard. Indeed, the Germans

Left: A Nazi book-burning ceremony. Only works regarded as acceptable to the fascist dictatorship were tolerated.
Far left: Hitler addresses a Nazi party rally at Nuremberg in 1938.

did carry out military manoeuvres with cardboard tanks back in the early 1920s before secretly importing and building their own real ones.

Meanwhile, France had the largest army and most impressive air force in the world. Most of its citizens prided themselves on the fact that Germany was unlikely to begin hostilities against such a superior force. As England viewed the Channel as an

Hitler unleashed a new and frightening brand of warfare called 'Blitzkrieg'

impregnable wall of defence, so France had the much-vaunted Maginot line. It took nine years to construct the frontier defences, brain-child of French minister André Maginot. The network of towers and

tunnels was remarkable enough in itself. Had the Germans attacked it directly, it might have served its purpose well, albeit that it stretched only as far as the Belgian border, and not beyond it.

This war, however, was going to be different to the first international conflict. Static trench warfare, which had claimed so many lives, was now an outdated concept – yet France and

Britain didn't realise it. When Hitler invaded Poland in September 1939, he unleashed a new and frightening brand of warfare into the world – called 'Blitzkrieg'.

First to feel the heat of this 'lightning war', Poland lurched back in helpless horror when the German army crossed it borders at dawn on 1 September 1939. It took only a few hours for the invading force to quell

BRITAIN'S FASCIST LEADER

Oswald Mosley became the creator of the British Union of Fascists in the early 1930s after having been a member of both Conservative and Labour parties and having been linked for a while with the Liberals.

He had a lively, sharp mind and a clarity of vision. He was even branded the best political thinker of the age. But his frustration at the confines of the accepted political doctrines cast him to the margins where he hit upon the fascism sweeping Europe.

The British, however, were not entranced with uniforms and salutes in the same way as the Germans, Italians or Spanish, among whom fascism flourished. He became a figure of fun, never taken seriously even after the outbreak of war. He was nevertheless jailed in 1940 for four years. Following his release, he was vilified in Britain and finally moved with his wife Diana Mitford and two small sons to France. He continued to exercise his mind around political problems but failed to find a platform for his views. He died in 1980.

Left: German soldiers survey the results of their fast-moving campaign in Poland.

Top: Britain was braced for attack months before it actually came.

Above: Germany used its tanks to thrust ahead during the Blitzkrieg it unleashed with great success against Poland, France and the Low Countries.

Polish defences. As the German troops and tanks rolled through the Polish countryside, the country's major cities were being bombed by the Luftwaffe and its ports were shelled by German ships.

Key to the success of Blitzkrieg was the use of tanks in large numbers and innovative style – they were still thought by Britain and France to be valid only as infantry support. The Panzer forces charged ahead independent of the troops, and wreaked havoc among defenders. Bursting through defensive lines, they harried the Poles from the rear, creating confusion and smashing supply lines.

The German air force had learned much aiding Franco during the Spanish Civil War, which ended in May 1939. Now pilots were putting this knowledge to good use and after a month Poland capitulated.

Poland's capital Warsaw held out for a few weeks longer than the rest of the country against the Third Reich. Heavy bombardment turned this once-grand city to rubble. As it surrendered, the Germans were triumphant. The hated Treaty of Versailles, which had condemned them to international servitude since 1919, was at last eradicated.

This time Britain and France refused to sit back and watch their ally being dismembered by Hitler. Both declared war on Germany almost immediately – although failed to do anything which would materially assist Poland – and braced themselves for the onslaught. Thankfully, it never came.

Despite the success of the Polish campaign, many German officers were concerned about taking on the might of the French army backed by Britain. Hitler was persuaded to abandon thoughts of an immediate push through the Low Countries into France, in favour of launching a spring campaign.

■ REALITY OF WAR ■

The reality of war was slow to strike home in Britain. When the feared air raids and gas attacks failed to materialise, there was an almost euphoric mood as people busied themselves sandbagging homes and putting up blackout screens in windows. The casualties in road traffic accidents caused by the rigorously enforced blackout far exceeded those caused in the war. Phrases full of mock indignation like 'put that light out' and 'don't you know there's a war on' typified the bureaucracy pervading

Above: A French cottage is destroyed by advancing German troops, who put French and British defenders to flight.

the country. Joblessness stayed high, war production lamentably low. Reservists were being signed up for army duty surely but slowly, doing drills with bayonets and gas masks – and sometimes wooden 'rifles'.

Nearly 200,000 soldiers in the British Expeditionary Force were sent to France where they dug in on the Belgian border. By now, Germany had mobilised six million men.

Hitler was concerned at the ease with which the British navy had managed to raid a German ship in Norwegian waters. On 9 April 1940 his troops moved into Denmark and Norway in what promised to be another short, sharp campaign.

Denmark was without an army and acquiesced the following day.

Norway, deeply anti-militarist by tradition, nevertheless put up a fight despite the evident popularity with which the Germans were greeted in some quarters. Churchill himself was looking at the possibility of occupying Norway to reap the rewards of its strategic position. The government would do no more than lay mines in Norwegian waters to disrupt a vital German supply line. In fact, the Royal Navy was doing just that when some of the invasion force from Germany sailed up. There was a skirmish in which some damage was inflicted on German ships. That was the only glimmer of optimism in what turned into an otherwise disastrous escapade.

> ### *Churchill himself was looking at the possibility of occupying Norway*

Britain sent landing parties to key points, hoping to steal a march on the Germans. But the small-scale campaign was ill-planned and improvised. The poorly equipped troops had no artillery and no air cover, whereas the Luftwaffe was in control of many Norwegian airstrips and was making full use of them. It wasn't long before the British, and the French forces with them, were forced to withdraw in disarray.

The debacle outraged many people and MPs in Britain, who feared the country was only making a half-hearted attempt at war. On 7 May there was a debate in the House of Commons in which Prime Minister Chamberlain made a statement on

◆ BLITZKRIEG IN THE WEST

From 14 May 1940, German Panzer forces bridged the River Meuse and poured into Belgium and northern France, driving all before them. The XIX Panzer Corps under Guderian crossed at Sedan, the XLI Panzer Corps (Reinhardt) at Monthermé, the XV Panzer Corps (Hoth) at Dinant, while Höpner's XVI Panzer Corps swept down from the north east. Within days, German tanks were at the Channel, but then paused. The British attempted a counter-attack at Arras, while the French planned a similar move from the south. These efforts came to little, however, and by the end of May, with German forces once again on the move, the British Expeditionary Force had its back to the sea at Dunkirk, awaiting rescue.

the Norwegian affair. The government won a vote of confidence by only 81 votes, too few for Chamberlain to continue.

The spring campaign got underway with a vengeance in western Europe

He resigned on 10 May, the same day that German troops made their first forays into Holland and Belgium. The spring campaign got underway with a vengeance as the horrors of Hitler's Blitzkrieg came to western Europe.

Airborne troops took the Belgian fortress of Eben Emael, chasing out the petrified defenders. At the same time in Rotterdam, 12 floatplanes landed on the River Maas. Out of each of them came an inflatable dinghy and a clutch of German troops ready to swarm over essential vantage points throughout the city.

■ HOLLAND FALLS ■

Also, there came the more orthodox methods of invasion, by Panzer forces over the borders. The French army and the British Expeditionary Force prepared themselves for a surge of German troops coming through northern Belgium. To their huge surprise, however, Panzer divisions had crossed the Ardennes, condemned as impassable by Allied commanders. Amid confusion, a division led by Rommel began a headlong rush west.

Holland capitulated on 14 May. It was another hammer-blow to the morale of the French. Without a dynamic leader – their commander in chief Gamelin was inaudible, indecisive and thought to be suffering

◆ EYE WITNESS ◆

Alf Turner joined a Territorial Army battalion in his home town of Barnstaple, North Devon, when he was 19.

In September 1940 we were stationed at Battle. Following Dunkirk it wasn't a case of "if the Germans invade", it was "when the Germans invade". So we had to put a minefield along the beach at Battle.

Not many people knew much about laying minefields. I was with a captain on the beach. We laid about four minefields and were starting on the fifth one. Our driver asked if he could help. The captain allowed him to lay a couple. The driver must have trodden on one and the explosion set lots of the mines off.

The captain and I were lucky to escape. A few days later our brigadier told us it was a vital area and asked us to go back to re-lay the minefield. I told the captain the chances of us coming out alive were only five per cent. Still, we had a job to do.

We re-laid about four and I was leading the way when the captain said he should go first. Soon after he took over he pointed to his right. In the middle of a crater lay the head of the dead driver. The shock must have unbalanced him.

Then the ground seemed to open up and I felt I was going into a great big pit. Yet actually I was being blown upwards. Our new driver was waiting on a shelf some 40 feet above the beach. He saw me go into the air above him and go back down again.

I was cross-eyed, had a perforated ear-drum and an injured arm. Still, I managed to get out of there. I was put under sedation for 24 hours, during which time I jumped out of bed three times. They even asked me to go down to the minefield again. I went – but this time they decided it was too dangerous to tackle again.

I was given a week's leave. The medical officer said if I had had any more, I wouldn't have come back. Going home in the blackout was hard. I had to race across pools of darkness, imagining all the time that parts of a body were coming out at me.

A fellow lance corporal blamed himself for the captain's death. He was a religious man and prayed very hard for me, knowing it was a dangerous job. But he didn't pray for the captain and he felt guilty about that.

Above: Crammed onto the decks of a small steamer, weary troops of the BEF reach a British port.

Below: Bewildered soldiers and frightened civilians roam the streets of Dunkirk as the Germans close in.

acutely from the ravages of venereal disease – the French army fell away, their lack of commitment a world away from the fighting spirit they showed so often during World War I.

The British forces found themselves racing back to the French coast, barely keeping a step ahead of the German advance. Despite an attempt to counter-attack at Arras in northern France, it soon became clear the situation was hopeless. Their commander, General Lord Gort, ordered his men to Dunkirk where they would await evacuation.

■ DUNKIRK ■

Luck was on their side. Hitler ordered his most advanced Panzer divisions to halt, wishing to conserve the cream of his troops for the invasion of Paris. It gave the British valuable time to install a defensive shell around Dunkirk –

albeit fragile – behind which they could stage a daring, dangerous and vital evacuation.

Courageous rearguard campaigners held off the German advance while the Royal Navy sent in ship after ship to remove the stricken forces. By 31 May the news blackout on 'Operation Dynamo', the code name for the operation to save British servicemen, was lifted and scores of small boats set sail for France to give aid to the Royal Navy. Experienced mariners set off alongside weekend sailors to pluck as many men as they could from the beach. It was a tough voyage on small craft but each skipper was imbued with a grim determination.

Before the remaining defenders of Dunkirk surrendered on 4 June, 338,226 men – British, French and Belgian – had been carried back to safety. It was no mean feat, given that the official estimates for the evacuation were 45,000. Disastrously, most of Britain's armoury was left behind. There were too few guns remaining in Britain to arm the country's soldiers.

■ PARIS OCCUPIED ■

French soldiers, supported in the west by some British fighters, continued a disorderly retreat. Two weeks after Dunkirk, Paris was occupied and region after region continued to fall. When French prime minister Reynaud resigned on 16 June, his successor Marshal Pétain immediately sued for peace.

The final humiliation for France came on 21 June when Hitler had its leaders sign an armistice in the same railway coach where the German surrender was authorised following World War I. Now Britain stood alone against the might of the Third Reich with only 21 miles of English Channel to save it from invasion.

JAPAN'S LIGHTNING WAR

With the success of Pearl Harbor under their belts, the Japanese were eager to capitalise on the supreme advantage of surprise. Defending British, Australian and American forces were caught off-guard throughout South East Asia and the Pacific as Japan began a 'Blitzkrieg' of its own.

Key targets were Hong Kong, the Philippines, Malaya, Singapore, Burma, Thailand, the Dutch East Indies and the stepping stone islands of Wake and Guam. Each offered the new Japanese empire mineral or agricultural wealth that was badly needed, or was a necessary land-base to protect precious cargoes.

Hong Kong was the first of the British domains to fall. Only 400 miles from Japanese air bases in Formosa (now Taiwan), it was vulnerable from the outset. The defence of Hong Kong and other prestigious British outposts had suffered thanks to the war effort in other parts of the world. During 1939 and 1940, troops, ships and aircraft were sent to trouble-spots like North Africa and the Mediterranean at the expense of the far-flung colonies, which appeared to be in no imminent danger.

By August 1940, Churchill accepted the view held by service chiefs that Hong Kong was practically indefensible and that the garrison on the island could be better used elsewhere. Japanese intentions were far from clear at this point. However, perhaps with growing indications that Japan was possibly hostile, no one acted further on the recommendation. In fact, the following year the Hong Kong garrison was strengthened by the addition of two Canadian battalions. In the event, they only added to the huge numbers of prisoners taken during those early Japanese exploits.

An initial strike made by the Japanese on 8 December proved to be devastating. The Allied troops were driven back to Hong Kong city within a matter of days. For a week, the Japanese were held at bay across the water barrier. Under the cover of darkness on 18 December, the inevitable Japanese landings on Hong Kong island began. Following Churchill's declared policy, resistance was slight. A wedge was driven between the defending forces. On Christmas Day one arm surrendered. Their comrades gave up the fight a day later. For the loss of 3,000 dead and wounded the Japanese had captured Hong Kong, together with its force of nearly 12,000 men.

The Philippines were to have suffered their first Japanese air bombardment on 8 December. Although not an American possession, they were reliant on US support before becoming independent. In fact, morning fog grounded the aircraft based in Formosa, delaying take-off.

The Americans, meanwhile, were debating whether or not to carry out a bombing mission in Formosa. The indecision proved fatal. In the early afternoon, when the US B-17s were finally being prepared for a sortie, the overdue Japanese aircraft finally

For the loss of 3,000 dead and wounded the Japanese had captured Hong Kong

arrived. With the American planes presented on an airfield, the Japanese pilots did their destructive worst. A number of the planes intended to protect the Philippines were wrecked.

Left: **Victorious Japanese troops enter Rangoon after quickly annihilating opposition troops in Burma. The Burmese people gave them an indifferent welcome.**

Above: **Dejected British soldiers file through the streets of Singapore after the disastrous fall of the colony to the Emperor's forces.**

RATIONS

Rations were boosted – and cut – for Britons on the home front throughout the war. Here is a typical weekly allowance per person.

8oz sugar, 3oz cheese
3oz cooking fat, 4oz bacon or ham
2oz jam, 2oz sweets, 2oz tea or coffee
1 egg, 3 pints milk, 1lb meat

Bread, fish and sausages, although not rationed, were scarce. Although there was no restriction on fruit and vegetables, many were impossible to get. Lemons, bananas, onions and even pepper were rarely, if ever, seen during the war years in Britain.
    Inventive housewives made chocolate truffle cake from potatoes, and banana pudding from parsnips.

Right: **General-Marshal Homma makes an assisted landing on Luzon in the Philippines on 24 December 1941, ousting defending American troops.**

The Japanese 14th Army quickly captured off-islands and made landings on Luzon, the largest Philippine island, as early as 10 December. There were continuing probes until the main landings, which took place on 22 December.

Coastal defences, comprising poorly trained and fearful Filipinos soon crumbled. A core of American troops was kept in the capital, Manila, by commander General MacArthur until it became clear that the defence of the island was an impossibility. He then ordered a withdrawal into the Bataan Peninsula in the hope the 31,000 troops could mount an adequate defence.

The Americans did manage to repel a number of raids. Then both sides became severely weakened through rampant malaria. Morale sank further in the American ranks when it became clear there was little or no effort being made to evacuate them. When the Japanese offensive began again on 3 April it took only six days to force a surrender.

There remained almost 15,000 Americans on the nearby island of Corregidor. The fight for this scrap of

Coastal defences, comprising poorly trained and fearful Filipinos, soon crumbled

an island was to be fierce. The Japanese carried out daily artillery bombardments across the straits from Luzon as well as waves of air attacks. When much of the American artillery had been knocked out, the Japanese mounted an invasion with 2,000 troops. More than half were lost in the battle that ensued during the night of 5 May. But despite their losses, the Japanese managed to land some tanks, enough to crush the remaining resistance.

A surrender bid by American General Wainwright was hampered by guerrilla action adopted by the Americans. By 9 June, however, all resistance was crushed.

The loss to the Americans had been considerable; likewise to the native forces. A combined total of 95,000 were taken captive by the Japanese. Yet the defenders had held out for six months with no outside assistance, a significant achievement given the domino fall of islands in the rest of the area.

On paper, it appeared the British defenders of Malaya and neighbouring Singapore were more than a match for the invaders. There were about 100,000 Allied troops taking on just 30,000 incoming Japanese. In Britain there was confidence that Singapore particularly was a fortress with stout defences. It was unthinkable that the stronghold would be overrun. As so often happens during wars, the unthinkable happened – at speed.

The defeat of the British and Allied forces at the hands of the Japanese was a shocking one for which few at home were prepared. Yet there were shortcomings in the defences of the countries invaded which allowed the enthusiastic Japanese to run rampant.

Despite the signs of militarism evident in Japan, the British government remained convinced this small country would not take on the combined might of America, Britain and Russia. After the war, Churchill admitted he among others had underestimated the threat posed by Japan, particularly in its air power.

The Allies had no tanks with which to blast the enemy while the Japanese rolled over the inhospitable terrain with something in the order of 300. And while the Allies possessed more than twice the amount of artillery, much of it was in Singapore facing seawards to repel a southerly invasion. The Japanese flooded in from the opposite direction.

▪ OPPRESSIVE HEAT ▪

As for aircraft, the Allies had only a sixth of the number of aircraft that the Japanese had at their disposal. In a war which proved air might was imperative, the British were left seriously underequipped.

Moreover, Japanese troops were trained for jungle warfare and the dense vegetation and steamy atmosphere did not daunt them. The British and Australians were quickly wearied by the oppressive heat.

In command of the Japanese was General Tomoyuki Yamashita, a devoted servant of Emperor Hirohito and a military marvel. Among his troops, he was known as 'the tiger'. The Allies, meanwhile, were under General Arthur Percival, held with such low regard by his men that he was called 'the rabbit'.

On the day that the prize British capital ships Prince of Wales and Repulse were sent to the bottom of the sea, Japanese forces marched into Malaya. With waves of air cover, they were quickly able to force the British down the Malay Peninsula in a rolling retreat. The highly organised invaders cut quickly through any defences they encountered. About 4,000 British troops and their equipment were stranded in central Malaya when Japanese tanks broke through their lines and seized a road

Below: **Seasoned jungle warriors, the Japanese troops found far less difficulty operating in the tropics than their beleaguered enemies did.**

WAVELL VICTORIOUS

When British and Commonwealth troops under the command of General Sir Archibald Wavell drove Italian troops into a spectacular retreat early in 1941, there was rejoicing at home at the first glimpse of meaningful victory. The *News Chronicle* wrote:

'It is still too early for any complete estimate of General Wavell's happy and glorious achievement; but from what we already know two factors stand out and demand the most generous praise: the perfect co-ordination of land, sea and air forces and the superb Staff work that preceded the attack and made the co-ordination possible.'

Somewhat prematurely, it ended:
'Rapidly the Axis is becoming a meaningless phrase: an axis requires two ends, and, if it is to function, each end must perform an equal task. Otherwise the whole thing crumbles away. One day that will happen, and General Wavell, by his care and genius, has brought that day nearer than two months ago we dared hope.'

bridge, curtailing their withdrawal. The capital, Kuala Lumpur, was abandoned by the Allies on 11 January and still the retreat continued to gather pace.

■ MALAYA FALLS ■

It took the Japanese just 54 days to overcome the resistance in Malaya. Their casualties amounted to around 4,600, compared with the loss of 25,000 Allied troops, many of whom were now prisoners of war. Thousands of Indians recruited to fight for the Empire already had doubts about the wisdom of risking their lives for the country which oppressed their own. Now many took the opportunity to join brigades organised by the Japanese and were fighting against former comrades.

Fleeing British and Australian forces made a dash for Singapore and blew up the bridge connecting the island with Malaya as they went. Japanese forces mustered threateningly on the other side.

Singapore was bombed on the day the war with Japan began. The casualties were mostly among the civilian population yet it forcefully illustrated the intentions of the Japanese. Perhaps for the first time, Churchill realised the folly of leaving the island of Singapore so woefully lacking in defences.

In January 1942, he declared: 'Not only must the defence of Singapore Island be maintained by every means but the whole island must be fought for until every single unit and every single strongpoint has been separately destroyed. Finally, the city of Singapore must be converted into a citadel and defended to the death. No surrender can be contemplated.' On 8 February the Japanese troops put his words to the test by swarming across the Johore Strait which had so far barred them from the island. Some used small boats and dinghies. Others simply swam across. The Australian defenders in the region might have been expected to use the spotlights especially installed to light up their targets and blast the invaders out of the water.

Yet the order to switch on the lights never came. The soldiers were

> ### *The soldiers were left firing at darkened objects in the night*

left firing at darkened objects in the night. Not only that, the troops were soon ordered to fall back rather than to counter-attack. It was a symptom of the faulty lines of communication that dogged the short campaign by the Allies to keep Singapore. The standard of leadership among the

Right: A Japanese artillery detachment making its way through the jungle in late 1941 during the Singapore campaign. They found little standing in their way.

Above: US soldiers surrender to Japanese troops. Ahead of them is a gruelling march to a harsh prison camp.

Allies was also continually poor, with tactical blunders being made time and again. Ill-thought-out orders to withdraw from strongly held positions around the coast gave the Japanese an open door. All of this did nothing to buck the spirits of the beleaguered Allied soldiers wondering why they were left without the benefit of air cover.

■ SINGAPORE SHAME ■

Nor did the sight of thick black smoke rising over Singapore city do much to improve their state of mind. It plumed from oil tanks set alight by the British themselves in the harbour area to keep them from falling into Japanese hands. From it came a pungent black rain which fell across a wide area. A flurry of activity by Japan's supporters in Singapore added to the chaos and confusion in the city.

Food stocks were running low and the water supply was under threat by the time street battles commenced. Percival realised that to proceed with the fight was futile. A package air-dropped to his headquarters in a cascade of red and white ribbons invited him to surrender. It bore the following sinister sentence from Yamashita: 'If you continue resistance, it will be diffcult to bear with patience, from a humanitarian point of view.'

He chose to ignore Churchill's orders to fight to the bitter end. Percival marched to meet the triumphant Yamashita with a Union Jack and a white flag, held aloft side-by-side. The close proximity of the national flag and the symbol of surrender did nothing to endear him to the establishment at home. His signature ended the British domination of Singapore at a conference held in the Ford factory on Bukit Timah hill. Some 80,000 British, Indian and Australian troops were snared, forced to face four years of gruelling captivity under the harsh Japanese regime. With the loss of Singapore came the bitter realisation that Britain's proud boast of being able to defend its colonies no matter where they were in the world was now a sham.

Afterwards, it was described as 'the greatest military disaster in [British] history'. For years Percival was an outcast, held personally responsible for the loss of a glittering prize. While his leadership was certainly flawed, he was only one of many Allied commanders who found themselves bowled over by the Japanese steamroller.

The extent of the Singapore debacle was only revealed fully after the war when Yamashita revealed he considered himself on the brink of losing the vital campaign: 'My attack

Right: Japanese soldiers soon adapted in the jungle, making use of local elephants to forge a path through dense vegetation. The Allied defenders could not match the invaders proficiency in jungle warfare.
Below: General Tomoyuki Yamashita, one of Japan's most successful military leaders, pulled off a dramatic coup when he captured Singapore.

on Singapore was a bluff. I had 30,000 men and was outnumbered more than three to one. I knew that if I had been made to fight longer for Singapore I would have been beaten. That was why the surrender had to be immediate. I was extremely frightened that the British would discover our numerical weakness and lack of supplies and force me into disastrous street fighting. But they never did. My bluff worked.'

December 1941 also saw the invasion of Burma. It was inadequately protected, with Malaya and Singapore seen as having greater requirement for military resources.

Once again, Japan had by far the most effective air force. It was to be another story of inglorious retreat, this time over 1,000 miles into India.

The Burmese capital Rangoon was being bombed by Christmas. The British forces were once again forced back under the onslaught of the 35,000 invading Japanese troops, who proved themselves faster and more adept in jungle warfare. On 6 March 1942 the order came to evacuate Rangoon.

■ MONSOON SEASON ■

After both sides had reinforced, the British, assisted now by Chinese forces, defended a 150-mile line south of Mandalay. The Japanese merely sidestepped the line and enveloped the troops manning it. By now it was April and the British troops not only had to consider the advance of the enemy but also the onset of the monsoon season, due in May, which would turn the roads vital for retreat into mires. Burmese soldiers, always unhappy about the colonial control of their country, were deserting in droves to join the

new national army that was fighting with the Japanese invaders.

British rearguard forces held up the Japanese advance before making the final dash for safety themselves. The tanks of the 7th Armoured Brigade made repeated counter-attacks to delay the enemy campaign.

Burmese soldiers, always unhappy about the colonial control of their country, were deserting in droves to join the new national army

A week before the monsoon season began, the majority of the British forces fell back exhausted and relieved behind the Indian frontier. They had lost much of their equipment and had suffered three times the number of casualties that the Japanese had incurred. But given their circumstances, it was a miracle that any succeeded in escaping at all.

◆ EYE WITNESS ◆

Hugh Trebble, a local newspaper journalist, joined the Civil Air Guard before the war when it offered the chance to learn to fly for one penny per minute. In 1940 he was recruited into the Royal Air Force, in which he was a clerk.

❝I was posted overseas in June 1941 and got to Singapore by August. From there I went to RAF Butterworth, overlooking Penang Island in north west Malaya. One of our first instructions when we got to Butterworth was that between 2pm and 4pm you were either in bed or out of barracks. It was impossible to raise a British officer during that time on the peninsula.

There was a lot of personnel in Malaya and Singapore but no equipment. At Butterworth we were still flying old-fashioned Bristol Blenheims. I never saw any combat aircraft the entire time I was there. Our junior officers were principally Australian.

After the Japanese invaded down the east coast we were pulled back to Kuala Lumpur to a base called Sungeibesi. A few weeks later General Wavell flew in to assess the situation. As soon as his Hudson took off we blew it [the base] up. We retreated via a rubber plantation down to Singapore.

There, we were put in a camp at RAF Seletar. There were hundreds of us that couldn't be gainfully employed. The last flight of so-called bombers that set off from there was made up of obsolete Vickers Wildebeest, twin-engined bi-planes. They took off but they never landed. They were destroyed before they could put down.

There was a desperate atmosphere in Singapore, even more so after the battleships *Prince of Wales* and *Repulse* were sunk. When they left port it was with a total absence of air cover and destroyer cover. They should never have been sent out in the first place.

In Singapore there were fixed guns facing over the sea – when the Japanese came overland. They didn't need fifth columnists in the city to help them. Japanese soldiers easily overpowered anything we had.

Some Allied soldiers got off troop ships and were taken prisoner virtually straightaway. They never fired a shot in anger. They had nothing to do any fighting with anyway.

On 13 January 1942 I was among many who were evacuated from Kepple Harbour on the *Empire Star*, a Blue Funnel ship, heading for Java. Clearly, we were sent to Singapore for propaganda purposes – nothing else.❞

The Dutch East Indies came under attack in December 1941, too. This arc of wealthy islands, at its easterly point just 300 miles from the coast of Australia, was rich in oil and thus an important target for the oil-starved Japanese. In a bid to halt the Japanese, the defending Dutch, Australian,

British and American forces were put under a single command, known as ABDA, led by Britain's General Archibald Wavell.

Although the Dutch resistance was soon annihilated, the Australians proved a more formidable foe. Yet there was little they could do to protect the scores of tiny islands from Japanese occupation.

After the disastrous Battle of the Java Sea, which the Allies lost in February 1942, the Japanese could count the Dutch East Indies as their own.

■ EYES ON CEYLON ■

Other casualties in the Japanese lightning war were Guam, Wake Island and the Gilbert Islands, which fell before the end of 1941. In the spring of 1942, the Bismarck Archipelago, the Solomon Islands and north eastern New Guinea all succumbed to Japanese forces.

Britain now feared attack from the Japanese navy in the Indian Ocean, where Ceylon was a prime target. Strategically, it was crucial to the British. On 5 April 1942 the British braced themselves for attack following an air strike by more than 1,000

> *Britain now feared attack from the Japanese navy in the Indian Ocean, where Ceylon was a prime target*

planes at Colombo, the capital of Ceylon. Two British cruisers were sunk and the port was badly damaged. The distances were too great for an invasion to be sustainable, however, and the Japanese knew it. They withdrew behind the lines of their expanded empire and concentrated on defence.

THE EASTERN FRONT

Winter weather had brought the German advance in Russia to a standstill. Yet Stalin knew that freezing temperatures and snow flurries alone would not be enough to defeat the might of the Third Reich's army.

He was neither a gifted tactician nor a seasoned campaigner, unlike his enemy Hitler. In personal command of his army, Stalin was isolated at the top. The blunders he made as the barbarous campaign against his country got underway cost millions of lives. He would soon learn by bitter experience about how to run a war.

He enjoyed a certain degree of good luck and, in time, he used it well. To his advantage, he had a seemingly inexhaustible supply of men.

After Pearl Harbor, Stalin realised Japan was too embroiled with its actions against America to now threaten Russia. So the men tied up with defending its eastern rear were at last free to man the German front. In addition, there were countless thousands of reservists, recruited from all over the Soviet Union, to replace fallen comrades.

It was this perpetual sacrifice of men above all other factors that

Above: **The half-frozen mud is littered with the bodies of dead Russian soldiers. Total Soviet losses, military and civilian, in the war may have exceeded 20 million.**

D-Day could not have gone ahead without the Russian front diverting German resources

changed the course of the war. If Stalin had found his people with less resolve and more ready to capitulate, Hitler might have won on the Eastern front. And a victory there would have ensured him triumph in the west. D-Day, the single most decisive action of the entire war, could not have gone ahead without the Russian front diverting so many German resources.

Somehow this massive country survived its appalling casualty rate. It

prompted the frustrated German chief of staff Halder to comment: 'We estimated that we should contend with 180 Russian divisions; we have already counted 360.'

Wherever possible, the Soviet Union's heavy industry was moved nut by nut and bolt by bolt to the east

Left: **Resignation is etched on the face of a German soldier on the Eastern front, more than two years after 'Barbarossa'.**

Zhukov joined the Tsar's army as a conscript at the outbreak of World War I, aged 18, winning two medals before the Bolshevik revolution. By 1919 he was in the Red Army and a Communist Party member. A personal rapport with Stalin saved him during the military purge of 1937. He remained one of the few generals able to speak his mind to the Soviet dictator, although on at least one occasion he was demoted as a result of doing so.

of the country to prevent it being swallowed up in the German advance – from here productivity was now stepped up. While the Germans suffered from privation, with inadequate supplies being ferried along overstretched lines beginning in occupied Poland and beyond, the Russian forces had their needs seen to swiftly and without hindrance along railway tracks still running into Moscow despite the conflict.

Key among the Russian supplies was the new T-34 tank, heavily armoured, fast and tough. It was equal if not superior to the tanks being driven by the Germans. By 1943 Russian industry was able to produce twice as many tanks as its German counterpart.

■ MARSHAL ZHUKOV ■

Russia also received fresh stocks from the Allies. Perhaps the most significant of these was a mammoth consignment of trucks from America. It enabled Stalin to move men around his huge country at increased speed. He had a fine commander in the field in Georgi Zhukov, whose military genius shone out from the floundering incompetents left at the top of what remained of the Red Army.

Above: **A smouldering tank is stopped in its tracks during the campaign, its crew almost certainly dead inside.**

> ## When they arrived they would face a quick court martial before being shot

Below: **Marshal Zhukov (left) pores over a battle plan as high-ranking Russians grapple with modern warfare techniques.**

■ RETREAT AND DIG ■

Not all the other Russian generals were so lucky. After war broke out, Stalin habitually telephoned commanders who had been compelled to pull back their armies and summoned them to Moscow. When they arrived they would face a quick court martial before being shot for dereliction of duty. Stalin was the only leader of World War II who continued with the outdated notion of shooting generals for failure in the field.

That was not the only old-fashioned element of warfare evident in Russia. Russian generals were forced on the offensive by Stalin no matter what the odds, as it was the

RICKY

In the treacherous task of clearing minefields, the British invasion force used specially trained dogs. When the dog sat down it was clear to his handler that a mine had been sniffed out.

Welsh sheepdog Ricky was clearing a canal bank in Holland when a mine blew up just three feet away from him. Ricky was wounded in the face while the blast killed the section commander. Regardless of his injuries, Ricky returned to his duties and found several more mines before retiring for treatment.

His courage won him the Dickin Medal, created by the People's Dispensary for Sick Animals, to recognise the courage of animals in the front line. Inscribed on it are the words 'For gallantry, we also serve'. Ribbons attached to the disc are green, brown and blue to represent sea, land and sky.

only way he knew of achieving victory. Devoid of any inspiration until the arrival of Zhukov and his protégés, they would send waves of men 'over the top' to hurl themselves at the Germans, much as soldiers did during the trench warfare of 1914-18. The unfortunate troops were cut down in waves.

It took Stalin at least a year to realise that his strategies were fatally flawed. When he began lending an ear to the new breed of generals, he finally realised that technique was everything in modern warfare. It was then that Russia began to turn the tables on its foe.

■ MOSCOW REPRIEVED ■

After an inconclusive Russian counter-offensive out of Moscow in December 1941, both sides suspended operations until May 1942 to give themselves valuable time to recoup men and hardware. Moscow was at least saved from occupation but its people still suffered the deprivations of war.

While Stalin was convinced Moscow remained the Third Reich's prime target, Hitler had other ideas. The need for more resources for his spiralling war effort became more pressing. He eyed the Soviet oilfields in the Caucasus greedily, knowing that success in capturing such prized

Below: **Prepared for invasion. Moscow was lined with anti-tank devices to halt Hitler's progress in the capital.**

assets would not only buoy Germany but would deprive Stalin of precious fuel resources as well.

Code-named 'Operation Blue', Hitler's drive east began at the beginning of May. In characteristic style, the thrust was dynamic and 170,000 Russians were taken prisoner in the first week. Two Russian counter-attacks ended in disarray. The first German objective, to take the tank-making town of Kharkov, was achieved by the end of June.

But frustration followed victory as the Germans lost the initiative when they became involved in a battle for the city of Voronezh. Russian fighters, released from the order to stay their ground by Stalin, could finally strike and then melt away, causing the maximum damage and nuisance to the Germans.

It delayed the German stab towards Stalingrad, the gateway to the Caucasus, which Hitler had earmarked as his own.

In October the German 6th Army finally reached Stalingrad and launched a bloody offensive with the aid of endless strikes by the Luftwaffe. Russian defenders of the city adopted the tactics of guerrilla warfare, going underground to snipe at the oncoming Germans.

■ OPERATION URANUS ■

Even as the winter set in, German commander Paulus braced himself and his men for a final effort, during November 1942. Although the killing went on, he achieved little.

But now the Russians were to bring into play some of the devastating tactics they had learned the hard way, at the hands of the invading Germans. Paulus found his flanks surrounded by a mighty Russian force ready to put a noose around the weakened 6th Army. This was Stalin's 'Operation Uranus', devised

between himself, Zhukov and Chief of General Staff Vasilevsky.

When he heard about the disaster, Hitler was furious. He pledged supplies would be dropped by the Luftwaffe to the beleaguered Paulus

and organised a relief column. But he refused to give Paulus the lifeline he needed for himself and his men – the order to break out of the encirclement or retreat.

■ GERMANS BESIEGED ■

At Stalingrad the outlook for the Germans was bleak. Only a fraction of the food and medical supplies needed were being flown in. Injury or sickness accounted for as much as one fifth of the 100,000-strong force.

The Russian commanders were confident enough to offer Paulus an opportunity to surrender as early as 8 January 1943. Paulus knew the Führer would be maddened so he stood fast.

Left: German pilots notched up some stunning successes on the Eastern front despite facing grim flying conditions.

◆ **EYE WITNESS** ◆

Dennis Golding, of Gosport, near Portsmouth, England, was a British rifleman with the King's Royal Rifle Corps. As a light infantryman he was engaged in hand-to-hand combat with German troops throughout the 1944 advance across western Europe.

'There are still so many myths about the war. If one of our men was wounded in an attack we didn't all stop and gather around him like you see in the movies. We didn't have time to think about it. We just carried on and completed our assignment.

Of course, you would help if you could. But it took four men to deal with one man wounded and you could end up going nowhere.

Then again I saw soldiers who didn't even realise they had been hit. It was only when one of their mates pointed out blood seeping through their uniform that they felt the pain.

Cracking up under fire is another aspect surrounded in mythology. Everybody thinks of these guys running away. I saw one lance corporal who just got up and wandered, babbling, straight into enemy fire. He was what we called bomb happy, or shell-shocked. We never found his body.

I came across the same symptoms affecting Germans who surrendered to us after we took the Falaise Gap. Almost an entire German division was wiped out there and there were thousands of bodies and animal carcasses just heaped up in the streets. That was a sight no man should ever have to see.

The German troops had been shelled and bombed for days without end. By the time the Canadians and ourselves got to them they had no fight left. You could tap them on the shoulder and they would follow you; they didn't know or care where you were taking them.

We always had to be alert. Once when we were clearing a forest a German infantryman popped out of his fox-hole a few yards away and levelled his gun at me. I heard one of my mates shout 'Look out Den' and then that man opened up on the German and killed him.

I'll never forget staring at his body and watching this very pale white cloud emerging from his chest, so faint you could hardly see it. Some soldiers later told me I'd seen the man's soul departing. I don't know about that. Maybe it was just another myth.'

Above: **Stalingrad proved a vital turning point for Germany in the war. Flouting Hitler's wishes, Third Reich troops surrendered to the Russians following a gruelling and costly winter battle.**

Another heavy bombardment rained down on Stalingrad a few days later, leaving the depleted fighting force even more demoralised and desperate. In a last-minute frantic gesture, Hitler promoted Paulus to the rank of field-marshal. Paulus knew well enough the politics behind the honour. No German field-marshal had ever surrendered. The message was clear, fight to the death.

In the misery of snow and ice, Paulus must have glanced around at some of the bodies of the thousands of German soldiers who died in those hellish weeks and wondered why.

Now Paulus found the courage to be the first field-marshal to wave a white flag. At the close of January his headquarters was overrun and he surrendered to the elated Russians. He went on to join a turncoat regiment of Germans who, following

capture, fought for the Russians. For the victors there was the prize of 110,000 prisoners. For the defeated, it was unmitigated disaster.

Germans were on the run elsewhere in Russia as well, chased by an increasingly confident Red Army who were at their best in winter. It was far from the end of the war at the Eastern front. But it was the beginning of the end for Germany even if Hitler remained blind to the fact for months to come.

Now Paulus found the courage to be the first field-marshal to wave a white flag

---

The subsequent drive by the Russian army between January and March was fruitless. Crack German commander Field-Marshal Erich von Manstein staged a determined recovery. This small consolation did little

for Hitler's morale. He was broken by the Stalingrad debacle, losing his self-confidence and intuition.

Fighting continued in explosive spats until the scene was set for a major confrontation at Kursk. Hitler allowed the planned offensive, 'Operation Citadel', to be delayed time and again while his commanders struggled to get sufficient numbers of tanks in position.

It was 5 July before the battle commenced. By 12 July there were some 2,700 German tanks and 1,800 German aircraft ranged against almost 4,000 Soviet tanks. It was the largest head-on tank battle in history, an epic test of firepower which would leave both sides battered and worn. Tank after tank went up in flames, its crew having little chance of escaping the inferno. At the end of the day there were 300 German tanks smouldering. Still more Russian tanks were burnt out but the German advance had been halted. It spelled defeat once more for the Reich. And the dramatic loss of so many tanks would take Germany many more weeks to recover than it would Russia, leaving their armoured divisions sorely lacking in firepower and mobility.

Now it was for Hitler to contemplate withdrawal. It was alien to his nature to pull out of territory fought over and won two years before. But the Red Army was flexing its muscles and was already chasing the German army out of the Crimea and the Baltic lands. The plan favoured by commanders like Manstein, to pull back to a single defensive line, soon

Below: **The tank battle at Kursk was an epic trial of strength. In the end it was the Russians who triumphed.**

DIEPPE

Twenty-one years after the disastrous raid at Dieppe which cost the lives of hundreds of Canadian servicemen, an investigation was launched to probe whether an advertisement for soap flakes gave the enemy vital advance information.

The commando raid at Dieppe in August 1942 involved 5,000 Canadians, 1,000 British, 50 American Rangers and some Free French fighters. Only half returned. The rest were killed or captured after being pinned down on the beach by the Germans. A week before it took place English newspapers carried an advertisement for Sylvan soap flakes under the title 'Beach Coat from Dieppe'. The copy afterwards read: 'How could you have known when you bought it that sunny day before the war that such a flippant little coat would be so useful about the house in war-time?'

There was speculation that in the advertisement was hidden the message 'Beach Combined Operations at Dieppe'. The woman pictured carried secateurs. Were they in fact wire cutters? Scotland Yard and MI5 swooped on the advertising agency Graham and Gillies and on the manufacturers of the soap flakes. They were persuaded it was a horrible coincidence. But no one knows whether the Germans had read the advertisement and seen secret codes where none in fact existed.

became the only option. If only there had been enough materials and men to build the defences envisaged by Hitler, perhaps the gains he made would have been preserved at least for a while. But the Germans were unable to dig in along the 2,000-mile front and provide an effective defence. Their greatest protection to date, the ineffectiveness of the Red Army, was no longer relevant. Hitler's dream to take Russia had

turned into the same nightmare that afflicted Napoleon 150 years before.

By January 1944 the Red Army was at last able to lift the siege of Leningrad. The city had been encircled since November 1941, suffering months of artillery bombardment. When liberation came after 900 days, only one third of the original population of three million were left alive.

Just as the winter of 1941-42 caused devastation among the

invaders, so it brought misery and despondency to the hemmed-in people of Leningrad.

Rationing was down to just nine ounces of bread per day for working people and half that amount for those too young or too old to be employed. Cats, dogs, even rats, were eaten in a bid to stave off starvation. In front of the desperate people lay the no-man's land of defences against the Germans. Behind them lay frozen Lake Ladoga, over which there was a narrow trail into free Russia.

When liberation came after 900 days, only one third of the original population of three million were left alive

Minimal supplies found their way across the trail at first and even the smallest relief attempts were harried by German aircraft. By the spring, the residents had learned a harsh lesson. Every available inch of land was cultivated and there were fresh

Above: The sight of Russian tanks lying uselessly by the roadside provide a grim spectacle for passing troops.

Right: Many German soldiers died as they vainly struggled to repair vehicles frozen in the snow.

vegetables available throughout the rest of their imprisonment. Electricity was also rationed, the sewers were brim full and even clean water was in short supply.

When the saviour army lifted the blockade, they were greeted with a weary relief by the Leningraders.

Between March and April the Red Army reclaimed 165 miles of territory. Their greatest push was yet to come, however, in the form of 'Operation Bagration', which began in June, just as Hitler came under acute pressure from the D-Day landings in Normandy. Before it began, the partisans working for the Russians behind German lines set to work by setting off a series of disabling explosions.

The operation was characterised by now-familiar tactics employed by the Red Army. A burst of artillery fire to 'soften up' the enemy followed by the rapid advance of the infantry. Thousands of German soldiers were taken prisoner as Minsk fell once again to the Russians. Their humiliation was to walk down the silent streets of Moscow on their way to prison camps, watched through the narrowed, loathing eyes of the city residents. Now the German forces in the east were stretched to breaking point. Stubbornly, Hitler refused to let his troops pull back even when they had been overrun. The Führer's behaviour only offered more to the Russians by way of enemy casualties and prisoners.

By August, the Russian troops were on the Polish border. They had been forced to contend with more than three times the number of troops facing the Allies in Normandy and had proved themselves equal to the task. For the first time, the war was to be carried into Reich territory.

A FORGOTTEN ARMY

Just like the British fighters in Burma and the American soldiers assisting the Chinese, the troops who fought to regain Italy believed themselves to be 'a forgotten army'.

Theirs was a protracted campaign remembered mostly for its mud, miscalculation and unexpectedly high casualty rate. Churchill had described the Italian peninsula as 'the soft underbelly' of the Third Reich. Fierce German resistance proved his judgement to be wildly awry.

After nearly a year of strenuous fighting, the Allies took Rome on 4 June 1944. The trumpeted D-Day operations which began the following night swallowed the limelight. Forces who felt they had lost the recognition they deserved joked wryly thereafter about themselves being 'D-Day dodgers in sunny Italy'.

The opportunity to open a second front in Europe occurred when the fighting in North Africa was brought to a victorious close in 1943. For months, the Americans had been pushing for a campaign on the continent. Their chosen siting was northern France. But Churchill and his commanders felt it was prema-ture, preferring instead to squeeze the Germans from the south.

By July 1943, the invasion of Sicily, code-named 'Operation Husky', was prepared. Montgomery was to lead his weary but able 8th Army in one assault while General Patton, heading the US 7th Army, came via a different route. The aim was to trap the defending German forces in a pincer movement.

During the course of the invasion, Italy swapped sides in the war, having overthrown the dictator

Little did they know that the resolve of the Germans was harder than ever

Mussolini. Despite the chaos that this caused among the Germans, a staggering 40,000 were able to slip through the British and American trap and escape to the mainland.

Nevertheless, Sicily was in Allied possession by 17 August. An armistice was signed on 3 September as the 8th Army crossed the Straits of Messina to land in Calabria, in 'Operation Baytown'. The effect of the revelation of the Italian volte face on the troops poised to continue with the invasion of the mainland was disastrous. There were cheers and celebrations before the operation had even begun. The men believed south-

Far left: The sky is decorated by a fireball, following a German dive-bomber attack on an American cargo ship during the invasion of Sicily.

Left, inset: Allied DUKW amphibious vehicles, nicknamed 'ducks', are loaded aboard a landing ship at Salerno harbour in preparation for the next phase of the invasion of Italy.

Above: Weary from a foot-slog in Sicily, US soldiers prop themselves up at the foot of an Italian memorial to the soldiers of World War I.

ern Italy was theirs for the taking. Little did they know the resolve of the German defenders to stop them was harder than ever, and they were mentally ill-prepared for the brutal fighting which awaited them.

■ SALERNO LANDINGS ■

On 9 September the next phase of the invasion began. A total of 165,000 British and American servicemen spilled out of 500 ships in a large-scale amphibious landing. The landings at Salerno, code-named 'Operation Avalanche', were scheduled by US commander General Mark Clark to last three days. He had supreme confidence in the ability of the troops to secure a quick victory. Within just 72 hours he expected Naples to have fallen, giving the Allies a crucial harbour facility. In fact, it took 21 days of gruelling battle. An attack staged at Taranto designed to divert the Germans failed. Crack German troops held the British and Americans at Salerno until reinforcements had been brought forward.

The fastidious and highly critical Montgomery, who expressed doubts about the planning of the campaign

By 15 November the campaign was brought to a halt, hampered as it was by winter weather. Relations between the British and American commanders were equally chilly.

The next tactic to bring about a breakthrough took the form of the Allied landings at Anzio in January 1944. In 'Operation Shingle', the beachheads were quickly secured, yet

cans, Japanese settlers in America who had been reviled at home after Pearl Harbor, made several vital strikes on behalf of the Allies.

■ MONTE CASSINO ■

The road to Rome was marked by the architectural treasure of Monte Cassino, a sacred Christian site founded in 529 by Saint Benedict. It was filled with cultural riches gathered through the centuries, kept lovingly in archives by the monks who lived and worked at the abbey.

Perched high on a mountainous ridge, Monte Cassino looked down into the town of Cassino and away across the plains. Monastery and town were connected by a funicular railway which climbed the sheer rocky face of the peak with ease.

Cassino was in the hands of the Germans in January 1944, a major strength in its defences known as 'the Gustav line'. It became the target of Allied plane attacks but even a heavy

from the outset, encountered tough resistance as he and his men tried to fight their way up the toe of Italy to rendezvous with the rest of the invasion force. He was horrified to find the German positions had been reinforced. Clark's and Montgomery's troops finally made the planned link up on 16 September. In those weeks 25,000 soldiers and civilians died.

Although a first vital and substantial foothold in Italy had been carved out, the fighting didn't get any easier. The terrain of rocky peaks and steep escarpments favoured defensive positions, all of which were held by the Germans. Time and again, the Allied soldiers found themselves fatally exposed.

Above: Allied artillery in action against targets in Italy. The gunners, from 97 Heavy AA Regiment, Royal Artillery, feel the heat.

the Allies had difficulty spearheading an advance. Indeed, they only narrowly missed being driven back into the sea by a determined German counter-offensive. Soon Anzio was under seige. Conflicts there were bitter. The Allies were desperately seeking routes to push forward.

By now the Allied reinforcements consisted of British, American, French, Canadian, New Zealand, South African, Greek and Brazilian troops. Even the Japanese were playing their part. The Nisei-Ameri-

> *The Americans then took one of the most controversial decisions of the conflict – to bomb the delightful monastery*

pounding failed to eradicate the defenders. Soon, it became clear the Germans were using the abbey as a defensive stronghold, unassailable at the mountain top.

The Americans then took one of the most controversial decisions of the conflict – to bomb the delightful monastery which was consequently smashed to smithereens.

Little was achieved. Still Allied forces were left clinging to the mountainside, scrambling forward a few yards whenever they could. It

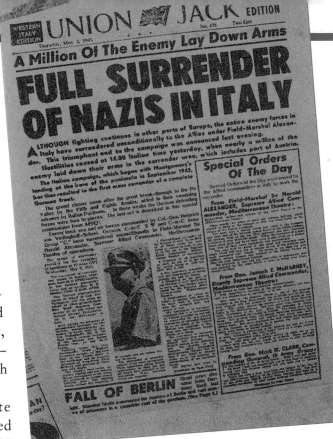

Right: The German forces in Italy finally surrendered to the Allies on 2 May 1945.

wasn't until May that the Allies by-passed the hazard, leaving the ruins of the abbey to fall to the Polish army in the rear. With heavy casualties, the Polish, assisted by a British contingent, took 1,500 prisoners – men of the German 4th Parachute Regiment.

To capture Monte Cassino, the Allies used 27 divisions with 1,900 tanks, together with 4,000 aircraft. Casualties on both sides were appalling, with some 105,000 Allied soldiers killed or wounded alongside 80,000 Germans.

■ FALL OF ROME ■

Although Rome fell soon afterwards and the incoming troops received a tumultuous welcome from its citizens, it was not the end of fighting in Italy. Still Germany threw men and ammunition at the advancing Allies. Pockets of resistance around Rimini and Bologna held the advance until the winter months, when by necessity it all but ground to a halt. Allied troops were forced to dig in during the inclement weather, experiencing the same dreadful conditions that faced their forebears in the trenches of World War I.

As late as 9 April 1945, the Allies were compelled to begin another offensive. It wasn't until 2 May that a surrender was negotiated with the weary and disillusioned Germans.

Right: **The fierce battle at Monte Cassino left the monastery a shattered wreck.**

Casualties were appalling, with some 105,000 Allied soldiers killed or wounded

◆ EYE WITNESS ◆

Lieutenant-Colonel Alex Borrie was in a New Zealand brigade involved in the battle for Italy and later wrote *Escapades around Cassino*. In his diary dated 18 March 1944, he wrote:

Our C Company moved past Castle Hill to attack Cassino. Their main objectives were 'Hotel des Roses' and 'Hotel Continental'. They were to retreat to a cave above part of the Monastery Road at 6pm. I was sent up the hill with a team of soldiers carrying food and medical supplies. The 4th Indian Division was beyond our Company on Hangman's Hill. Passing from Castle Hill to the road, the Germans put up many flares. We felt most conspicuous but the experienced soldiers said: "Stand still!" No shots were fired. At 9.10pm we reached the cave spot on time. I called out "Any Kiwis here?"

"Ssh, quiet, we just arrived ten minutes ago. There are Germans everywhere." On the way down, supplies had been dropped by parachute. Someone once said to me: "Parachutes make wonderful underpants." I tore off plenty but back at the R.A.P. it was red thick cotton – useless.

OVERLORD!

It was the day that Europe had been waiting for, when Allied soldiers would tread again on French soil. In the event, many had to step over the bodies of fallen comrades lying lifeless in the Normandy surf before their feet touched Nazi-occupied France.

The Americans had been pressing for an assault on occupied Europe virtually since their entry into the war. Cautious British commanders, stung by heavy losses during the trial foray onto the French coastline at Dieppe two years previously, at last thought the time was right to begin the liberation of the continent. A defeat could have been a death-blow to Britain's war effort, leaving her without an army. The commanders were finally convinced that victory was likely to be theirs.

The Germans, too, had been waiting with trepidation for the day that their enemies would try to get a foothold once more in Europe and had fortified the French coastline accordingly. Construction on the lines of tunnels, guns and bunkers to protect Hitler's Europe stretching 3,000 miles from Holland to the south of France began in September 1941 and got underway in earnest when Rommel took charge of the huge task in 1943.

German intelligence was good yet they still had no idea when and how the invasion would come. Norway, the Balkans and Calais were all strong possiblities. The imminence of the invasion, however, was beyond doubt in anyone's mind.

Hitler hoped it would be Disaster-Day for the Allies, with the German defenders casting the invaders back into the sea. He guessed rightly that the outcome of the attack would decide the war. Fulfilling everybody's expectations, the invasion came in early June. 'Operation Overlord' was the culmination of more than a year's

Left: **When Utah beach was secured, troops and supplies flooded ashore from the scores of ships in the Channel.**

Right: **Dwight Eisenhower sent a 'good luck' message to all those who took part in 'Operation Overlord', the Allied invasion of occupied France.**

work. It was an elaborate plan involving thousands of soldiers, sailors and airmen. The troops who would be scrambling up the foreign shores and overwhelming the German opposition could only guess at what fate held in store for them when they set sail across the Channel for France.

The shortest route from Britain would, of course, have been from Dover to Calais, where German and British troops could already spy each other on clear days. For this reason, German defences were tight on that section of the French coast in readiness for an Allied invasion.

Despite the advantage of the brief crossing, the beaches around Calais posed too great a threat to the

Further west, they found the answer – the long, golden beaches of Normandy

troops. Allied commanders had to look elsewhere. Further west, they found the answer to their conundrum – the long, golden beaches of Normandy. Here the German defences were comparatively thin.

Before 'Operation Overlord' got underway, there were key factors to consider which would help the Allies win the battle – and triumph in the

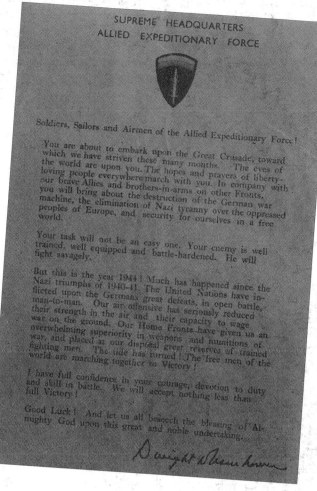

SUPREME HEADQUARTERS
ALLIED EXPEDITIONARY FORCE

Soldiers, Sailors and Airmen of the Allied Expeditionary Force!

You are about to embark upon the Great Crusade, toward which we have striven these many months. The eyes of the world are upon you. The hopes and prayers of liberty-loving people everywhere march with you. In company with our brave Allies and brothers-in-arms on other Fronts, you will bring about the destruction of the German war machine, the elimination of Nazi tyranny over the oppressed peoples of Europe, and security for ourselves in a free world.

Your task will not be an easy one. Your enemy is well trained, well equipped and battle-hardened. He will fight savagely.

But this is the year 1944! Much has happened since the Nazi triumphs of 1940-41. The United Nations have inflicted upon the Germans great defeats, in open battle, man-to-man. Our air offensive has seriously reduced their strength in the air and their capacity to wage war on the ground. Our Home Fronts have given us an overwhelming superiority in weapons and munitions of war, and placed at our disposal great reserves of trained fighting men. The tide has turned! The free men of the world are marching together to Victory!

I have full confidence in your courage, devotion to duty and skill in battle. We will accept nothing less than full Victory!

Good Luck! And let us all beseech the blessing of Almighty God upon this great and noble undertaking.

Dwight D Eisenhower

war. First was the training of the men involved. Although amphibious landings had already been tried and tested during the war, nothing of the same magnitude had ever been attempted. British, American and Canadian soldiers were posted around Britain for rehearsals.

Coastal resorts like Woolacombe, Gosport, Westward Ho!, Salcombe, Studland Bay and Slapton Sands played host to hundreds of soldiers sent to practise beach landings in an environment similar to that which they would encounter in France.

Slapton became a scene of disaster when live ammunition killed some of the soldiers taking part. Then, on 28 April 1944, mass devastation was wreaked when German E-boats slunk into a convoy in training off the coast, sinking two landing craft and killing 749 soldiers and sailors.

◆ 'OPERATION OVERLORD'

During the night of 5/6 June 1944, the armada carrying 21st Army Group – the 'Operation Overlord' strike force – approached the coast of Normandy. The assault was to be concentrated on five beaches: the two in the west (code-named 'Utah' and 'Omaha') were the responsibility of the Americans under Bradley; the three in the east ('Gold', 'Juno' and 'Sword') were the target of the British under Dempsey. The army group was under the overall command of Montgomery. Early in the morning of the 6th, the reconquest of continental Europe began as the first Allied forces hit the beaches and struggled to establish beachheads. German resistance was tough, but the liberation was underway.

Support for the soldiers and sailors promised to be greater than anything known before. Construction firms all over the United Kingdom set to work on a top secret engineering project, each company manufacturing a different component for a giant concrete jigsaw. Few of the workers involved could guess that they were building massive harbours called 'Mulberries', to be towed across to France for docking purposes by 150 tugs. Now the invading forces didn't have to capture a ready-built harbour, always a costly exercise in terms of human lives. Tanks, trucks, big guns and supplies would roll along the Mulberries with ease.

■ PLUTO ■

A pipeline under the ocean (code-named 'Pluto'), made from steel or sometimes steel and lead, was installed to bring essential fuel quickly from Britain to France; it was laid on the sea bed by slow-moving tugs. After the war, it was salvaged to provide plumbing for 50,000 houses.

Reconnaissance was meticulously detailed. Air force pilots flying Spitfires stripped of ammunition to make them as speedy as possible photographed as much of the coastline as they could. In addition, an appeal for holiday photographs and postcards of the region reaped thousands of pictures of the area. Further aided by maps provided by the French Resistance, cartographers began to build up a three-dimensional impression of the targeted Normandy beaches.

Midget submarines went on dangerous nightly missions to the Normandy coast. Their occupants braved the water and the German patrols to bring back soil and sand samples and up-to-date information on the position of German defences.

Last but not least the British authorities embarked on a highly detailed decoy campaign to fool the Germans, who were equally involved in reconnaissance.

Along the Kent coast, some 150 miles from the British heart of 'Overlord', there was an impressive collection of armour and shipping being prepared. Only on close inspection was it revealed that the tanks were rubber and the ships were made from plywood. Lines of tents were empty apart from army cookers puffing smoke through the chimneys to make them appear authentic. The oil depots, planes and jetties that

Only on close inspection was it revealed that the tanks were rubber

mushroomed in the area were also shams, designed to convince the Germans that the Allied thrust would be launched against Calais.

'Operation Fortitude', as it was code-named, was vital to the success of the invasion. The Allied forces could still be driven back into the sea if the might of the Third Reich descended on them within the first few days of the assault. With a variety of bogus intelligence messages, the commanders behind 'Fortitude' managed to convince the Germans that the invasion in Normandy was only a diversion and that the real attack was coming at Calais. Given that information, the Germans refused to move their forces from Calais, thereby saving the Allies from an onslaught.

◆ EYE WITNESS ◆

William Ryan, of the US 16th Infantry Regiment, was in the first wave to land at Omaha beach. At 18, it was his first action. He went on to serve 30 years in the army and is a veteran of the Korean and Vietnam wars.

❛ We loaded up the transports at Portland, Weymouth, about 2 June. We were supposed to attack on 5 June. They cancelled it due to weather. We were on the ship all those days.

Everyone was sea-sick. At about 2am on 6 June we loaded on to small 36ft LCVPs, we were 12 miles out. They wanted to surprise the enemy. The seas were six or eight feet high. By now most of the men were so sick they didn't care whether they lived or died. They were too sick to be scared. Even coxswain was sick. I ran the boat for five miles until he started to feel better.

My company was assigned six boats. We lost two boats almost immediately – they were swamped with heavy waves. Heading for the beach the coxswain lost his bearings. When he realised we were off course he had to try again.

The guys from the next sector blew over into our beach – their boats filled the beach so we couldn't get in. We had to circle around like sitting ducks. When we finally started into the beach we lost all four boats with the fire from the German 88s.

I was blown over the side and knocked unconscious. I was told later that two of the men in the boat with me dragged me through the water and propped me up against an embankment. Otherwise I would have drowned.

At first there were five or six wounded with me. Then there were hundreds. I laid on the beach in that same position from about 8am until 10pm when they evacuated us. I had concussion in addition to shell fragments in my head, shoulder and leg. All this time I was going in and out of consciousness, looking down on Omaha beach. It was just a madhouse.

Troops were pinned down by the gun emplacements. Eventually a US Navy destroyer came in as close to the beach as possible without running aground and started firing at all the German emplacements. In a little while two or three other destroyers started shelling as well. In my opinion, that is what saved Omaha beach from defeat.

I heard afterwards the skipper on the ship was ordered to go back to a safe position. Apparently he said he wasn't leaving while US soldiers were pinned down on the beach. He could have been court martialled for what he did. But he should have got a medal.

I didn't have anything to eat all day. In the afternoon a US soldier came over the hill with a couple of bottles of French red wine which he gave to us. You are never going to beat Americans in war. They are crazy. ❜

Right: D-Day would not have succeeded had the Allies not had mastery of the skies. A B-26 Marauder returns home after carrying out a bombing mission unchallenged over Normandy.

A double stood in for Monty and made a public departure for Algiers – when the real Montgomery was safely ensconced in 'Overlord' headquarters, which was Southwick House, Portsmouth.

The initial landings were to be made by 156,000 men, mostly Britons, Americans and Canadians. With them was an impressive turnout from occupied Europe. The line-up included an armoured division from France, a Belgian brigade, a Dutch brigade, a Polish division, as well as multi-national seaborne forces. In the skies, the main air forces were joined by squadrons from Norway, Czecho-slovakia, France, Poland, Australia and New Zealand.

More men and equipment were held in reserve for future operations in Europe. It took an armada to ferry the men for the first action across the Channel. By late May, 359 warships, 1,000 minesweepers and associated vessels, 4,000 landing craft, 805

Local people became used to the sight of tanks and trucks lining the streets, as major military traffic jams built up

merchantmen, 59 blockships and 300 other small craft were at the ready.

Overhead, more than 11,000 aircraft were assembled. Some would be towing gliders to be released over France. Each of these carried some 30 troops, tasked with tackling inland enemy positions, including vital landmarks which would halt a German advance, like Pegasus Bridge. The seas and the skies belonged to the Allies. Montgomery had promised his men that the invasion would not go ahead until that umbrella of protection was firmly in place.

Anyone living on the south coast of England could have had no doubt that an invasion was poised to go ahead. Local people became used to the sight of tanks and trucks lining the streets, as major military traffic jams built up on the main roads to Portsmouth. Now there were 1,500,000 American troops alone massed on British shores. Then, one morning, they were gone.

Beginning on 2 June, the hordes of men and machinery bound for Normandy boarded their ships. The weather had been unseasonably poor. High winds and rain had lashed southern Britain, putting the entire operation at risk. It had to be postponed once from 5 June. General Dwight Eisenhower, supreme Allied commander, considered a further postponement in the face of the driving winds and rains which could wreak havoc with a seaborne landing force. The next date in June when the tides and the light were compatible was not for almost another two weeks. Some commanders favoured waiting. Others, like Montgomery, believed the strike should go ahead. It would, after all, be impossible to keep aboard ship those men already embarked. Each soldier and marine had already been interned in a camp for at least three weeks and was primed and ready for

Above: A US ship returns to a British port loaded with 'Overlord' casualties, while in France the action continues.

action. Any postponement could only have led to a deterioration in their mental and physical fitness. Anyway, the risk of them talking once they got ashore – and giving the game away – was too great.

Eisenhower smoked and read Westerns while he pondered the dilemma. Finally he made his decision. Heartened by predictions of a break in the weather, he signalled the go-ahead for 6 June, with the words 'OK, let's go'.

■ IKE SPEAKS ■

Eisenhower, fondly known as 'Ike', gave this message to the departing men of the Allied Expeditionary Force: 'You are about to embark upon the Great Crusade, toward which we have striven these many months. The eyes of the world are upon you. The hopes and prayers of liberty-loving people everywhere march with you. In company with our brave Allies and brothers-in-arms on other Fronts, you will bring about the destruction of the German war machine, the elimination of Nazi tyranny over the oppressed peoples of Europe and security for ourselves in a free world.

'Your task will not be an easy one. Your enemy is well trained, well equipped and battle-hardened. He will fight savagely.

'But this is the year 1944! Much has happened since the Nazi triumphs of 1940-41. The United Nations have inflicted upon the Germans great defeats, in open battle, man-to-man...The tide has turned! The free men of the world are marching together to Victory.'

The only message to reach the expectant public that day was a short, sharp statement, reading: 'Under the command of General Eisenhower, Allied naval forces, supported by strong air forces, began landing Allied armies this morning on the northern coast of France.'

As the soldiers and sailors bobbed in darkness on a choppy sea, they were nervous, tense, euphoric and excitable. Some were sea-sick, some prayed, many fought an overwhelming feeling of doom. Still more found enough spirit to tell jokes. The huge size of the armada involved in 'Operation Neptune', which got them across the Channel, only served to inflate their confidence.

The troops heard the drone of aircraft overhead – a big boost to their morale. Not only were the planes going to bombard enemy positions along the coast in preparation for the landings. Some were carrying paratroopers who, in the first leg of 'Overlord', were being

◆ EYE WITNESS ◆

Henry 'Marty' Martin, from Chicopee, Massachusetts, USA, witnessed the tragedy of 'Operation Tiger' at Slapton Sands while training for D-Day.

'When the German E-boats attacked we just thought it was just part of the exercise. I was right in that exercise and I didn't find out for another 43 years that 749 men had drowned. These guys were wearing their life jackets around their waists when they should have been up around their armpits. With 30-35lb packs on their backs they were just tipped upside down in the water and couldn't right themselves.

I can understand why the government kept it secret at the time because the news would have been a terrible blow to morale. I only question why it took so long for the facts to come out.'

Right: Allied soldiers pause to inspect a French memorial to those who died in the carnage of World War I, before continuing with the liberation of western Europe.

dropped at 2am into east and west flanks of the landings.

When they approached the beach, they saw what appeared to be men walking on water. These were crew members of the midget submarines used to guide in the flotillas of landing craft. Men lashed themselves to the masts of their tiny submarines, which floated low in the water to signal to the captains of much larger vessels.

■ H·HOUR, D·DAY ■

Just a few hours later, naval big guns were joining the aircraft in the pounding of enemy positions. Before 6am, the first men were ashore, putting months of rigorous training to the test.

British and Canadian troops were destined for the easterly beaches between Arromanches and Ouistreham. The three beaches earmarked for landings were code-named Gold, Juno and Sword.

In the west, the Americans tackled beaches Utah and Omaha, stretching between Les Dunes de Varreville and Colleville. On each of the beaches there were barbed-wire hazards, anti-tank stumps entrenched in the sand and other menaces. First to come off the boats were the commandos who were to knock out the pill-boxes, and the sappers, charged with clearing a safe path up the beach.

The operation surprised the Germans, who at first believed the landings to be a diversionary tactic. Rommel, in charge of defending the Atlantic Wall, was so unprepared for the Allied arrival that he was in Germany celebrating his wife's 50th birthday when the landings occurred. After Rommel heard of the invasion

at 10.15am, he began a frantic drive back from Germany to his post. 'If I was commanding the Allied forces right now, I could win the war in fourteen days,' he confided to a colleague on his staff.

After the war, Rommel's son Manfred recalled how his father had told Hitler many times that the invasion battle could not be won. Hitler refused to listen. 'All my father could do was to pull the front further and further back and, until he was wounded, carry out his duty.'

When he was told of the early-morning events of 6 June, Hitler ordered his troops to clean up the beachheads before nightfall. He knew the only way to save his extended

---

The Führer refused to release two Panzer divisions from the east of France

---

empire was to throw the Allies back into the sea. But convinced it was a false alarm, the Führer refused to release two Panzer divisions from the east of France to counter the Allied attack until 3.40pm.

Troops on Sword, Juno and Gold made solid progress in spite of

casualties, although many soldiers landed without their guns and ammunition, which were lost in the water. They had to wait in huddles until the beach was taken before resuming their war. Blasting in their ears was the non-stop sound of the naval guns. On Utah beach, the German defences found it impossible to keep the swarms of Americans at bay. It was speedily taken with fewer than 200 lives lost.

■ HELL OF OMAHA ■

Unfortunately, on Omaha the poor weather combined with strong currents and fierce resistance to make the landings a hellish nightmare. Here the failure of the air forces to knock out large artillery was keenly felt. There was also the unexpected presence of a German division posted to Normandy on defensive exercises.

More than 2,000 men lost their lives. They were drowned when they were swept away by a changing tide with heavy equipment strapped to their backs. Some died when they trod on mines. Others perished from artillery, machine-gun, mortar and rifle fire from beach pill-boxes and from positions on cliffs above the beach. Wounded men strewn on the beach were in danger of being run over by tanks. There was little shelter and no escape.

◆ EYE WITNESS ◆

George Ross, from Glasgow, was called up in 1939 when he was 19 years old. He recalls how as sergeant major of 101 Company, 5th Beach Group, he landed on Sword beach in the early hours of D-Day.

' We didn't know what we were going to come up against. The crossing was rough. Our craft was led by a chief petty officer. He had been at sea 25 years and never been sea-sick. But he was sick as a dog that morning.

Coming ashore, the first thing we noticed was a camouflaged pill-box. We got underneath the slits and launched a grenade attack. Our job was to establish a route where our tanks could come through. I honestly cannot say I was nervous. I was anxious but I had been warned about what to expect during six months of lectures beforehand.

There were bodies in the water of both British and Germans. One of the officers told us afterwards how, when he was walking up the beach, he felt he was walking on cushions. It was bodies of dead soldiers he was walking on. '

Lieutenant-General Omar Bradley considered a withdrawal. It would have been disastrous for the invasion, offering an opening for the Germans to attack both British and American flanks. Yet hardy US Rangers finally scaled the coastal heights to tackle the problem guns and alleviate the problems on the beach.

■ LONGEST DAY ■

Some of the men on the beaches were battle-hardened veterans. There was, however, a large contingent of raw soldiers, particularly among the Americans. They were pitched into the most intense, violent battle-ground, and forced to pick their way among the dead and dying amid the roar of big guns overhead and the sensation of small-arms fire whizzing past their ears. The air was filled with the pungent smell of flesh, blood and cordite.

Particularly on Omaha but also true of the other beaches, the first wave of men forced to fight their way ashore were cut down. Preparing to take to the beaches, the second wave witnessed the carnage then ran past the bodies of their comrades, hoping they didn't meet the same miserable fate.

Alongside panic there was determination – each flash of cowardice displayed by frightened, confused men was matched ten times by instances of heroism and stoicism. Minor troubles and petty differences lay forgotten. Each man was focused only on surviving for the next minute, the next hour and into the following day.

Ahead of them lay the task of capturing German-held towns, some of which fell more quickly than others. Russians who had been forced into German uniforms after being captured on the Eastern front were eager to lay down their arms. French

Below: A Sherman tank, affectionately nicknamed 'Betty', goes ashore to fight the battle of Normandy.

people rushed out to greet the liberating Allies, offering drinks, flowers and greetings. A few French residents near the beaches braved the conflict to aid the wounded and dying.

Tales of outstanding courage filled the newspapers for months and years afterwards. One commando corporal led his men up the beach past enemy pill-boxes, bellowing encouragement. He fell only when he had passed the pill-boxes – he had received more than 50 wounds.

The defending Germans were mostly in chaos. One senior commander reported in panic that American gliders were landing Volkswagen cars in Normandy which were driven by American troops in German uniforms. Arguably, the day was as much lost by the confusion and indecision that paralysed many Germans as won by the heroic efforts of the Allied troops.

By the end of 'the longest day', 10,000 Allied soldiers had fallen. The figure was a third of that estimated by Allied command. But there was no turning back. The Allies had achieved the Normandy landings. Nothing and nobody was going to force them out of France again.

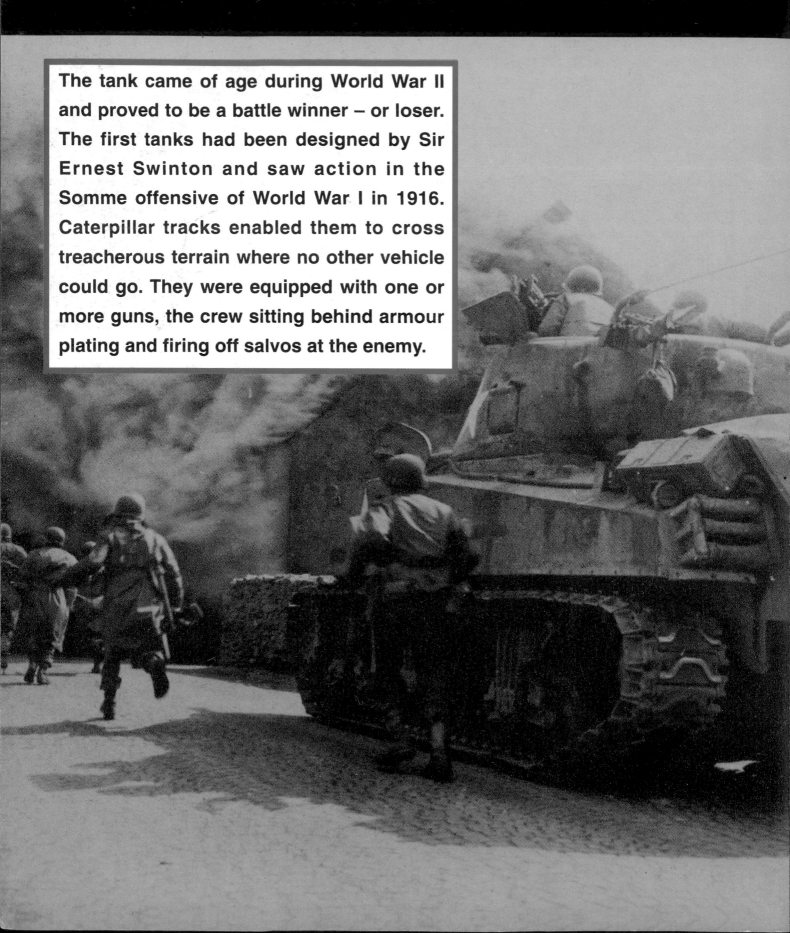

TANKS COME OF AGE

The tank came of age during World War II and proved to be a battle winner – or loser. The first tanks had been designed by Sir Ernest Swinton and saw action in the Somme offensive of World War I in 1916. Caterpillar tracks enabled them to cross treacherous terrain where no other vehicle could go. They were equipped with one or more guns, the crew sitting behind armour plating and firing off salvos at the enemy.

Now German general Heinz Guderian used the outbreak of World War II to put his own theories about the use of tanks to the test. Tanks should not be pinned down to flanking foot soldiers, he argued. Their purpose was to break out against the enemy, putting a speed into land-based warfare which it had never known before.

With that in mind, he formed his highly efficient Panzer divisions. The tanks were fast but lacked adequate protective armour. Nevertheless, they were an integral part of 'Blitzkrieg', the lightning war, a tactic with which Hitler easily won Poland, France, Holland and Belgium.

The technique took Britain and France by surprise. Although France had an enormous number of tanks at its disposal, 2,475 to be exact, their effectiveness was muted because of the old-fashioned way in which they were deployed. Instead of combining the firepower as Guderian did, each tank was evenly spaced down a long defensive line. In time Allied

When a tank 'brewed up', the escape hatches were wholly inadequate, or blocked

commanders mimicked Guderian to get the best out of their tanks. Used individually, they were easy targets.

If tankmen in World War I were better protected than their colleagues in the infantry, the same could not be said of their counterparts 20 years on. In fact, there were few infantrymen who would willingly change places with tankmen. For while tanks

stole a march on the enemy in the the killing fields of Flanders, technology had now caught up. Now there was a wide range of anti-armour artillery designed to knock tanks out. Men inside a stricken tank had little or no chance of escape.

And for the first three years of the war, German tanks and anti-tank weapons were appreciably better than their British counterparts. For example, the Mark II Matilda was known for its weak steering clutches, the Valentine offered only limited vision to its commander, the Crusader was mechanically unreliable. It took only an armour-piercing shell from one of the new breed of anti-tank guns used by the Germans to finish them.

That's when infantrymen remained heartily glad they had the job they did. For when a tank caught fire, or 'brewed up', the tiny escape hatches on the tanks were wholly inadequate and, in any case, were often blocked. Sometimes there was a matter of seconds before fire took a hold and

Above: **Tank crews during World War I were rightly delighted with the new hardware, which provided them with ample protection. But in World War II, a variety of anti-armour weapons existed to make life hell for the tankman.**
Far left: **The men of an armoured division running through the smoke-filled streets of the German town of Wernberg.**

the tank's ammunition began to explode. Sometimes there was not. Nicknames for tanks during the war included 'steel coffins', 'tommy cookers' and 'Ronson burners', because, like the products of the same name, they would always 'light first time'.

■ BLACKENED DOLLS ■

One witness gruesomely detailed the effects on the men trapped inside: 'Little blackened dolls about two feet high have been found in tanks. Once these were men.'

As the war progressed, the Germans learned about the shortcomings of their tanks, which were

Left: **Matilda tanks were favoured by the British military but they failed to match the firepower of German Tigers, pictured below.**

A later generation of Allied tanks, including Shermans and Churchills, began to overcome some – but not all – of the difficulties. Yet no design, no matter how superior, could compensate for the problems thrown up by the terrain the tanks were working in. Every theatre of war offered its pitfalls to tanks. In Europe the rain

lacking in firepower and suffered from flimsy armour. Their most painful lesson came on the Eastern front when their troops encountered the fearsome T-34 tanks of the Russian armoured divisions.

Accordingly they introduced the Panther, in July 1943, and the Tiger, in September 1942, which were battle winners thanks to the enormous range of their guns, quite outstripping the British models, which were unable to get close enough to counter-attack effectively.

■ THE DEADLY 88 ■

By the time the British developed the six-pounder gun, the Germans had in their armoury the heavier 75mm weapon. As the Americans caught up, with their own 75mm gun, the Germans leaped ahead again, fitting the deadly 88mm guns, which were originally designed as anti-aircraft guns but wreaked havoc when mounted on the Tiger tank.

As an illustration of the immense advantage kept in hand by the Germans in terms of tank technology, a single Tiger tank operating in Normandy knocked out 25 British tanks, 28 armoured vehicles and killed an additional 80 infantrymen.

It seemed as if the British had learned nothing from their experiences in the desert a full two years earlier. The poor state of British and American

The poor state of Allied tank technology was little short of a scandal

tank technology was little short of a scandal. It left Allied tank crews disheartened and reluctant, a malaise which never affected the Germans.

made the earth unacceptably boggy; in North Africa the desert dust clogged engines and sharp stones tore the tracks; in Asia, where there were few tanks, the humidity affected the engineering. In nine days of fighting in Germany in 1945 the 9th Royal Tank Regiment and the 147th Regiment suffered 85 tank casualties – and only 17 were due to enemy action. No less than 36 succumbed to mechanical problems while 32 got stuck in the mud. Nevertheless, while tanks did much to speed the progress of Germans into France, they also helped to chase those same invaders out of France. This time the innovators were the British. A series of modified tanks were used to breach the beaches at Normandy. Witnesses reported that some German soldiers threw down their guns and ran at the sight of this bizarre new breed.

Behind them was Major-General Sir Percival Hobart. Like his brother-

> ## *A series of modified tanks were used to breach the beaches at Normandy*

in-law Montgomery, Hobart was outspoken and did not suffer fools gladly. His forthright manner won him few friends at the War Office and by 1940 he was retired. It was only the personal intervention of Churchill which installed Hobart back in the fight against Hitler.

■ HOBART'S FUNNIES ■

Mindful that Allied troops would encounter all manner of defences during the landings, his priority was to install tough armour to protect the troops. Then he looked at ways of tackling an amphibious landing, crossing a minefield, blasting a well-fortified pill-box and travelling with heavy vehicles across boggy ground.

To get hefty tanks ashore from landing craft, he came up with the Duplex Drive, an amphibious tank with propellers and a canvas skirt to protect it from the water. When the tank made it to the shore, the canvas was lowered.

An adaptation of the Churchill tank helped to combat the threat of minefields. On the front he installed a large rotating drum hung with heavyweight chains, turned by power from the engines. This 'Crab' would

ROMMEL – DESERT FOX

Erwin Rommel, courageous soldier and gifted leader of men, became known as the Desert Fox thanks to his cunning in North Africa.

The son of a teacher, Rommel joined the army from his home town of Württemberg as an officer cadet and proved his early promise during World War I. Between the wars he taught at Germany's military academies and authored a book about infantry strategies which was published in 1937.

When war broke out, Colonel Rommel was put in charge of the troops guarding Hitler. Frustrated with his behind-the-lines role, he seized the opportunity early in 1940 to command the 7th Panzer Division which he took into action in France before it was occupied, striking as far north as the Channel coast.

A year later he was put in charge of the German troops sent by Hitler to bail out the beleaguered Italians in North Africa. He shone in his new role, despite his misgivings about his wavering Italian allies. His impressive early victories won him the rank of field-marshal.

He was held in high esteem by his men for his initiative and bravery. In an example of his charismatic leadership, he once leapt from a car to address a division of men: 'There is an English Armoured Brigade getting ready to attack you from the north and in the south there is an English mixed force which is advancing. Take care that you are finished with the first before the second arrives!'

Yet he was all but ready to pull out his exhausted men when Hitler ordered a strike on Cairo in Egypt. Once again, he found remarkable success until his supply lines became hopelessly overstretched as he ventured further into British-held territory. Weakened by lack of essentials and wearied by months of fighting, he was finally defeated and pursued out of Africa.

In 1944 Rommel was ordered by Hitler to secure the French coastline against Allied invasion. Even though he was already convinced the war was unwinnable, he tackled the unenviable task with a deep professional pride. Yet he received little practical support from the Führer despite his warnings that all would be lost if the enemy penetrated the insubstantial coastal defences.

Although at heart he was non-political, Rommel was recruited by plotters who wanted Hitler replaced. The popular and realistic Rommel was their chosen leader. It is unlikely, however, that he knew about plans to assassinate the Führer for he was deeply opposed to killing for political ends.

In any event, an attack by British bombers put Rommel in hospital with serious injuries when the abortive coup took place. Hitler himself was reluctant to expose Rommel as part of the plot against him. He knew only too well that he was vulnerable to the grass-roots affection won by Rommel. So he dispatched two generals to see his reluctant adversary to offer a deal. Rommel and his family would escape the shame of public exposure if he would take poison and eliminate himself as a threat to Hitler. On 14 October 1944 Rommel did as his leader asked and was buried with full military honours.

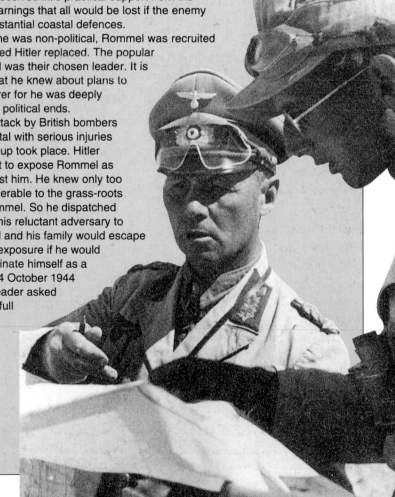

Right: **Rommel (left) confers with a subordinate during the desert campaign.**

explode the hidden mines without causing damage to the tank or its crew and could beat a path up a beach for soldiers to follow.

Another anti-mine device was the 'Plough', a harrow attached to a tank which would uproot mines before

> **When SS troops captured the crew of a Crocodile, they would shoot them**

they could do any damage. The 'Ark', a tank with four long beams at each corner, became a bridge to span small ravines and enable troops and armoured cars to cross.

Providing a roadway for troops and vehicles through soft ground became the job of the 'Bobbin' tank. It had a large, rolled, heavy-duty canvas roadway attached to its front. As the tank trundled along, it unfurled the roadway for following traffic. But

perhaps the most fearsome of his designs was the 'Crocodile', another modified Churchill tank, this time designed to throw a scorching flame for 120 yards. Attached behind was its own fuel depot on wheels. Its effect on the enemy was instant. So feared was this flame-thrower that when SS troops captured the crew of a Crocodile, they would shoot them straightaway. Inappropriately, the stable of inventions was called 'Hobart's Funnies' – although they offered little to the enemy to smile about.

■ RIFLES AND GUNS ■

These were not the only technological advances that assisted the Allies. In just four years, the advances in gun capabilities had been enormous. When the war started, the Allied stock of rifles dated mostly from the previous world war or before. Bolt-action guns like this were slow and cumbersome to carry and use.

Now rifles were smaller and lighter than ever before and fired faster too. Rates of fire were up in

machine guns as well. The British Bren could now dispense an astonishing 500 rounds a minute, the same as the US Browning. New mortars were light enough for infantrymen to carry with them into battle.

But just as these assisted the battle in one respect, they were a hindrance in another. The pack of equipment loaded onto the back of the infantryman was heavier than ever. Soldiers had to rely on good, old-fashioned mules in some cases to transport the guns to the top of high, hostile escarpments in rugged terrain.

Even then the pre-prepared defences installed by the enemy were strong enough to resist the firepower of such weapons. Only bombs would have a sufficiently devastating effect and that called for air support.

Left: Versatile Jeeps were put through their paces in Normandy during the autumn of 1944. Medics even used these rugged, four-wheel-drive vehicles to transport the wounded.

Left: **Allied soldiers in Burma used newer, more powerful weapons to get the better of their enemy.**

advantage over their Japanese enemy through the regular supplies dropped in by aircraft. In Europe and Africa, improving methods of amphibious landings allowed the trucks which were being turned out by the thousand in America to reach the battle fronts and replenish the men.

■ WILLYS JEEP ■

Transport had to be reliable and tough to be of any use. In 1940, the Jeep made its debut, its name derived from the full name first given it – general purpose (i.e. 'GP') vehicle. First constructed by the Willys Overland Company, this legendary creation had speed and agility and was an instant hit with the army. It could tackle even the roughest terrain and was useful for transporting troops, small arms and other light loads. It further helped to make horses redundant on the battlefield.

Given the firepower, the men made use of it, expending thousands of rounds of ammunition a day. The prospect of ammunition shortage, not to mention shortage of fuel for tanks and food for men, was a daunting one. As all armies discovered during World War II, a fighting force was only as good as its supply line.

In Burma the Chindits had an

◆ EYE WITNESS ◆

Sydney Hartley suffered a badly injured leg when he was in the third of three tanks sent forward to pinpoint the whereabouts of the enemy during a battle in the Tunisian campaign. It was later amputated just above the knee. He was 28 years old.

❝ I knew the dangers of crossing open ground on enemy territory but I clearly remember thinking that, with a bit of luck, we might again just get out of this unscathed with us being the last tank in a line of three.

After about 150 yards I heard the voice of the squadron leader come through my headphones. "Third troop, halt. Turn right and engage the enemy tanks." As we turned we realised we had run into a trap. Just coming into their final positions were two German tanks or self-propelled guns. We were all taken by surprise.

I knew this was the moment of truth, life or death. I quickly estimated the range, our big 75mm gun was loaded, I put the sights on the target and fired. It was impossible to follow the tracer bullet because the sun was lying just behind the target. Then it didn't matter as I saw the German tank's gun flash and a split second afterwards our world exploded. Everything suddenly went black and I felt what seemed like a red-hot poker against my right leg.

Flames were rising and I knew I had to get out quickly. I tried to pull myself out of the turret but at waist high I realised something was holding me back, because I was still wearing my headphones. Then I made a superhuman effort and flung myself the eight-foot drop to the ground. I knew something was terribly wrong with me. I heard this soul-destroying scream – it could have been any one of us. I dragged myself away. Looking at my right leg, the shock was more mental than physical. The armour-piercing shot had taken away half of my calf and broken up the calf bone. The foot was dangling from what flesh remained.

I took out a large field-dressing from my pocket and made a tourniquet. It looked like the driver and co-driver hadn't made it out of the tank. The next tank in line was burning although the crew got out safely. Mortar bombs were dropping all around. The troop corporal carried me to the rest of the men which was excruciatingly painful. I had morphine tablets but felt faint from blood loss. I didn't know which was most painful, my leg or the burns on my hands and face. The top skin of my hands peeled back like roller blinds. I had a very bumpy ride on a Bren-gun carrier back to the echelon alongside an injured German soldier and his friend.

I was laid out on a stretcher, looking up at the sky, when I saw a Messerschmitt 109 come into view. It appeared to be heading straight for me. He started machine-gunning us. It was the first of three aircraft attacks before I was put in the ambulance and driven away. ❞

REICH IN RUINS

By the end of 1943, the Germans were on the run from Stalin's forces. The Battle of the Atlantic had ended in their defeat and U-boats were being systematically blown out of the water. Germany itself was suffering a barrage of bombing campaigns, Italy had changed sides and, to many in the Nazi hierarchy, it seemed the war was already lost.

The following year brought little by way of relief. The long-awaited landings of thousands of Allied soldiers finally occurred in Normandy in June. When German soldiers were unable to defend the beaches, it was clear the destination for the Allies was nothing short of the German Fatherland itself.

During their first few weeks on French soil, the Allied armies encountered some strong resistance, particularly centred at Caen. Here was a professional SS division and a green German unit culled from the Hitler youth. Although some fighters were as young as 16, they were fired with enthusiasm and proved to be formidable opponents.

The British forces failed to capitalise on their surprise attack to gain their D-Day objectives and paid the penalty for their short delay while regrouping, as the Germans dug in with a vengeance. It took two major pushes, code-named 'Epsom' and 'Goodwood', to oust the few hundred Germans in residence, costing hundreds of Allied lives.

Countless numbers of French civilians died, mostly in the enormous air raids launched by the Allies which reduced the historic town of Caen to rubble. Fires raged in Caen for 11 days after the main bombing attack. Estimates put the number of French dead as high as 10,000. Still the German resistance held fast. The net effect of the air raids was simply to provide new hazards, like blocked roads, for the Allied ground forces.

■ TANK BATTLES ■

There were bitter tank battles between the newly landed British and Canadian forces and the Panzer units which rushed to the area from eastern France and Poland. Supplies began to falter when a gale blew up in the Channel on 19 June, wrecking the Mulberry harbours, onto which the Allies were unloading.

Churchill and the American leaders were filled with angry frustration. There was talk of sacking Montgomery for his failure to move forward. But while German reserves were embroiled in the battle, other Allied divisions were given a free hand elsewhere on the coast.

The Americans were making more headway. Having captured the Cherbourg peninsula, troops broke out to make a sweep through central Normandy. US troops discovered too the horrors of fighting in the Normandy bocages. This was the ancient hedgerow and field system covering the countryside providing havens for German snipers and hazards for Allied tanks and infantrymen.

Churchill and the American leaders were filled with angry frustration

The German reinforcements, which had at last made their way to Normandy, created more firmly held pockets of resistance, which were tough to shift. Falaise, Metz and a number of other towns formed serious blockages in the arteries of the Allied invasion.

Soldiers who on D-Day had never fired a shot in anger or seen a dead body were within a matter of weeks brutalised by the harshness of conflict. If they were fearful, they hid their feelings. Many were overwhelmed with elation when they killed an enemy soldier. As one US Ranger explained: 'It was not joy that I had killed him but that he hadn't killed me.'

Far left: French inhabitants and US soldiers rejoice after Cherbourg is won from the Germans.
Left: German soldiers surrender to the US military near Toulon, in southern France, following the invasion of the south of the country in August 1944.

By 15 August 1944 the Germans found southern France was also at risk. 'Operation Dragoon' got underway 10 weeks after D-Day, with the forces of the US 7th Army making landings between Toulon and Cannes and meeting only mild opposition.

The advance through France was known as the 'Champagne Campaign'

Among the soldiers to land at the beaches south of St Tropez was a 20-year-old Audie Murphy, later to be a Hollywood hearthrob, who single-handedly wiped out an enemy machine-gun nest.

The US forces drove up France, keen to link up with their comrades swinging down from the north. Such was the ease of the advance, and the joy of their reception by the French, it became known as the 'Champagne Campaign'. Paris was liberated by Free French forces on 25 August.

■ ARNHEM ■

By September, Montgomery and American general Omar Bradley had thrust through Belgium and Luxembourg. The fighting remained gruelling with British paratroops experiencing horrific losses when they tried to take Arnhem, Holland, at the end of September.

Finally, the successes of the Allies began to take their toll. The front line forces were running out of ammunition and other supplies while enemy soldiers were making stronger

Right: **Although General de Gaulle was never popular among Allied war leaders, he won the undying adoration of his people for his uncompromising views.**

◆ EYE WITNESS ◆

Rudolf Valentin was among the German soldiers who fought at Monte Cassino, and revealed some of his experiences to New Zealand author Alex Borrie. He saw some tough fighting as the Germans tried to recapture Hangman's Hill.

Our situation was not an enviable one. Whoever came out of cover during the day became a sure victim for the Indian sharp-shooter. The Gurkhas on Hangman's Hill were in a similar position. They also had to make themselves scarce during the day otherwise they drew German fire.

The set of circumstances meant that almost all attacks were switched to night-time. Just after the onset of darkness, we had to repel the first attack and two others followed. With the beginning of the new day, we had to creep into holes again which we enlarged with the spikes of our jack-knives. We had to survive the armed attacks in these holes.

In the evening the murderous close-combat began again. During this one often had to let the enemy advance until only metres away before one was able to recognise him by the shape of his helmet. In addition to this, hunger and especially thirst were also becoming factors.

At dawn on 19 March the 1st/FJR 4 [a German paratroop unit] came out to us with about 120 men from the monastery with the order to capture Rocca Janula again. After approximately 10 minutes of machine-gun fire and shelling our comrades overwhelmed the Rajputanis at the lower hair-pin curve and stormed the walls.

A terrible hand-to-hand combat flared up there. The Germans were attempting to scale the walls. They succeeded in blasting a hole in the wall. But the enemy from the Essex Battalion fought with the same determination and beat off the attack causing heavy casualties. Courage and the willingness to make sacrifices did not help at all. The castle could no longer be captured. This attack cost the lives of half the comrades, the rest had to retreat.

But the English and the Indians also suffered such heavy casualties that they had to abandon their intentions to capture the monastery in this way. On this day a ceasefire lasting several hours was agreed upon in order to recover the dead and wounded. It was at this point that we exchanged cigarettes with the enemy and helped each other out with bandages. The English even lent us stretchers to transport our wounded to the monastery. At the same time the Gurkhas took their wounded through our positions. A short time later the men who helped each other out in such a comradely fashion were once again the bitterest of enemies. What madness!

Right: German soldiers came uncomfortably close to succeeding in their objective of reaching the Belgian port of Antwerp during the Battle of the Bulge.

stands than before. Waiting for relief, the Allied initiative ground to a halt in December 1944 before going on to make headway in Germany.

The infantrymen were heartily relieved. It had been a long, arduous haul which cost many lives. Combat exhaustion as well as other maladies were striking the servicemen who had survived the fighting. Seemingly ceaseless rain and acres of mud weighed their spirits down.

■ SLOW ADVANCE ■

Many soldiers were weary of the inch-by-inch advance they had experienced in some of the fiercest battles waged on the Western front, which resembled the trench warfare known by their fathers two decades earlier. A rash of self-inflicted wounds began bringing waves of soldiers to the sick bays. Anyone who was suspected of having deliberately injured himself was instantly court martialled.

Their commanders, meanwhile, were frustrated in their desire to push relentlessly onwards. Hitler seized the

The fury of the American and British air forces was brought to bear on the Germans

opportunity to strike back. Choosing the same route which had served him so well some four years earlier, he proposed a surprise attack through the Ardennes with the intention of driving a wedge between the Allied forces and capturing Antwerp, the

Belgian port through which vital Allied supplies were being brought.

Luck was with the Germans as the bold offensive got underway on 16 December. Low cloud was keeping the Anglo-American reconnaissance aircraft on the ground. The Allied commanders had no idea of what was coming until it arrived.

Field-Marshal von Rundstedt commanded the German forces, comprising ten armoured divisions and 14 other divisions. However, only the 6th SS Panzer Army was up to full strength and adequately equipped. When the weather cleared, the fury of the American and British air forces was brought to bear on the Germans. Fighting raged on over Christmas and into the New Year, with the Allies gradually gaining the upper hand. The Battle of the Bulge, as it was called, was over by 23 January when the Allies took St Vith, the last remaining German stronghold. Another, less substantial German thrust into northern Alsace which began on 1 January 1945 was also quickly suppressed.

The cost of the two German assaults was high. Both had weakened the German defences elsewhere, a fact that didn't go unnnoticed by Allied commander General Patton. At last the fortified Siegfried line, built to protect Germany, was in danger.

February saw a further big offensive in north west Europe from the Allies. In a series of pushes the Allied armies managed to link up to form a formidable front line.

■ REMAGEN ■

They were bucked when a sharp-eyed US sergeant spotted a railway bridge left intact by the retreating Germans, spanning the Rhine at Remagen. The Germans had viewed the Rhine in much the same way as the English saw the Channel, a vital line of defence which would be hard to penetrate. Now troops forged along the bridge while further up- and downstream their comrades made less comfortable crossings on swiftly assembled pontoons. The defences of the Fatherland had been breached.

Airborne troops landed on a large scale helped capture stalwart German towns. By early May, key regions including the Ruhr, Hamburg, Bavaria and Austria were in the hands of the Allies. Yet the battles had been grim. The German defences were cleverly conceived and included mines and booby traps.

Frequently, the morale of troops was low. In addition to seeing bloody action and burying their friends, the infantry had to endure apparently endless hours of foot-slogging. Their rations were pitiful, consisting mostly of tinned spam, corned beef and soya sausages. Despite the strong cameraderie of men forced to suffer unspeakable hardships, there were numerous instances of insubordination and desertion in the field.

Meanwhile, Russian troops had been pouring into Germany from the east, their target Berlin. Even the most hopeful of German commanders must have realised the end was near when a tidal wave of Russian

Right: US army engineers attempt to put rails across the bridge at Remagen. Four hours after the picture was taken, the bridge collapsed into the Rhine.

troops overran the Silesian industrial basin in January. Albert Speer, head of war production, wrote a memo to Hitler, beginning with the words: 'The war is lost.' Speer realised that Germany could not sustain its industry or defence when the region which produced 60 per cent of its coal had been snatched from it. But Hitler refused to listen.

■ RED FLAG RISES ■

Russian generals Zhukov and Konev encircled Berlin by 25 April and began another relentless advance towards the very heart of the Reich. Fierce street fighting raged as loyal Nazis battled to stop the Russians closing in on their beloved Führer. Loyal members of the Hitler Youth aged 12 to 14 joined in. Despite their efforts, a Red Flag was raised over the Reichstag on 2 May 1945.

As for Hitler, he finally summoned his long-time mistress Eva Braun to be at his side in the middle of April, realising that his days were numbered.

His 56th birthday on 20 April was marked by more catastrophes in the field. Nazis including Goebbels, Göring, Himmler, Ribbentrop and Bormann joined him for the muted celebrations. They urged him to flee

south but Hitler refused to leave Berlin. In fact, he rarely left the 18-room bunker beneath Berlin's Chancellery that had become his home. With him were the commanders who had remained close to him, and his most valued aides.

He slept for no more than three hours at a time, partly as a result of the pounding of the incessant air raids. Incredibly, Hitler still talked of inflicting defeat on the Allies. The next day he ordered a last-ditch stand

> *Albert Speer, head of war production, wrote a memo to Hitler beginning with the words: 'The war is lost'*

against the Russians, bellowing that every last man should be thrown in. The counter-offensive never had a chance to get off the ground.

When Hitler finally realised there was no hope, he erupted in a volcanic fury, accusing all his closest commanders of cowardice and treachery. For the first time he spoke of killing himself. Still, he refused to abandon

Above: Soldiers of the US 9th Army flush out German soldiers in a battle-scarred town over Germany's western border. Meanwhile Russian troops bore down on Berlin from the east.

the war effort, a stand which cost the lives of countless German soldiers left fighting against atrocious odds around Germany.

Inside the bunker the nervous exhaustion and psychological tension among its occupants reached new heights. Although he was sometimes calm, Hitler exploded in rage when he heard that his hitherto faithful lieutenants Göring and Himmler were both making advances to the Allies for peace.

On 27 April, Hitler carried out a macabre rehearsal of his suicide and the deaths of the faithful still at his side. However, it wasn't until 29 April that he dictated his will to his secretary. There was no expression of remorse for the misery and death he had caused worldwide, only the same tired tirade against those he held responsible for his misfortunes: 'More than thirty years have now passed since in 1914 I made my modest contribution as a volunteer in the First World War which was forced upon the Reich. In these three decades I have been actuated solely by love and loyalty to my people . . .

'It is untrue that I, or anyone else in Germany, wanted the war in 1939. It was desired and instigated solely by those international statesmen who were either of Jewish descent or who worked for Jewish interests.'

The last paragraph in Hitler's will read: 'Above all I charge the leaders of the nation and those under them to scrupulous observance of the laws of race and to merciless opposition to the universal poisoner of all peoples, international Jewry.'

■ HITLER'S END ■

In the early hours of the same day, Hitler married Eva Braun and had a champagne celebration with Bormann, Goebbels, his secretaries and his cook. Within hours he heard of the death of Mussolini, shot with his mistress Clara Petacci and then hung by the ankles in a square in the centre of Milan.

On the afternoon of 30 April, with the Russians just a street away, Hitler said his final farewells, retired to a sitting room with his wife and shot himself. Eva chose to end her life by taking poison.

The instructions he left for the disposal of his body were carried out, with his remains being burned by petrol fire in the yard of the bunker. With Hitler turned to ashes, his successor as Führer, Grand Admiral

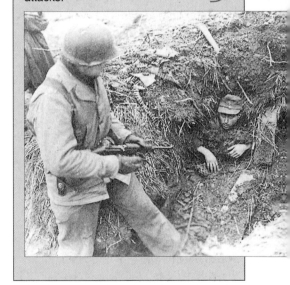

Karl Dönitz, commander in chief of the German navy, tried to negotiate a peace settlement, but the Allies were unimpressed. They wanted nothing short of an unconditional surrender. And so, as pockets of German resistance capitulated around the former Reich, the surrender was finally signed on 7 May 1945.

BLACK SANDS OF IWO JIMA

America's mighty war machine was now in top gear. In the field the US had the latest and the best military equipment. At home its colossal industrial muscle provided seemingly endless supplies of hardware. There were ranks of young men drawn from all over the States queuing up for action, full of grit and determination.

In opposition, an over-extended Japan was war-weary. The country's battle losses in ships and planes far outstripped the number of replacements being produced on the home islands. Japan itself was being starved of the materials it desperately needed by the naval blockade imposed by America. Its industry was targeted for devastating air raids. Long-term jungle fighting had taken its toll among the surviving troops, despite their rigorous training.

Yet still the Japanese soldiers were threatening and tenacious. Against all odds, they were determined to hold back the American advance. In-bred in the Emperor's men was an oriental code of honour which dictated that they must fight to the death. In most cases, this is just what they did, costing many Allied lives. The hallmark of the Pacific campaign was prolonged savage fighting and huge loss of life.

Right: Admiral William Halsey, commander of the 3rd Fleet, sits deep in thought on the bridge of the USS *New Jersey* en route for the Philippines.

were a selection of Japanese strongholds on New Guinea still to be beaten.

Meanwhile, Admiral Halsey, of the South Pacific sector, already had the Russell Islands, Vella Lavella and Bougainville in the Solomon Islands under his belt.

Both MacArthur and Halsey recognised the value of leap-frogging many Japanese-held islands and outposts, picking for attack mainly those that were inadequately defended. The rest were left to 'wither on the vine', increasingly isolated from Japanese lines of communication.

■ TARAWA ■

Now nine crucial atolls under Japanese control, collectively known as the Marshall Islands, had to be taken. A taste of the fierce fighting to come occurred on one of them, Tarawa, defended by 5,000 Japanese. When a similar number of US Marines landed

on the island on 21 November 1943 they found themselves pinned down on the open beach. Before night had fallen, 500 of the Americans were dead and a further 1,000 wounded. Japanese gun positions were only silenced when their entire crew was killed. Only an additional landing of

The hallmark of the Pacific campaign was prolonged savage fighting and huge loss of life

With a victory established in New Guinea by the start of 1943, Allied commander of the South West Pacific General Douglas MacArthur was already pondering his route to the Philippines, a campaign dear to his heart. Before he could take it, there

Left: General MacArthur remained determined to push the Japanese out of the Pacific. *Right:* An island beach devastated by gunfire becomes a depot for US troops.

troops won victory for the Americans. In all 1,000 Marines died along with virtually all the Japanese.

The Americans learned a valuable lesson. When it came to taking another atoll in the group, Kwajalein, there were no landings until a heavy bombardment neutralised much of the defence.

Fleas, flies, lice and mosquitoes were liable to be carrying appalling disease

Although the American campaign was fast, there was immense hardship for the troops brought about by the conditions. Fleas, flies, lice and mosquitoes plagued them. More than just pests, they were liable to be carrying appalling disease. It wasn't until 1944 that DDT sprays were introduced to combat the insect swarms.

Once an island was taken, it became a top priority to bury the dead on both sides. For the corpses attracted not only flies but also rats, which came in droves.

■ MARIANAS ■

Truk, a key naval outpost for the Japanese navy, came under fire on 18 February 1944 in a raid orchestrated by Vice-Admiral Marc Mitscher. There were 30 separate strikes at the base which destroyed 275 aircraft and 39 ships.

Next stop was Saipan in the Mariana Islands, a fearsome task given that 32,000 Japanese soldiers were garrisoned there. Nevertheless, it was a dual disaster for the Japanese. For soon after the American landings on 15 June came the Battle of the Philippine Sea, in which their Fleet Naval Air Arm was decimated.

◆ EYE WITNESS ◆

Ito Masashi spent 16 years in hiding in the jungle of Guam after it was overrun. He describes his reason for not surrendering in his book *The Emperor's Last Soldiers*.

'By the start of October the only sound we heard was the shell fire so far off that it sounded like distant thunder. But the fighting continued. The enemy no doubt considered it simply mopping up but for us it was a full-scale and bloody battle.

We had eaten what little there was of our portable battle rations of dried bread and now we lived on what berries and fruits we could find. We kept up a vain defiance with nothing left to help us but our grenades. But now the vital will to fight was absent. Our commanders sent messages advising us to end the senseless resistance, to give up our arms and pack it in. But somehow we didn't. We were afraid to.

Afraid that our useless rifles and guns – marked with the noble crest of the Imperial Chrysanthemum – might fall into enemy hands, we buried them deep in the ground. And we prepared, quite resignedly, for death as the only possible outcome. For us soldiers of Japan, the only thing left to our way of thinking was to deck out our last moment as nobly and bravely as we could.

By now there was no supply base for us to go back to and we didn't know whether there still existed any company or battalion headquarters where we could have got orders. So we formed sad and sorry little squads, hardly alive, now hiding ourselves away in the jungle, now moving aimlessly along the paths and lanes. We had been reduced to the status of a ragged band of stragglers. Even during this period however there were a number of incidents when we tangled with Australian troops backed by tanks or fell foul of a line of pickets. Fortunately, we always managed to get in our grenades and escape. But on every occasion the number of our already small band would dwindle by the odd one or two.'

And by July the defenders of Saipan were running short of ammunition. They chose to kill themselves by the score, along with the 22,000 civilians who had been living on the island since before the war, when it was a Japanese dominion. American troops looked on helplessly as women and children joined their menfolk in plunging from high cliffs to be dashed on the rocks below rather than face the ultimate shame of surrender. Saipan was under US control by 9 July.

The islands of Tinian and Guam were the next to go. Then the Palau group of islands. Although it didn't take nearly as long to achieve victory here as it had done on Saipan, the fighting was every bit as ferocious. It frequently included suicidal rushes at secure American positions by shrieking Japanese soldiers, who were duly mowed down in their masses. With fighters refusing to surrender in even the most hopeless of battles, the Americans were forced to use armoured flame-throwers to clear well-protected pockets of resistance.

By October 1944 the Americans were ready to redeem the Philippines. The island of Leyte was their chosen point for invasion, poorly defended by just 16,000 men. While a memorable victory was quickly carved out for the Americans at sea,

the land-based struggle for supremacy lasted longer, with the Japanese counter-attacking in December. The losses on both sides were heavy. The Americans mourned 15,500 fighters, while the Japanese suffered the body-blow of 70,000 deaths. Yet once Leyte was won for the Americans, the rest of the Philippines fell to them with gratifying ease.

At Iwo Jima the US Marines were cut down in droves by the defenders

Now it was time to approach the Japanese home islands. Choosing to by-pass several strongholds, including Formosa, the Americans decided to take the Ryuku Islands, less than 400 miles from Japan itself. A stepping-stone island between the

Above: US Marines hold their weapons aloft as they wade ashore on the stepping-stone island of Tinian, unsure about what awaits them beyond the beach.

Philippines and the Ryukus was deemed necessary as a rendezvous for American planes. Iwo Jima in the Bonin Islands was selected for invasion in February, while an operation to capture Okinawa, the largest of the Ryuku Islands, was timetabled for April.

At Iwo Jima the US Marines were cut down in droves as they tried to penetrate the complex defensive system constructed by the defenders. Bombardment by battleship prior to the landings had not obliterated the defences as hoped. In fact, the Japanese were so deeply entrenched it had made little noticeable difference.

Amphibious landing transports were beached and blown up and the Marines found themselves without an iota of cover on their route up the

'FRIENDLY FIRE'

'Friendly fire' took its toll during World War II, particularly during the Normandy campaign.

Bombers had failed to dislodge German gun emplacements before D-Day. This should have acted as a warning against so-called precision bombing. Yet American heavy bombers were called on in July 1944 to target the German lines. Instead, the bombs fell on US troops, killing 25 and wounding 131. The next day, the same mistake was made again, only this time 111 American servicemen were killed and 490 were wounded. Among the dead was US Lieutenant-General Lesley McNair, the highest-ranking Allied officer to be killed in the Normandy campaign.

Three weeks later, 'friendly fire' claimed more Allied victims from above. This time 77 Canadians and 72 Polish soldiers died. 'Friendly fire' incidents occurred through poor weather conditions, imprecise briefings, lack of training and sometimes through nervous fingers being on the trigger.

beach. There was also little opportunity to remove the wounded from the firing line.

Japanese commander Lieutenant-General Kuribayashi's order to his men was acidly clear: 'No man must die until he has killed ten of the enemy.' He added that each of his men must think of his defence position as his graveyard. It was widely considered to be the worst landing the Marines experienced in the war. Iwo Jima finally fell into American hands on 16 March after they had used bulldozers to bury defenders in their bunkers. The tally

Below: **Pinned down by mortar fire, Marines of the 5th Division inch their way up the slopes of Mount Suribachi, determined to seize Iwo jima.**

of dead among the Americans amounted to 6,821 but yet again there was a far more devastating number for Japan as virtually all the 21,000 troops were killed.

On 1 April the landings by the Marines on Okinawa, as part of 'Operation Iceberg', were in stark contrast to the blood-bathed beaches of Iwo Jima. An estimated 50,000 Americans got ashore barely hearing a shot and for the following five days there was hardly a skirmish. It was a deliberate lull engineered by the Japanese before they unleashed a storm of incredible violence.

The Japanese had drawn up a defence plan code-named 'Ten-Ichigo', which involved thousands of 'kamikaze' missions. The Japanese commanders

were even prepared to sacrifice their prized battleship Yamato in a suicidal attack. On 6 April the ship left its base with sufficient fuel for a one-way journey to Okinawa. Its aim was to wreak havoc there among the landing forces.

■ KAMIKAZE ■

However, soon picked up on radar, the great warship came under fire from 280 US aircraft until she was finally crippled and sunk on 7 April with her 2,300 crew still aboard.

Meanwhile, swarms of kamikazes were setting about the US Navy as it cruised off Okinawa. On the first day, three destroyers, two ammunition ships and an LST (Landing Ship Tank) were destroyed. It temporarily halted the drive forward, through lack of ammunition. On the next day a battleship, a carrier and two destroyers were hit. Of the 16 destroyers sent forward to give early warning of kamikaze raids, 14 were sunk before the end of the campaign even though they were of minimal stragetic value. The story goes that one destroyer's crew erected a poster complete with arrow bearing the words: 'To Jap Suiciders.'

Right: On Okinawa, advancing Americans were forced to use fire power to oust tough Japanese resistance.

Carriers are that way.' And still kamikaze fliers descended on the fleet.

During the battle to secure Okinawa, which raged between April and August, there were an estimated 2,000 kamikaze raids carried out by both army and navy aircraft as well as about 5,000 conventional sorties. In total 20 ships were sunk by kamikazes, often under a barrage of attacks by suicide pilots, against six sunk by other aircraft manoeuvres. Kamikaze planes notched up a further 217 strikes against ships.

Yet inevitably the Japanese resources were wilting under the strain. After two months of sustained kamikaze raids, there were few aircraft left for such missions.

On land the fighting was equally horrific. In one of the early battles, to win the off-island of Ie Shima and its landing strip, more than 4,700 of the 5,000 Japanese defenders died in battle. Towards the end of the eight-day confrontation, local women,

some with babies strapped to their backs, draped demolition charges around their necks and rushed at American positions.

It took until the last days of June to eradicate the last of the Japanese land-based resistance on Okinawa. Total American losses amounted to almost 7,000 men as well as numerous ships and 763 planes. Unusually, the Americans found themselves taking prisoners, some 7,400 in all. Many of these were too sick or severely wounded to kill themselves.

Meanwhile, 110,000 died in battle, with all the senior officers committing ritual suicide in their offices, and there was carnage among the population. The Japanese stood the loss of 7,800 aircraft.

> **After two months of sustained kamikaze raids, there were few aircraft left**

The hostilites in South East Asia were just as gruesome for the troops involved. Following the Chindit offensive into Burma and a second, unsuccessful, attempt by the British to re-enter Burma at Arakan, the Japanese commander in Burma, General Renya Mutaguchi, decided that going on the attack against the British in India was probably the best form of defence.

On 6 March 1944 the 'U-Go' offensive opened, with three Japanese divisions setting off for Kohima and

Left: Billowing smoke marks the path of a kamikaze plane which caused devastation on the USS *Bunker Hill*, hit off Okinawa on 11 May 1945.

Imphal, high in the Assam hills. For the first time in the conflict, British troops stood firm against Japanese aggression in defence of India.

■ KOHIMA ■

Both Kohima and Imphal were under siege by the first week in April. There followed some of the harshest fighting of the war.

Japanese soldiers were in the majority but the Commonwealth troops were in no mood to be routed this time. The bitterest of the fighting was at Kohima. Japanese soldiers had killed everything in their path until they reached the tennis court of what was once the Deputy Commissioner's bungalow. They dug in on one side while the defenders were holed up just 20 yards away.

Grenades and mortar bombs rained down on the Commonwealth forces, taking a toll on the troops. However, they repelled the frequent Japanese charges with surprising ease. Each one was accompanied by the traditional 'banzai' cry and screaming. The Allies were able to open fire and cut them down. There was little opportunity for the Allies to collect their dead. Bodies lay rotting on the ground, emitting a terrible stench. Sometimes they were buried where they had fallen, in shallow, inadequate graves, with arms or knees left exposed. A cloud heavy with the pungent smell of burning flesh hung over the Allied position as the Japanese cremated fallen comrades.

Both sides were racked with tiredness and riddled with disease

Both sides were racked with tiredness and riddled with disease. Any minor abrasion could quickly become life-threatening through septicaemia and gangrene. After 16 days of gruelling fighting the defending regiments were relieved by the 1st Royal Berkshire Regiment.

They left behind 1,419 dead, among them 19-year-old Lance

Above: **After a siege by the Japanese, the British 14th Army was finally able to open the Imphal-Kohima road.**

Corporal John Harman – born and bred on the tranquil island of Lundy – a strapping soldier who ran up to a Japanese machine gun, shot the crew and hoisted it up on to his shoulders to bring it back behind his own lines.

Further, he stormed a bakery held by the Japanese, set it on fire and came back to his dug-out with a wounded Japanese soldier under each arm. It was as he was returning from one of these astonishing feats that he was fatally wounded. He was awarded the Victoria Cross posthumously for his incredible efforts.

Airlifts by the American air force and RAF continued to aid the defenders of Kohima and Imphal. The Japanese soldiers had pitiful rations by comparison. It was a staggering 80 days before the Japanese were compelled to withdraw, with just a quarter of the original force left on their feet. Over half the casualties were claimed by sickness.

War at Sea

GRAF SPEE

When war was declared, the British people expected an instant torrent of bombs to fall from a sky blackened by enemy aircraft. The wail of the air raid siren sent people scurrying for shelter clutching their gas masks in fear of being enveloped in a cloud of poisonous chemicals.

It didn't happen and soon the opening stages of the war were labelled 'the Phoney war' or even 'the Bore War'. The sceptics at home who believed the war would be over once Hitler had his way in Poland had to wait nearly a year to see action over Britain. But at sea it was an entirely different story.

A lone U-boat set the tenor of the sea-farers conflict when the liner Athenia sailing out of Glasgow was sunk off Ireland the day after hostilities were officially opened. U-boat captain Fritz-Julius Lemp believed he had an auxiliary cruiser or troopship in his sights. In all, 112 lives were lost including 28 Americans. There was shock at such an atrocity, even in Germany, and it prompted fresh orders to the U-boat commanders, to target only freighters and Navy ships. It was only a matter of months before the tighter rules which governed the U-boats were disregarded once more, however.

> **More than 800 sailors died when a U-boat slid into Scapa Flow and destroyed a battleship**

The brutal attack on Athenia sparked an Allied blockade of Germany in which ships were stopped and searched at the rate of 100 a week. Although the Royal Navy did capture some German ships this way, it caused acrimony between Britain and other neutral countries who resented the intrusive action.

By the end of September 1939, 20 Allied ships had been floored by U-boats, including HMS Courageous,

lost in the Atlantic with 515 men. Even neutral boats heading to Britain bearing vital supplies were not safe from the prowling German submarines. Already the spectre of life without the benefit of essential sea-borne trading links was looming in Britain.

■ MAGNETIC MINES ■

Britain's mariners fared little better in October. More than 800 sailors died when a U-boat slid into Scapa Flow, the anchorage of the British Fleet 10 miles off the north coast of Scotland, which was thought to be a safe haven, and destroyed a large British battleship. Under the command of Captain Gunther Prien, the submarine manoeuvred through a narrow, unguarded channel leading into the

harbour area and dealt a deadly blow to the Royal Oak. Claims that the battleship's armour could withstand a torpedo attack proved to be nothing more than a pipe dream. Just 396 members of the 1200-strong crew survived.

Shipping not only had to contend with the phantom U-boats. Germany was laying hundreds of mines, with devastating effect. The Reich had pioneered a deadly magnetic mine which could be dropped by air on to the sea bed, to later rise and attach itself to any passing ship, with deadly consequences. It was far superior to the mines being laid by Britain, designed to defend its shipping.

Fortunately, one of the mystery mines was jettisoned in error on land. Thanks to one courageous naval officer who tackled the explosive, its secret of success became known. The antidote was 'de-gaussing', with an electric cable fitted to ships which neutralised magnetism. The plague of the magnetic mine at least to British ships was quickly overcome.

Above: After the Battle of the River Plate the *Graf Spee* limped into Montevideo for repairs. However, it could not escape its predators for long.
Left: U-boat Captain Gunther Prien was hailed a hero in his homeland for penetrating Scapa Flow.

Above the waves were the determined ships of the Reich's navy equally adept at picking off British vessels. Among them was the pocket battleship Admiral Graf Spee. By agreement before the war, the Germans were only supposed to build ships up to a certain size. These were tagged pocket battleships, larger than cruisers but smaller and less effective than battleships.

The Graf Spee slipped out of port just before war was declared, sidestepped the ensuing Royal Navy blockade and headed for the South Atlantic. It was then the pride of the German navy with its high speed and thick protective plating. In the first three months of the war, it had notched up nine British ships, including the liner, Doric Star.

Canny British commander

HMS Exeter, and two light cruisers, Ajax and Achilles, one from Britain and one from New Zealand.

■ CRUISERS DAMAGED ■

Graf Spee's captain, Hans Langsdorff, reckoned he could outgun the opposition, believing the heavy cruiser was accompanied only by destroyers. He opened fire, inflicting serious damage on the Exeter and the Ajax. The reply from the British ships crippled his own. With smoke pouring from the German ship, there was a chase led by the Graf Spee which was heading for the safety of Montevideo in Uruguay.

Although Uruguay was a neutral country, it was inclined to support the Allies. In international law, the Graf Spee was only entitled to stay in its capital, Montevideo, for 72 hours

waiting for a kill. Indeed, he believed the mighty Renown and Ark Royal had joined the pursuit when they were, in fact, hundreds of miles away.

Langsdorff deemed the situation hopeless and asked Berlin for permission to scuttle his ship, rather than have it fall in to enemy hands. Consent duly came.

Crowds had gathered on the waterfront eager to witness the great sea battle

---

On 17 December the Graf Spee set off slowly for the middle of the harbour. Crowds had gathered on the waterfront eager to witness the great sea battle that would surely follow. But they were disappointed. When the majority of the crew had safely disembarked, a huge explosion wrecked her and she sank to the estuary floor.

Langsdorff considered the incident a grave disgrace. Three days afterwards he wrapped himself in the flag of his beloved fatherland and put a bullet through his head.

■ NEUTRAL NORWAY ■

Churchill, First Lord of the Admiralty, instantly trumpeted the achievement of his navy even though it was gained by luck and misunderstanding on behalf of the enemy. Yet while Britain celebrated the triumph, it was far from the end of its troubles at sea.

Within a week in January three submarines, HMS Grenville and destroyer HMS Exmouth were sunk. There was little more by way of encouraging news for the British until February when HMS Cossack carried out a top secret raid on a German supply ship shelter in the waters of

---

◆ EYE WITNESS ◆

Bill Gamble, from Derbyshire, joined up in 1939 when he was 22. The following year, he became one of the thousands of men of the British Expeditionary Force evacuated from Dunkirk.

❝The Germans kept the beach under fire. I had never been under shell fire before. The Luftwaffe planes were strafing the beaches. There were rows and rows of fellows waiting to get on a boat. There was no panic because officers were there. They would have shot you if you had panicked.

I have got a vivid memory of the Welsh guards who formed the rear guard action which helped us escape. They were courageous men. I don't think I had properly fired a rifle until then. We didn't have half the equipment we should have had and there had been no training. We were just like civilians in uniform.

I was dead scared. Finally, I got on to a little barge and then on to a destroyer. When the waves came up we had to jump from one to the other. I landed in England on June 2. A few days later that destroyer got blown up. All those brave lads on the ship died.

At least when it came to D-Day, I wasn't bothered about it. By then I was properly trained. I had a job to do and I did it.❞

Commodore H. Harwood guessed that it was only a matter of time before the Graf Spee was lured to the River Plate, Uruguay, attracted by the rich vein of British shipping there.

At dawn on 13 December the Graf Spee was spotted at the river estuary. Lined up before it were the ships in Harwood's force; the heavy cruiser

and the Uruguayans stoutly refused to extend its deadline.

It gave Langsdorff enough time to transfer his injured seamen to a German merchant ship. The most pressing repairs were carried out. But Langsdorff knew that outside the protection of Uruguyan territorial waters lurked a bevy a British ships

Above: With Hitler's consent the pocket battleship *Admiral Graf Spee* was spectacularly scuttled off Montevideo.

neutral Norway. Aboard the *Altmark*, concealed in filthy conditions in a hold, were 300 prisoners taken by the *Graf Spee*. Regardless of international regulations which banned such action, the *Altmark* was boarded and the prisoners released. Norway protested about the violation of its neutrality. Its objections sounded somewhat lame, however, in the light of the fact that Norwegian authorities had apparently already searched the ship and apparently not found the captives. The daring feat persuaded Hitler that Norwegian waters should be under German control if his navy was to get the protection it deserved.

The Royal Navy continued its efforts to contain the U-boat threat and the activities of the German fleet until May 1940 when a task of much greater importance beckoned.

At the start of May, German forces had moved into Belgium. With characteristic speed, the Reich's forces overran Belgium, Holland and northern France. The lightning pace of the attack left everyone gasping for breath, not least the British Expeditionary Force, numbering some 200,000 men, which was sent to France at the outbreak of war to bolster French defences. The British

---

The Reich's forces overran Belgium, Holland and northern France

---

soldiers were driven relentlessly back amid some bloody fighting. With them was a section of the French forces, weary and disenchanted with apparently no hope of escape.

Commander of the BEF, General Lord Gort, had quickly realised there was no option but to withdraw his men by sea. The best and shortest route would have been from Calais to Kent, but the French port was almost in the hands of the Germans already. Dunkirk seemed to be the single remaining point from which any kind of meaningful evacuation could take place.

British and French soldiers staggered on to the beach at Dunkirk in groups or sometimes singly. All semblance of order was gone after the hasty retreat in which bands of men lost sight of their units. Communication between commanders and their men was cut inland. The soldiers, now acting on initiative, got to Dunkirk as best they could.

The French forces' commander in chief, General Gamelin, had been bemused by the German advance. His tanks, evenly spaced down the frontier, were unable to provide a striking action against the rear of the Germans. So while the Panzer armies were tiring and running short of supplies, there was no one to exploit their vulnerability.

Ironically, it was Hitler himself who called a halt to the German

Right: The *Altmark* lurking in Norwegian waters was holding British POWs when HMS *Cossack* attacked.

march. Concerned that vital tank divisions were at risk if they went into action against the by-now concentrated strength of the Allies on treacherous marshlands and would be unable to complete the invasion of France, Hitler stopped the key Panzer advance. He was made even more anxious by the counter-offensive of sorts that the Allies had managed to stage at Arras.

■ DUNKIRK ■

The strategy was perhaps sound. Hitler's decision came on 24 May when a comprehensive rout of the enemy seemed assured. Its unavoidable side effect was to give Allied troops two days' grace without which an evacuation from Dunkirk would surely have been impossible. Historians have subsequently speculated that, had the BEF been lost in northern France, Britain would have sought peace at any price as there would have been no army left to fight with.

As early as 20 May, Admiral Bertram Ramsay, the Flag Officer at Dover, had been gathering a small fleet capable of crossing the English Channel to rescue soldiers. At this stage it was believed just 35,000 men would be saved.

Still more and more men were straggling on to the beach until the ragged throng numbered 38,000. Many were by now unarmed, picking up weapons where they could which had been discarded en route or fallen from the hands of recently killed comrades. There were still rations of sorts, but many soldiers had been without sleep for days. Between periods of calm and order there was panic as the instinct of self-preservation got the better of men with

tattered nerves and a deep-rooted fear of what the future might hold if they were not rescued.

Each hour brought the Germans nearer. The shelling grew ever closer. Dunkirk itself was being blown to bits, offering little by way of protection for the British and French forces. There were attacks by the Luftwaffe, too. The low whine of oncoming aircraft followed by the clatter of its guns sent men diving to the ground for cover. Many never got up again.

'Operation Dynamo', the evacuation at Dunkirk, was officially begun on 26 May 1940

There was a feeling of resentment among many that the Royal Air Force was not doing its bit to aid the plight of the soldiers. In fact, its pilots were going up time and again, helping the rear guard defenders of Dunkirk or hampering the Luftwaffe high above the clouds. But the pilots' role was invisible to the eyes of the stranded soldiers – who were looking for someone to blame for their appalling predicament.

In peacetime Dunkirk had ample harbour facilities from which a major evacuation could have been carried out with ease. Now the town was rubble and the harbour installations in tatters. The only useful jetty left was wooden planking extending a mile into the sea. Yet it was valueless to the big ships for embarkation. Even the mildest wind would have blown the vessel into its concrete foundations causing damage below the waterline. As time went by it became clear that men would have to be taken off the beaches, no matter how cumbersome the task.

Operation Dynamo, the evacuation at Dunkirk, was officially begun shortly before 7pm on 26 May although in fact some support units had already been brought back to Britain. Before midnight fewer than 8,000 men had been brought home.

When the depth of the dilemma facing the bulk of Britain's army became clear, a flotilla of small boats was called upon to assist. Such boats already had to be registered with the government. Now they were recruited for the still-secret operation, with many civilian captains being allowed to stay with their ships.

The British public finally got to hear about 'Operation Dynamo' on

31 May, when about 194,000 British troops had been brought back under the guidance of the Royal Navy. When news about the crisis was broadcast, many more owners of small boats set sail immediately. This was the brave face of Dunkirk that haunts history.

◼ CIVILIAN COURAGE ◼

Their task was no easier than that faced by the Royal Navy. Bombardments by the Luftwaffe continued claiming the lives of servicemen and civilians alike. On 1 June the courage of the civilian boat owners reaped dividends when 64,429 soldiers were rescued. Having ferried their battle-worn cargo to safety, boat owners turned back to face the risks all over again in a bid to haul yet more soldiers to safety. Not least of their worries were the minefields that lay between them and their destination.

By any standards, the rout of the British army in France by Hitler's

---

The courage of the civilian boat owners reaped dividends

---

forces was nothing short of outright defeat. Yet the way in which the cream of the British army slipped through the Führer's grasp and the courage of the evacuation gave an element of heroism to the event, which set it apart from other ignominious military debacles suffered by the British, and has ensured it a special place in British military history.

The soldiers who made it back were full of criticism for the army that had sent them to France inadequately armed and supplied. Yet

within a few days or weeks, most were posted again, in many cases back to France where remnants of the British contingent were still fighting with the French to keep Hitler out of Paris.

The last Allied boat pulled away from the beaches of Dunkirk on 4 June with the remnants of the

338,000 rescued British and French soldiers aboard. Each man was precious and represented the future fighting force of Britain. Yet behind the retreating force lay its equipment, without which no army could fight. Before leaving, the BEF had sabotaged 63,900 vehicles, 289 tanks and 2,472 guns.

◆ EYE WITNESS ◆

Miner Wilf Cowie was 25 when he joined the army and was part of the British Expeditionary Force in France which evacuated from Dunkirk.

We were in France on the Belgian border for about six months with very little happening, just a bit of bombing and shelling.

When the retreat started, we had to make our way over fields because the Germans were patrolling the roads. The worst thing I ever saw were the refugees streaming out of Belgium pushing prams and carrying beds just machined gunned by German planes. Hundreds of them were killed.

I was one of the last to get out of Dunkirk. It was horrible on the beach. We were lying in bomb craters on the beach, expecting every day to get away. Every day seemed to take forever. Luftwaffe planes were firing at us and then there was the shelling. That was the worst thing of all. The shells screamed as they were going over the top of you and you never knew where they were going to land.

Once I took shelter in a bomb hole with three other lads. I was the only one who came out alive. The others were killed by a machine gun blast from an aeroplane.

There were hundreds of lads killed. We had to go and get the identity discs from the bodies and give them to our superiors. It was a bit upsetting but it was just a job that had to be done. We saw so many young men dead that in the end we didn't worry about it.

I came back in a trawler. It took 36 hours to reach the east coast after the skipper diverted to avoid mines. Several men on the boat died when they were hit by machine gun fire from Luftwaffe planes passing overhead.

Above: Devastation of the beaches of Dunkirk following the evacuation.

U-BOAT MENACE

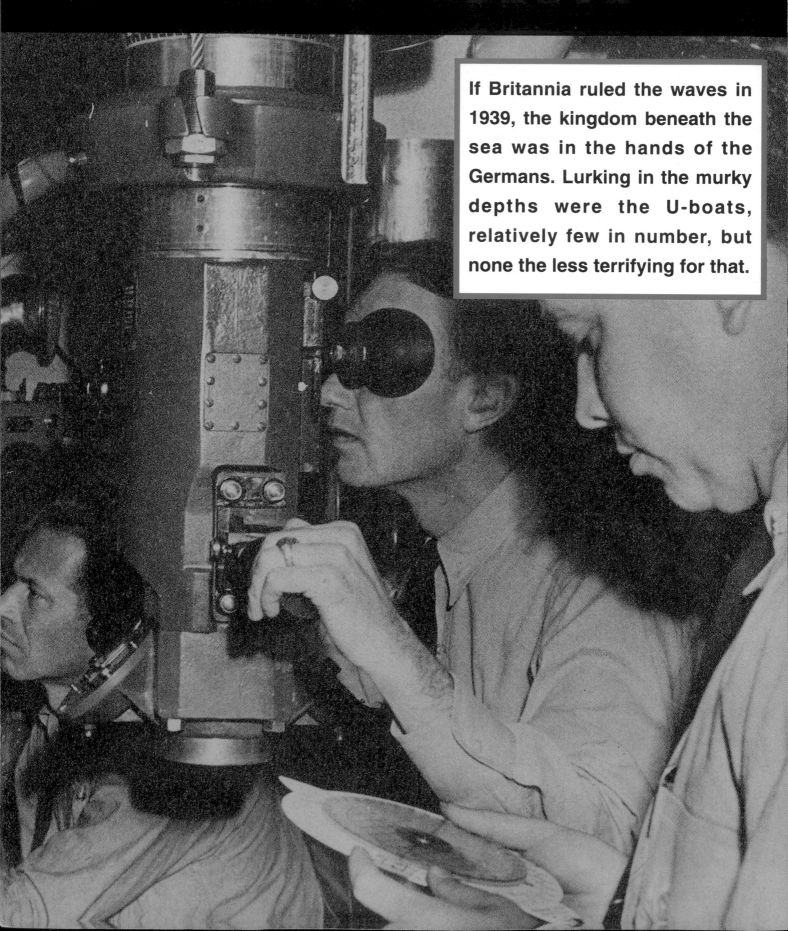

If Britannia ruled the waves in 1939, the kingdom beneath the sea was in the hands of the Germans. Lurking in the murky depths were the U-boats, relatively few in number, but none the less terrifying for that.

Just a mention of the name could strike fear into the stout hearts of the English sailors. Winston Churchill confessed later that the U-boat threat in the Battle of the Atlantic was 'the only thing that ever really frightened me during the war'.

For U-boats (Unterseeboot in German) had a habit of creeping up on British shipping and sinking it without warning. At first merchant ships seemed very much like sitting ducks if U-boats were in the area. There appeared to be little opportunity to dilute the threat.

Britain, Canada and America lost thousands of tons of cargo, not to mention scores of seamen, to the prowling U-boats. Bitter experience finally taught the Allies effective defences and, later, vital offensive tactics which would ultimately neutralise the stealthy foe.

U-boats soon began to hunt in 'wolf packs', an idea thought up in

Above: German U-boats came close to their goal of strangling Britain.

Germany in the mid-1930s in which a group of submarines orchestrated their attacks on convoys. At first, the concept was thwarted by a lack of boats. Sometimes, in the early stages of the war, there were only a handful of submarines to put to sea, the others being in dock for repairs or in use for training. The lack of air

By the summer of 1940 there were two 'wolf packs' operating in the Atlantic

support from the Luftwaffe to the U-boat service also slightly lessened their menace, since they were compelled to search, sometimes for days, for convoys.

However Raeder, commander in chief of the Kriegsmarine was conscious of the golden opportunity that was open to him. While finding it almost impossible to keep more than six U-boats in the sea at a time before February 1941, he devoted much time and energy to rectifying the short-coming. Before the year

was out the number of U-boats in his fleet had been increased tenfold.

By the summer of 1940 there were two wolf packs operating in the Atlantic, preying on the convoys as they made their way with precious food, goods and, later, troops to Britain from America. Submarine commanders could now pinpoint convoy positions thanks to the German Radio Monitoring Service (B-Dienst). Slung across the Atlantic, the U-boats formed a deadly chain from which the convoys could not escape. The aim was for the boat which first spotted the convoy to shadow it until other submarines could gather for a mass attack. In October, three convoys lost 38 ships to U-boats in the space of just three nights.

■ U-BOAT TECHNIQUE ■

The technique used by the U-boats continued to improve. At first, commanders attacked from positions both above and below the waves. Their firepower was far more accurate, however, when the U-boats were on the surface. It became

Above: Admiral Karl Dönitz knew the potential of his U-boat fleet. *Left:* The Allies also had submarines.

accepted procedure for the boats to sneak into the centre of a convoy, surface after dark and wreak havoc, disappearing before daybreak when the first of the Allied flight escorts arrived. On the surface, the sleek machines, powered by diesel engines, could outrun larger convoy escort vessels with relative ease.

> ## On the surface, the sleek machines could outrun larger convoy escort vessels

There followed a 'happy time', as it was known among German submariners, in which dozens of merchant ships were sent to the bottom. They were picking off targets with ease and the convoy escorts were floundering with exasperation, not knowing how to halt the rising casualty toll. In 1940, U-boats accounted for more than

Right: Sailors keeping watch from a surfaced submarine got a drenching.

1,000 ships while just 16 U-boats were knocked out. The following year followed a similar pattern with 24 U-boats being sunk.

■ AMPLE WARNING ■

Had there been a greater number of U-boats operating at that time, Britain would have been in grave danger of being throttled. Hitler was delighted with the success of the U-boats. Always sceptical of the power of his naval fleet, he became a

Above: One U-boat torpedo was enough to break a ship's back.

convert and lavished his favours on the U-boat arm. If he had devoted more resources to them in 1939 instead of waiting until 1941, the outcome of the war might have been very different. By the time his confidence was raised in the potential of the U-boats, it was just one of many services forced to get in line for the available resources.

As it was, technology came to the rescue for the Allies. Britain finally cracked the German radio code signals. Now operators could give ample warning to the convoys as to the whereabouts of the U-boats. Ships began to successfully bypass the waiting packs which were now forced to stretch out over huge distances, diminishing their effect.

Operators could give ample warning as to the whereabouts of the U-boats

Although the sinking of the liner Athenia at the beginning of the war did serve to tighten up the rules of engagement which governed U-boats, these were soon relaxed, in part because it was difficult for submariners to abide by such rules without putting themselves into considerable danger. Stipulations like the one laid down in the 1935

Below: **In 1942 the remains of a convoy approach beseiged Malta.**

 ◆ EYE WITNESS ◆

The following personal account of life aboard a patrolling British submarine in the Mediterranean appeared in the *Daily Express* in June 1942.

'The captain is wearing shorts with a sweater handy in case it is chilly. His favourite dress while submerged in action is a towel wrapped around his loins.

The crew are wearing overalls, shorts, shirts, vests – anything they fancy. There are no badges of rank and it is impossible to tell the captain from the cook.

Life goes on quietly, almost dully, for some days while the submarine continues towards her patrol station. There are only seven gramophone records, some of them scratched and indistinct through constant wear. The captain tells the first lieutenant he will brain the first rating to play *Frankie and Johnnie were lovers* – he swears he has heard it 3,000 times.

At midday the next day the captain is resting in his cabin. The first lieutenant is at the periscope. He swings it, sees smoke on the horizon. Without ceasing to look he says: "Captain, in the control room". The murmur is taken up and goes around the boat. Within a matter of seconds the captain is at the periscope clothed in his towel. He looks and says: "There is smoke on the horizon – a couple of masts."

Then the orders come fast. "Diving stations, full speed ahead together, starboard 25, steer 320." The hum of the motors can be heard through the otherwise silent submarine.

There are three merchant ships escorted by six Italian destroyers. The captain grabs his slipping towel as he snaps the range – 8,000 yards.

Excitement in the submarine is terrific and suppressed. Nobody speaks except the captain. At times the silence is so intense that a movement by a rating sounds like thunder.

As the torpedoes jump from the tubes the submarine shudders a bit. The captain's towel falls off. Nearby ratings chuckle at naked authority.

Stop watches have already started to mark the time the torpedoes take to reach the target. The captain's: "I'll have a cup of tea, please," is hardly necessary. The electric stove was switched on some minutes before. It is a ritual. Everybody in the service knows that you must have a cup of tea before the depth charging begins.

In 55 seconds the explosion which means the target has been hit rocks the submarine. The captain sits on the engine-room artificer's tool box, sipping his tea. Then the first depth charge arrives.

The captain's cup leaps off the tool chest. The submarine vibrates with the clangour of charges exploding nearby.

For two hours the racket of the depth charges goes on. The men behave as if they were on tiptoe. Barely a word is spoken. As the noise of the depth charges dies away the submarine creeps to periscope depth. The captain sees three destroyers picking up survivors from the sunken merchantmen.

One of the ratings off duty has already got hold of the "Jolly Roger" skull and cross bones flag of the submarine service and is preparing to stitch another chevron to the other battle honours. They will fly it when they get back from patrol.'

London Submarine Agreement that submarines must stop intended victims and order the crew into lifeboats before opening fire were soon forgotten. The hunter quickly became the hunted if he lingered too long trying to establish the identity and purpose of a ship in the Atlantic. Neutral shipping was also at risk from German U-boats. Some vessels flying the flags of unaligned countries were hit by accident. Others, suspected of aiding the British, were rammed or torpedoed on purpose.

In November 1939 neutral countries were warned by Germany that their ships could not be guaranteed a safe passage in waters around the British Isles. Meanwhile, secret instructions to U-boat commanders gave them the go-ahead to sink tankers and other, key commercial ships approaching Britain unless they were identified as Russian, Japanese, Italian, Spanish, Greek or American. To cover their tracks, the U-boat commanders were told to use only electric torpedoes which did not leave a tell-tale wake in the water. It meant the explosion could be blamed on an engine fault or a mine.

It wasn't only in the Atlantic that the U-boats plied their deadly trade. Six were broken into pieces and transported by road to Linz in Austria where the water was deep

enough for re-assembly and were then launched into the Black Sea. The first to go into action there took to the water on 28 October 1940.

Operation in the Mediterranean was difficult for the U-boats – which were known by numbers rather than names – as their dark forms could be quickly spotted in the shallow, clear water by aircraft above or nearby ships. Also, the fast flowing eastern currents assisted the U-boats as they

---

It wasn't only in the Atlantic that the U-boats plied their deadly trade

---

sailed into the warm seas but thwarted their exit.

Nevertheless, it was there that the U81 sank HMS Ark Royal on 13 November 1941, one of the prestige ships of the Royal Navy.

Above: Relief as a German U-boat and its crew return safely to port after a long spell on patrol.

Far easier was the task of the U-boats in the waters off America and Canada. Until Japan's attack on Pearl Harbor and Germany's subsequent declaration of war on America, Hitler had ordered that any ship bearing the stars and stripes standard be allowed freedom of the waters. There had been sinkings of US vessels before December 1941, but presumably these were in error.

When America and Germany were eventually pitted against each other, the U-boats seized the opportunity for yet another 'happy time'. U-boat commander in chief Karl Dönitz, the man who was later to take over from Hitler as Führer of Germany, knew his forces had to pounce before America became wise to the threat.

Five of the largest submarines, called Type IX boats, were dispatched from the Mediterranean

◆ EYE WITNESS ◆

Stoker Fernand 'Pedro' Guinard, 69, from Halifax, Nova Scotia, served on several Canadian warships including HMCS St. Laurent.

❝ My first contact with the enemy came early in the war when we picked up 27 survivors from the German submarine UB31. We were four days out of Newfoundland.

A lot of these guys were Czechs and Poles. They told me they'd been offered the chance to fight in the navy or go work in a slave camp. You couldn't really blame them for joining up. I got quite close to them because I had to detail them to hand pump the bilges.

Even that got me into trouble. When we docked and disembarked the POWs, two of the Germans came over to shake hands and say goodbye. That didn't go down well with the officers. I got warned in no uncertain terms not to fraternise with the prisoners.

We only killed one submarine in my first three years of service. But we saw plenty of attacks on our convoys. I remember one time when a wolf pack began torpedoing our boats at sunset. It was so sad to see these ships going down. There were people in the water everywhere but to be honest we didn't give a bag about them. There were guys in a life raft obviously looking for help and we just rode straight through them throwing out depth charges. All we cared about was getting the submarine.

Was I scared? I didn't have much time to be scared. I was part of a team and you just got on with your job. ❞

where they were then operating to North American coastal waters in 'Operation Paukenschlag'.

■ EASY TARGETS ■

Americans living along the eastern seaboard had so far been virtually untouched by the war. There were no blackouts, built-in defences, or restrictions on radio use. Even navigation lights remained helpfully in place. Not only did the U-boats have easy targets but, after the 'kill',

the pursuing submarine hunters were inexperienced and ill-prepared. There was little to stop the U-boats getting clean away. In 'Operation Paukenschlag', each boat averaged almost six 'kills' before returning to home waters. Some of the boats sunk were those who had traversed the Atlantic in a convoy to pick up a cargo only to be sunk, as the British saw it, through a reckless lack of defence on behalf of the Americans.

A further wave of 12 smaller boats did their utmost to match the grand total but, thankfully for the Americans, fell short of the target. Within a few months, America began using convoy systems in its home waters

and mimicked the successful British methods of hunting U-boats.

The tentacles of the U-boat campaign also spread into the southern oceans. There were plenty of ships carrying essential goods which

> ### *Within a few months, America began using convoy systems in its home waters*

Below: **Living conditions on a U-boat were cramped and uncomfortable, with restricted fresh food and air.**

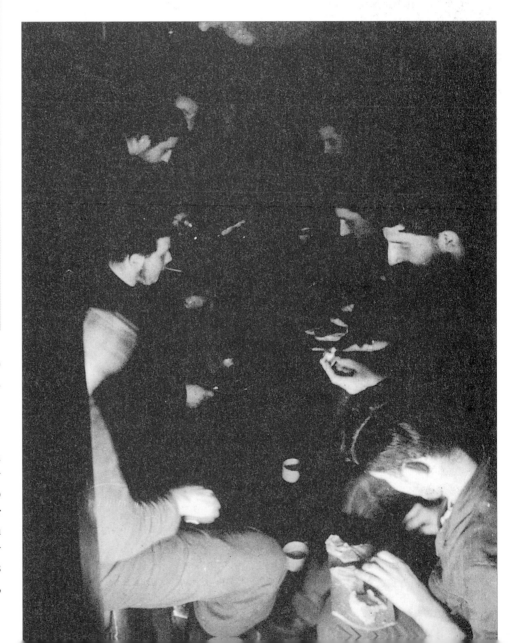

were poorly equipped to deal with U-boat attack. In addition, it further stretched the Royal Navy ships charged with hunting for submarines.

Not all of the 1,300 U-boats put to see by Germany during World War II saw action. Some were used for train-

> ## U-boat men got about double the rates of pay awarded to other sailors

ing, others for supplying the roving hunters. Still more U-boats were employed carrying goods from the far east to the Fatherland.

Men who served in the U-boat arm of the Kriegsmarine (German Navy) were considered the elite by their countrymen – although they were loathed and detested by the British. There can be little doubt that they had strong nerves and plenty of

Above: A U-boat in harbour is loaded with supplies before embarking on another lengthy ship-bagging voyage.

courage. Some were volunteers, attracted by the excitement the service appeared to offer. This was perpetuated by the public accolades awarded to U-boat aces like Gunther Prien and Joachim Schepke. U-boat men also got about double the rates of pay awarded to other sailors.

Other men who found themselves serving on the U-boats were naval recruits who had been drafted.

Yet aboard a U-boat, the day-to-day life was far from glamorous. Conditions were cramped. There was a curtained-off cabin for the captain but there were not enough beds for every member of the crew. Some men slept in hammocks, while others slept on the floor.

■ LIFE EXPECTANCY ■

Until hostilities began with America, the U-boat commanders had little idea of the distances their crafts were able to travel. They were pleasantly surprised to find they could cruise far further than they ever thought possible if they conserved fuel by keeping to reasonable speeds and travelled on the surface.

More supplies were needed on a long voyage, however. They took up valuable living accommodation, leaving the crew of about 50 even fewer comforts. Water was rationed

MASCOTS

Animals featured as mascots to the branches of army, navy and air force throughout the war. On HMS *Duke of York*, the ship's tabby cat was Whiskey who became famous for sleeping soundly through the battle which sunk the Scharnhorst. A cat called Susan made herself at home on a Royal Navy tank landing craft and even attended the D-Day invasion. A St Bernard by the name of Bamse was the mascot of the Norwegian fighting ship *Thorod*. He assured himself a place in the heart of his crew by rounding them up from shore leave by visiting their favourite bars and clubs – even boarding a bus to patrol the more far-reaching destinations.

One of the more unusual mascots of the war was a Syrian bear by the name of Voytek, adopted as a cub by the Second Polish Transport Company in Persia. He was thought of as human by his soldier pals who watched distressed as he cried like a child when his carer, Lance Corporal Peter Prendys, disappeared from sight. His love of water led to the shower room having to be locked to prevent him from exhausting the water supply. When he discovered an Arab spy, he was acclaimed a hero and allowed a morning's free play in the bath.

It was as a hero he was greeted in Scotland at the end of the war where he served the army until 1947 when his owner was demobbed. It was then he was handed over to Edinburgh Zoo where he had to get used to a new life behind bars.

and the opportunities for washing were few. The atmosphere was squalid, sweaty and unpleasant.

Early models were even more spartan than the rest. There was inadequate heating aboard. So men soaked from taking their turn on the watch when the boat was on the surface found themselves unable to dry their sodden clothes. Men wore layers of jumpers and still felt chilled.

When the most primitive U-boats were forced to submerge, the men

Above: A U-boat is armed with a giant torpedo before a trip.
Left: Sailors stood little chance when a U-boat was blown up.

had to wear breathing masks to prevent poisoning by carbon monoxide. Later, more sophisticated air purifiers were built into the wall of the ships, so masks became obselete.

Voyages lasted for months at a time and there was little chance to

The greatest shadow over a U-boat crewman was his brief life expectancy

breath fresh air. U-boat men operating in the darkened Arctic region during the winter months were known to queue up patiently for a glimpse of sunlight.

Perhaps the greatest shadow over the life of a U-boat crewman, though, was his brief life expectancy.

During the first two years of war, their existence was perilous due

Left: Depth charges were one antidote to roaming U-boats.

or fewer ships, many making no hits at all before they were sent to the ocean bed.

The U-boat force gradually became more impotent prompting the desperate Dönitz, by now admiral of the entire Kriegsmarine, to order a kamikaze-style attack by them following D-Day.

■ RECKLESS ATTACK ■

On 11 June 1944 he issued an order which read: 'The Invasion Fleet is to be attacked with complete recklessness. Every enemy vessel that aids the landing, even if it puts no more than half a hundred men or a tank ashore, is a target calling for all-out effort from the U-boat.

'It is to be attacked even at the risk of losing one's boat. When it is necessary to get to grips with the enemy landing fleet, there is no question of any regard to danger through shallow water or possible minefields.'

Even with the benefit of hindsight it is difficult to discern whether the U-boat captains, fired by their leader's words, carried out assaults

---

entirely to the shortcomings in their torpedo systems. Then, when they bore the brunt of Allied air and sea power, U-boats became an endangered species. Apart from torpedoes and mines, the only weapon the U-

German sailors grew into the habit of calling their craft 'iron coffins'

boats could use against their enemies was an undersized machine gun which could do little in the face of a concerted attack. German sailors grew into the habit of calling their craft 'iron coffins'.

After attacking, there are examples of U-boat captains displaying concern for their victims, passing on food and water and radioing their position so help could be sent. Survivors were never allowed on board, however.

Equally, there were tales that abounded in Britain of men from sunken ships being machine-gunned to death by callous U-boat captains

---

as they lay helpless in the water. While that may have occurred, there is the strong possibility such stories were used for propaganda purposes by a Ministry of Information which depicted U-boat captains as callous, dedicated Nazis.

The most successful U-boat was U48, which came into service in April 1939 and sank a record 59 ships before being sunk itself in October 1943. Many of the submarines, particularly those commissioned in the later years of the war, sunk five

---

ORAN DILEMMA

In one of the most controversial moves of the war, Churchill turned British guns against former ally France a little more than a week after the armistice with Germany was signed.

A British squadron led by Vice Admiral James Somerville encircled the pride of the French fleet harboured in the Algerian port of Oran on 3 July 1940 as part of 'Operation Catapult' and issued an ultimatum to the ships sheltering there to sail for Britain or America. When the order was refused, the mighty force of British ships including the ill-fated battlecruiser *Hood* opened fire.

Prestige ships, among them the *Provence*, *Bretagne* and *Dunkerque* were sunk or badly damaged and 1,300 French sailors were killed. The aim was to prevent the ships falling into German hands but it caused a major outcry in France and among French-speaking nations around the world.

Churchill said he regretted the loss of life but insisted the action was necessary. 'I leave the judgement of our actions with confidence to Parliament. I leave it to the nation and I leave it to the United States. I leave it to the world and to history.'

The French ships in British ports were confiscated with barely one shot being fired.

and were defeated or if indeed the U-boat force was already so depleted and poorly supplied that they were unable to take any meaningful action. Certainly, there is little evidence of U-boat activity in the Channel following D-Day.

Despite the Allied successes in combatting the U-boat menace, the Nazi hierarchy continued to pin great hopes on the success of a renewed campaign. Hitler, keeping faith with the U-boat service, was convinced the newest model designed by Germany was a war-winner. In his diaries, dated 6 March 1945, his loyal aide Goebbels reflected those optimistic opinions. With the Allies crossing the borders of Germany into the Fatherland itself, he wrote: 'There is

considerable hope for us here. Our U-boats must get to work hard; above all it may be anticipated that as the new type gets into action, far greater results should be achieved than with our old U-boats . . .'

Later, on 28 March, barely a month before the collapse of Hitler's Germany, he noted the Allied bombing campaign against the new submarines in dock at Bremen and penned with satisfaction: 'Clearly the revival of our U-boat war has made a great impression on the war.'

Below: Another convoy ship falls victim of U-boats, Hitler's underused war weapon.

BATTLE OF THE ATLANTIC

During World War I, German U-boats almost succeeded in severing the supply routes from America and Canada to Britain. Without shiploads of goods, including fuel, from overseas the prospects for Britain were dim.

Unable to support herself, Britain had for years relied on trade to keep her people fed, clothed and employed. If those vital links were cut during conflict, Britain would have been forced to capitulate – or see her population starve. Now in World War II the grim scenario was being played out once more. U-boats, in tandem with the German Navy or Kriegsmarine, were set to exploit the Achilles heel of the British Empire. They nearly succeeded.

Both Britain and Germany's navies had been unprepared for war. Navy chief Erich Raeder had far fewer U-boats at his disposal than he would have liked. In addition, the submarine construction programme was virtually at a halt. Hitler had little faith in his navy and earmarked only limited resources for it.

Meanwhile, Britain had a mighty fleet of Royal Navy vessels and numerous merchant ships. But the Admiralty appeared to have devoted little time or effort in the years between the wars in looking at ways to counter the U-boat threat. It still believed in the outdated notion that wars could be won with offensive action by battleships.

Putting their lives on the line alongside sailors in the Royal Navy were volunteer merchant seamen. It was their job to ferry the all-important supplies to Britain, mostly from America and Canada across the Atlantic. Instantly, they became targets for the roaming U-boats. Their pay was £9 a month with an additional two shillings and sixpence in danger money.

Instantly, the convoy system in which merchant ships banded together and travelled under armed

The major threat in the Atlantic was always from U-boats

escort was employed once again, as it had been with marked success in World War I. There were some drawbacks, however, which made shortages more acute on the homefront. For example, it took valuable time for a convoy to be assembled and some ships were compelled to travel by a longer route than they otherwise would have done. Speedier ships were impeded by the pace of slower vessels. Also,

Left: **Freezing weather in the Atlantic had the crew thawing out anchor chains.**
Below: **U-boats on far-flung missions were dependent on supply ships.**

dockyards became hopelessly congested when a glut of ships arrived all at once.

■ ESCORT SHIPS ■

Nevertheless, the accompanying Royal Navy ships at least offered some protection to the merchant fleet. At first, however, the short range of the accompanying ships meant that escorts could only be offered for some 200 miles out of Britain. The convoy was then on its own until it met with a reciprocal Canadian escort a few hundred miles from the other side. It offered a mid-Atlantic gap which was ideal for hunter U-boats.

Even the proximity of the armed destroyers at the outset and close of the voyages proved little deterrent to the U-boats in the opening years of World War II.

The major threat in the Atlantic was always from U-boats and sometimes from merchant ships fitted out with weaponry, known as armed raiders. Hitler was unwilling to risk his capital ships in the open sea after the Bismarck disaster. Lacking any aircraft carriers, the Germans were unable to launch air bombardments out of range of their airfields.

If they operated at night, the U-boats often went unnoticed by the escort ships even on the surface. Low

---

By the close of 1940, more than 4,700,000 tons of British shipping had been lost

---

in the water and much smaller than a surface ship, the most vigilant watch could be forgiven for letting the streamline craft slip by.

The only technology available to counter the threat from U-boats was Asdic, a sonar device which sent out

underwater impulses that could, by the sound of the echoes, indicate the presence of solid objects. Not only was it almost useless used at speed or against surface objects, but early models were also unable to produce an accurate range and operators were woefully inexperienced.

In a bid to flush out U-boats during the early months of the war, Royal Navy warships attempted sweeps of convoy routes. The U-boats would simply dive and wait for the danger to pass. Even if their presence was detected, there was every chance the depth charge dropped by a pursuing vessel would fall short of its intended mark.

As the war progressed, Germany eased the way for its U-boat captains in their task of sinking trans-Atlantic shipping by providing new ports from which they could operate. The fall of Norway and France offered plenty of fresh and friendly harbours

for repairs and restocking. In port, the U-boats were housed in specially built bunkers with two metre thick walls. That meant that although the docks came under heavy fire during Allied bombing raids the U-boats remained safe. It wasn't until 1944 that the Allies found sufficient fire power to shatter these solid defences.

By the close of 1940, more than 4,700,000 tons of British shipping had been lost in the form of 1,281 vessels, about one fifth of the pre-war merchant fleet.

◆ EYE WITNESS ◆

Dennis Bell, 67, of Water-looville, Hampshire, was one of the youngest seamen to sail with the D-Day invasion fleet. At 16 he was a galley boy in the merchant navy, serving aboard the converted troop ship _Liberation of Europe_. His pay was £2 per week, including £1 3s 4d 'war risk money'.

"I spent the early months of 1944 chugging along the south coast to drop off soldiers for secret beach-storming exercises. Looking back, I was incredibly naive about the whole business of war. I was only a kid and I knew nothing. I used to think I'd be all right because I was wearing my lifejacket.

By D-Day I'd already had a taste of the Atlantic War. At 15 I was galley boy aboard a crude carrier called the _Robert F. Hind_, bringing oil from the States to Britain and North Africa. Nobody would ever tell me what was going on – they would just shout at me to get back to the galley and work.

I soon cottoned on to the fact that none of the escort ships wanted to come too close to us. Obviously a tanker was a nice juicy target for the U-boats and if we'd gone up in flames we'd have lit up the sky."

Left: Crewmen on board an escort warship observe the progress of a south-bound convoy.

Above: Always alert, seamen knew the threat of attack was never far away.
Right: Germany housed her precious U-boats in sturdy concrete bunkers.

In May 1941, the first convoy to receive protection for the entirety of its voyage set sail. It was an important first step towards victory in the Battle of the Atlantic.

Soon after came the introduction of radar, still far from foolproof but a huge boon to the navy ships charged with spotting predators. Radar also

Now, at last, aircraft could be brought to bear against the undersea menace

aided Coastal Command aircraft as to the whereabouts of U-boats. Now, at last, aircraft could be brought to bear against the undersea menace and the planes posted to coastal duties appeared to be reaping a reward. Britain's Admiralty,

without a fleet air arm, was constantly battling to keep those few planes in place when many in the RAF and the war office thought they would be better employed bombing land-based targets in Europe. It took several years for the Germans in command to become fully aware of the danger posed by radar to its U-boats.

Also, the British cashed in on a fatal flaw of the wolf pack system

used by U-boats, in which a handful of craft operated together during a convoy attack. To alert nearby boats of the presence of a convoy, the German commanders had to use their radios. The prospect of the British being able to track the signals was dismissed out of hand by the Germans for months. But that is just what did happen when the High Frequency Direction Finder was pioneered, affectionately known as

'Huff-duff'. When the U-boat position was fixed by the radio operators, it gave Royal Navy vessels far greater scope in their attack.

Convoy defences were reorganised so that extra escort boats could loiter above a submerged submarine for up

1941 proved to be a key year for the Allies in their fight against the U-boats

to two days, waiting for the craft to surface for air. Then it was an easy target. Other vessels manoeuvred themselves around the precious convoy ships to fill the gap left by the

lingering vessel for fear that another U-boat would make merry in the unexpected opening.

In the British armoury, too, was the increasing ability of the decoders to pinpoint the position of U-boats. At the start of the war, the translation of the messages sent between the German admiralty and its ships was slow and provided only retrospective information. With practice, the 'tapping' system speeded up, providing accurate and detailed assistance for convoys and British ships on the whereabouts of the enemy. While the German commanders suspected a breach in security, they never identified where the leak was.

So 1941 proved to be a key year for the Allies in their fight against the U-boats. Although 432 ships were

Above: **A US destroyer pulls alongside HMS *Norfolk* to refuel mid-voyage.**

sunk, the total was down on the previous year. The U-boat arm lost 35 of its craft.

When the U-boats turned their attentions to the pickings off America in early 1942, the pressure on the Atlantic convoys eased. But when the U-boats returned to Atlantic waters, it was with a vengeance.

■ AIRCRAFT ATTACKS ■

At last U-boat manufacture was coming up to the levels hoped for by Dönitz. Every month, 20 new U-boats left the ship yards.

The boost for the Kriegsmarine was bad news for British sailors in the Atlantic who found themselves once more at the heart of a fierce battle for survival. Although the extended air patrols aided the safety of the ships and significantly improved the rate at which U-boats were knocked out, it was still a fearful fight to the death. U-boats began to attack once more during daylight hours, a sign of their boosted confidence.

During August and September alone U-boats – helped by the German advances in cracking British codes – found 21 convoys and sank 43 ships. By the end of 1942 Allied tonnage totalling 7,500,000 had been

Below: A cargo ship is lost amid smoke and flames following an air attack.

Above: When a convoy put to sea, the Atlantic throbbed with activity.

sunk, more than the combined totals for the three previous years of war.

Allied aircraft stepped up the numbers of attacks against U-boats during 1943 after the long-awaited allocation of more long-range

> ## Between March 1943 and the end of the war, air attack accounted for 290 U-boats

aircraft. Between March 1943 and the end of the war, air attack accounted for 290 U-boats alone. A surface U-boat could offer little by way of defence to an aircraft as its guns were so small as to be useless.

Suddenly, the campaign against U-boats was accelerating. That spring eight U-boats were lost in the battle to protect one convoy. During May alone 41 were sent to the bottom of the ocean, causing a concerned Dönitz to pull the ranks of remaining U-boats out of the Atlantic for a few

The importance of the Battle of the Atlantic suddenly loomed large for Hitler

months. Still, he failed to question the security of his cipher system.

The importance of the Battle of the Atlantic suddenly loomed large for Hitler, who had previously been wholly absorbed in his bid to conquer Russia.

In January 1943 Admiral Raeder was replaced as

◆ EYE WITNESS ◆

Swedish-born Nels Olson, 72, from Chicago, USA, was a gunner in the US Navy Armed Guard, responsible for manning 5-inch guns on Atlantic convoy merchant ships.

❛ There were 1800 of us in the Armed Guard and they split us up to around 25 per ship. I signed up in December 1942 and was assigned to the *Alcobanner*, built during World War I. Later I moved on to Liberty ships. The US built 2,700 of these during the war and it was just as well because the Germans sank so many. I guess we lost nearly 800 in the first eight months.

The Armed Guard took heavier losses than any other US naval unit. Merchant ships were a prime target because there was so little with which to defend them. We knew it was bad when we volunteered. They only took volunteers. No one was ordered to do it.

When the German submarines got in among a convoy it was a terrible sight. They always attacked at night and there was always pandemonium. I remember watching an oil tanker explode. It lit up the skies for miles around. And we had no target to fire back at. ❜

commander in chief of the Kriegsmarine by Dönitz. Hitler saw Dönitz with new eyes after the impressive successes of the U-boat war. Now Dönitz found it impossible to achieve similar standards.

U-boat production was still relatively

Left: **Young, fit men were always needed for the fight against the U-boats.**

healthy, despite an increasing shortage of manpower in the dockyards. However, the lack of crews was becoming a dilemma for Dönitz who was compelled to send barely trained men into action despite the fact he believed the success of the U-boats lay at least in part with a rigorous training for the men aboard.

■ LIBERTY SHIPS ■

The Allies, meanwhile, had the bonus of Liberty ships – rapidly made craft which went to replace the mercantile fleet decimated by U-boat action. By July 1943, the number of new ships coming out of the American yards

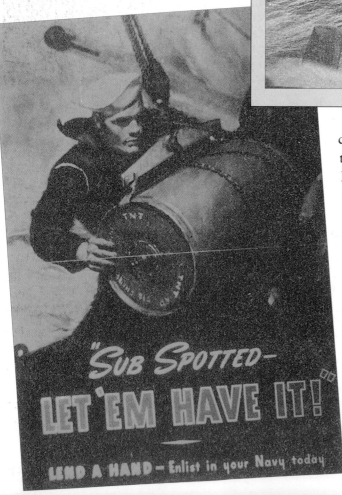

"SUB SPOTTED—
LET 'EM HAVE IT!

LEND A HAND - Enlist in your Navy today

was greater in total than the amount being lost.

With losses being so severe, the pack formation was abandoned in the autumn of 1943 and U-boats returned to the Atlantic hunting alone, cutting their effectiveness.

In looking at the Battle of the Atlantic, it is important to remember the contribution made by Britain's own submarines. During the war they sank 15 U-boats. Only three British U-boats were sent to the bottom by U-boats. Submarines were never sighted by their own kind until they were at very close range. For a successful attack to be presse home, the two could be no more than half a mile apart. The first U-boat fell victim to HMS Salmon as early as December 1939.

■ **COST OF CONFLICT** ■

In the last four months of 1943, the U-boats succeeded in sinking 67 ships at a cost of 64 U-boats. Clearly, the Battle of the Atlantic was lost by the Germans although it would be months before shipping in the Atlantic was completely safe from U-boat attack.

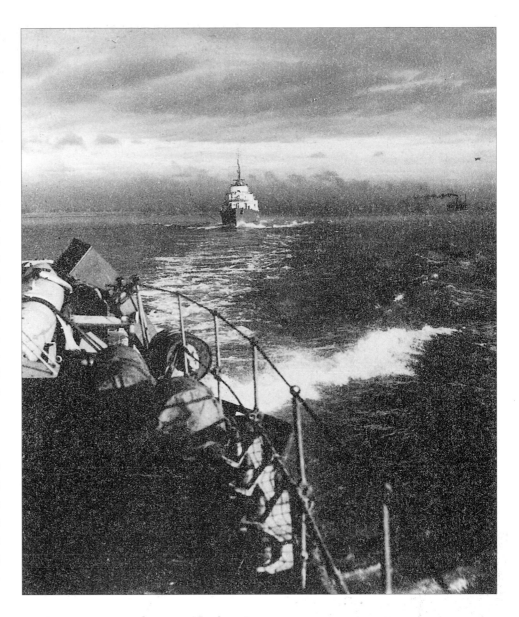

Above: A convoy reaches port, thanks this time to the Royal Canadian Navy.

At the end of the war, it became clear that the conflicts at sea – chiefly the Battle of the Atlantic – had been costly for both sides.

During the war, the Allies lost 5,150 merchant ships, 2,828 of them to U-boats. The number of merchant seamen who lost their lives amounted to 50,000. The U-boat tally also included 148 Allied warships.

As for the U-boat arm, 785 of its 1,131 strong fleet were lost, costing the lives of at least 27,491 crew and officers. About 5,000 were taken prisoners of war.

◆ **EYE WITNESS** ◆

J. H. Blonk, from Eindhoven, Holland, was blinded in one eye in 1941 when he was serving as an engineer on the cargo ship *de Friesland* which was hit off the English coast.

❛ We knew that if we were hit, we were on our own – the other ships would not and were not allowed to turn back otherwise they would be easy targets. The ship saunk so fast that we didn't even manage to get a float from the deck.

I can still remember how the wireless operator who I shared a cabin with was standing beside me. Then the water came and I never saw him again, I just felt his hand on my leg.

I was in the water for four hours. I held on to a panel from the deck that had gone overboard. An English communications officer was holding on to the other side. After an hour or so he said to me: "I think I'm going to let myself go, I'm so tired, I can't hang on any more."

I begged him to keep going. After he went, I lost all conception of time and that is the greatest danger for a drowning man – he thinks he is bobbing around for hours when in reality it is a much shorter time.

After four hours a trawler returned from the convoy to see if there were any survivors. Thirteen members of a 27-man crew were saved.

MATAPAN

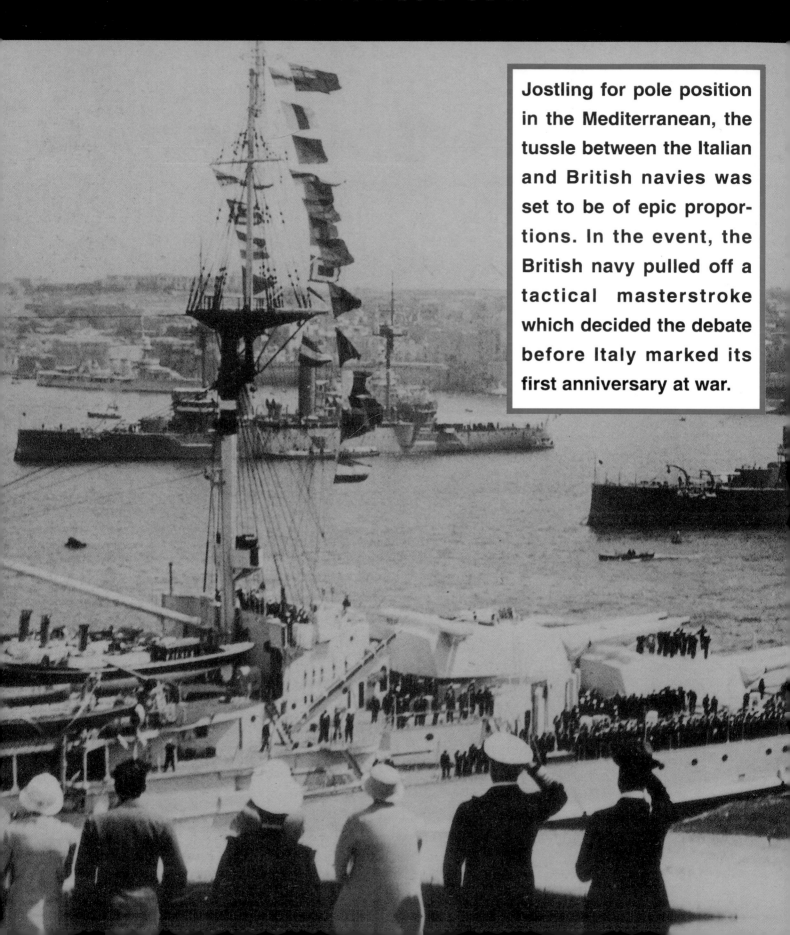

Jostling for pole position in the Mediterranean, the tussle between the Italian and British navies was set to be of epic proportions. In the event, the British navy pulled off a tactical masterstroke which decided the debate before Italy marked its first anniversary at war.

Britain had its own Mediterranean fleet. Key bases for Britain were Gibraltar, at the teeth of the Mediterranean, the hard-pressed island of Malta and Alexandria, the Egyptian port operating under Admiral Sir Andrew Cunningham, from which supplies were being shipped to Greece.

Italy had well-established ports of its home territory opening into the Mediterranean and the Aegean as well as control of Albania and Libya, on the northern coast of Africa.

When war broke out, the British had a grasp of Italian naval codes and gathered enough information to sink nine Italian submarines before the end of June 1940. But a fortuitous switch in cipher systems by the Italians in July prevented the British from cracking the codes again.

The Italian air force wasted no time in bombing the British big ships when they were at sea. Italian intelligence about British sea traffic was

The Italian air force wasted no time in bombing the British big ships

good. It enabled her captains to circumnavigate all convoys to Libya around the British forces.

Against this background, Cunningham was determined to punish his Italian enemies and put to sea 16 times between June and October 1940. Yet he only managed to track Mussolini's ships three times.

So it was a priceless morale booster for the British when, on 11 November 1940, the Fleet Air Arm

attacked Taranto, an Italian port. In port were six Italian battleships. A dozen Swordfish aircraft from the aircraft carrier Illustrious took off at dusk and flew 170 miles to deal the blow to the Italian navy vessels, struggling to gain height with their heavy load of explosives.

They notched up two strikes with hits against the battleships Cavour and Littorio. A second wave of Swordfish arrived less than an hour afterwards, directed to their target by the blaze now roaring at the base. Together, they damaged the battleship Duilio. At a cost of two aircraft, the Italian fleet was deprived of three valuable battleships – Cavour permanently; Littorio and Duilio until the late spring of 1941.

The Italian navy was still a force to be reckoned with, however. Admiral Cunningham was determined the threat they posed to Allied shipping in the Mediterranean should be rubbed out.

At the turn of the year, Fliegerkorps X, the Luftwaffe's anti-shipping force, transferred 200 of its aircraft to Sicily. By 10 January 1941

bombers from the precision corps landed six bombs on Illustrious and also struck Warspite, although neither ship was terminally damaged.

It demonstrated, however, the need for air superiority if the Allies were to control the Mediterranean. Unfortunately, there was a shortage of Allied aircraft in the area, worsened when the Illustrious was hit again while in dock at Malta. Air attacks against Malta were so heavy and so frequent that it proved impossible to carry out adequate repairs to the much-needed aircraft carrier there. Consequently she had to be withdrawn from the Mediterranean.

■ ITALIAN THREAT ■

The British resolve to eradicate the Italian naval threat hardened and its objective was carried out in spectacular fashion, off Cape Matapan, the most southerly point of Greece. On 27 March 1941, a British reconaissance plane spotted a large gathering

Above: Italian cruisers *Fiume*, *Gorizia* and *Pola* undergoing manoeuvres.
Left: HMS *Revenge* sets sail from Malta in 1939, before the siege.

of Italian ships. The squadron comprised eight cruisers, the prestige battleship Vittorio Veneto and a host of destroyers. Vittorio Veneto was the pride of the Italian fleet now her sister ship Littorio had been holed by the British at Taranto. Now she was poised with her support vessels to blow convoys destined for Greece out of the water.

Cunningham was instantly informed at his base in Alexandria. To back the aircraft sighting there were messages passed through the Italian secret service cipher which had been broken by the Allies. He

Below: **The big guns of the *Vittorio Veneto* unleash their fire power.**

DAKAR DEBACLE

Among the military calamities faced by Britain in the first half of the war was the debacle of Dakar. British ships sailed to the colony of French West Africa with the aim of landing Free French Forces who would wrest control from the Vichy regime.

As they anchored off the main port of Dakar on 23 September 1940, General de Gaulle broadcast a series of messages to the colony's governor stating his intention to land troops. All of the messages were ignored. Five messengers sent ashore with similar news were likewise rebuffed.

De Gaulle began threatening to use force. In reply, the coastal guns and ships at anchor in the port let off a barrage at the British ships, preventing the planned landing. The next day the exchange of fire continued with the British battleship *Barham* being struck. Twenty four hours later the battleship *Resolution* was hit, this time sustaining more serious damage.

At this the British commanders and de Gaulle realised that their carefully laid plans to steal a march on Vichy France was quite literally being shot to pieces. Consequently, the ships pulled out of the engagement and returned humiliated to Freetown, the capital of Sierra Leone. Apart from the damage to its ships, the British also had to endure a reprisal air raid by the leaders of Vichy France directed against Gibraltar.

abandoned the case and slipped back aboard the battleship Warspite in time for an evening departure. Fortunately, the British ships did not pull out until after the Italians had carried out aerial reconnaissance of Alexandria harbour which revealed all were still at anchor. Italian Admiral Iachino was satisfied the British posed no danger.

The two forces, both travelling in independent groups, first clashed in the morning of 28 March. After 40 minutes of exchanging shells, neither

The British launched wave after wave of aircraft to pester the Italians

side had scored a hit and the action was broken off. The British launched wave after wave of aircraft to pester the Italians who were themselves left virtually completely unprotected by their own air forces – which were stationed in easy range.

grouped together three battleships, the aircraft carrier Formidable, four cruisers and as many destroyers as he could muster. If trouble was coming, the Royal Navy together with its Australian contingent were prepared.

Admiral Cunningham then made a move to protect the secrecy of the British activities which has since gone down as wartime folklore. A keen golfer, he played regularly in the same club in Alexandria as the Japanese consul who reported every move made by the British Mediterranean Fleet to its enemies. Not only did Cunningham take his clubs to play golf that afternoon but ostentatiously carried a suitcase, clearly bound for a night ashore. Having duped the tell-tale consul, he

Above: Vittorio Veneto **was the jewel in the Italian navy crown.**

Vittorio Veneto was hit by one torpedo but still managed to escape the ravages of the air bombardment. However the cruiser Pola was stopped in her tracks by British firepower. Iachino, who was without the benefit of radar and still apparently oblivious to the presence of British big ships, ordered two other cruisers to assist her. That night all three were attacked at short range. Two were quickly sunk without firing a shot. Pola and two other vessels were also sent to the bottom.

■ TIMED EXPLOSIVES ■

The British ships in the vicinity picked up 900 survivors before being scared off by the arrival of Luftwaffe planes. A further 270 men were plucked from the sea in the subsequent days but still the Italian casualties amounted to a devastating 2,400. The Battle of Matapan had been the biggest naval engagement of the war so far and dealt a serious blow to the Italian navy.

Vittorio Veneto was not to escape for long. A British submarine torpedoed her again in December 1941.

Despite the inferiority of Allied air cover, the Royal Navy continued to carry out admirable harrassing manoeuvres against the Italians and the Germans in the Mediterranean. Most notable were the contributions made by the cruisers Aurora and Penelope operating out of Malta who targeted convoys destined for Libya with immense success. Hitler and Mussolini were counting the cost of the contribution to the North African campaign made by the small island.

But the British didn't have it all their own way. When U-boats arrived in the Mediterranean, the fleet was deprived of the aircraft carrier Ark Royal which was sunk in November 1941, as well as the battleship Barham and two cruisers.

If the Italian navy was down, it certainly was not out as its attacks against British ships berthed in the harbour at Alexandria in December 1941 amply illustrated.

In the naval armoury were minute submarines, nick-named 'pigs' by

their crew who were clad in frogmen's suits and sat astride the 22ft long craft. The 'pigs' were carried close to their position by regular submarines. Then it was the job of the crew to go in close to the target and attach timed explosives.

The Italians had made two abortive attempts using 'pigs' against the British during August and September 1940. This time there were to be no mistakes.

The Battle of Matapan dealt a serious blow to the Italian navy

After dark on 18 December an Italian submarine picked its way quietly and cautiously through mined seas to the approach of Alexandria harbour. There it off-loaded three 'pigs' and six crew, with a noiseless ripple on the water.

Now the Italian frogmen got to work. Beneath the waterline of the

Royal Navy battleship Queen Elizabeth, one team placed an explosive charge. Without being noticed, the two divers scrabbled ashore and posed as French sailors until they were seized by Egyptian police some time afterwards.

The second Italian team struggled to affix explosives to the side of a tanker. They were cold and stricken with sickness after spending too long underwater. But they didn't emerge from the water until their task had been completed. Egyptians arrested them as they attempted to pass the first control post of the harbour.

Below: Vittorio Veneto smokes after attack by British Albacore planes.

One member of the third team passed out but bobbed back to the surface and clutched a buoy until his partner finished the job in hand. The latter was having problems of his

---

The men were still there when an explosion sent the ship lurching to portside

---

own, meanwhile, with a torn diving suit exposing him to lethal cold. Then the 'pig' plunged to the sea bed. Despite the growing effects of exposure, he dived to retrieve it,

Above: Probably the last photo taken of the Italian big ships before Matapan.

manhandled it 60 feet back to the base of his target, the Valiant, and set the detonator.

He and his partner, now recovered, were picked up out of the water by a British motorboat and interrogated aboard Valiant. When they refused to speak about their operation, they were sent into the bowels of the ship close to where the charge was planted. The men were still there when an explosion sent the ship lurching to portside. They witnessed the effects of the blasts on the Queen Elizabeth and the tanker, too, with satisfaction. All the vessels would be

MALTESE CROSS

Malta was awarded the George Cross in April 1942 after four months of continuous bombardment by the Axis air forces. As the Royal Navy battled to get convoys containing vital supplies through to the island, they were hampered by U-boats and airborne attacks which wrecked merchant shipping. It wasn't until August 1942 that a convoy arrived intact. With the volley of bombs coming from the sky the people of Malta and the beleaguered defending forces were subject to the most appalling privations. Yet Malta was a key point in the Allied defences. Had it fallen into the hands of Germany, Rommel would probably have won the battle for North Africa and the outcome of the war might have been different.

out of action for some considerable time to come.

The Italian navy with Luftwaffe assistance continued to blockade Malta, the island which held the key to victory in North Africa. In December 1941 the Germans flew 169 bombing raids over Malta. In January 1942 the number rose to 262. Of course, the devastation took effect and Axis convoys began seeping through once more as Allied ships were put out of action, deprived themselves of fresh supplies.

Nevertheless, Churchill was determined to keep Malta in Allied hands at all costs.

■ DAILY BOMBINGS ■

It wasn't until March 1942 that a British convoy managed to slip through the Italian net bringing in vital supplies. Attempts to get supplies to the island in June failed. Yet still the vicious air bombardment continued. Much of the island was laid waste by the daily bombings as Hitler and Mussolini plotted an invasion.

In answer to a pressing need for raw materials, the Allies planned a convoy of unprecedented size and strength in 'Operation Pedestal'. Setting off from Gibraltar to guard the supply ships were three aircraft carriers, two battleships, seven cruisers, 34 destroyers and eight submarines. The US carrier *Wasp* was also in evidence to bring new air forces to the island. The convoy departed on 10 August 1942 and came under repeated air attack. Both the Luftwaffe and Italy's Regia

Churchill was determined to keep Malta in Allied hands at all costs

Aeronautica launched endless attacks with dive bombers, torpedo bombers and fighter aircraft.

In the four day battle which pursued the convoy, the carrier *Eagle* was lost when it was sunk by U73, the cruisers *Cairo* and *Manchester* and the destroyer *Foresight* were sunk and ten out of the 15 merchant ships were floored. Many of the surviving escort ships were damaged. The Italian navy, denied air cover by its own airforce, refused to join the offensive and fell victim to a British submarine as it made its way back to port.

■ CRITICAL LOSSES ■

But even though the losses were critical, Malta was saved. Supplies that did filter through, amounting to some 30,000 tons, allowed the islanders and its battered forces to rebuild. It continued as a vital Allied base and deprived the Axis powers of a toehold which would have given them access to North Africa and the Middle East.

Woollen skull cap covered with a fine mesh camouflage net

Mouthpiece and airtube

Rubber tunic, water tight at the wrists, neck and waist

Under water breathing equipment and oxygen bottle

Rubber trousers

Frogmen feet

SINKING THE BISMARCK

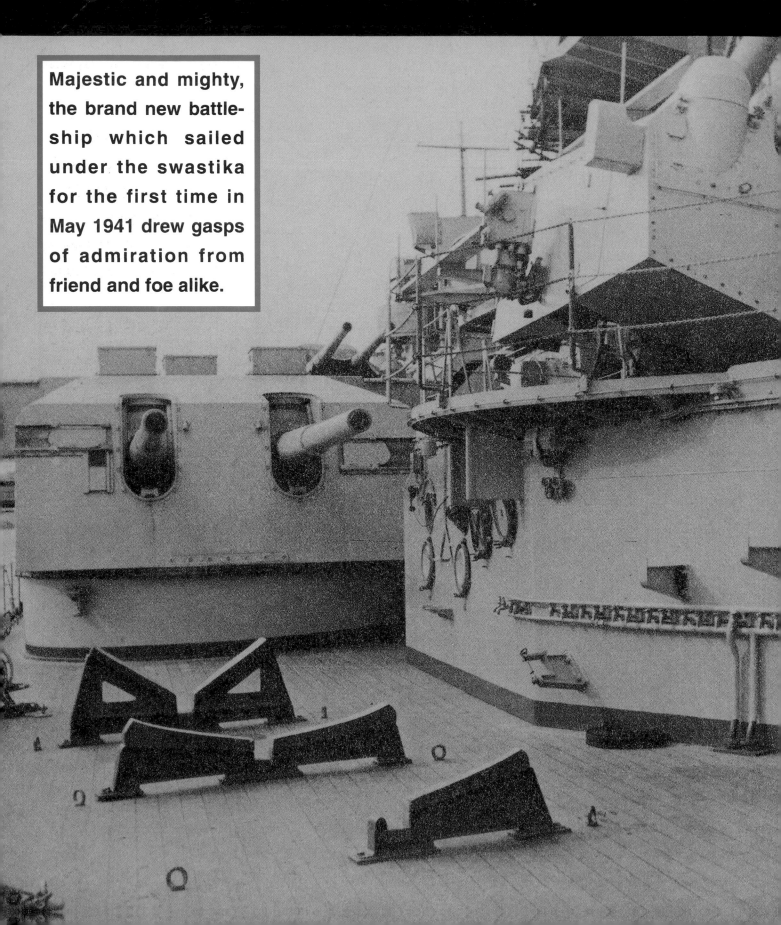

Majestic and mighty, the brand new battleship which sailed under the swastika for the first time in May 1941 drew gasps of admiration from friend and foe alike.

The Bismarck cut an awesome sight as it sped through the waves. More than 800 feet long and almost 120 feet wide, it was heavy with armour plating and bristled with giant guns yet was still sleek and fast. Who could blame the proud Germans for believing it was unsinkable?

It was down to the Royal Navy to send the great ship to the ocean floor and it was an urgent task which they were eager to undertake. A powerful battleship like the Bismarck posed an enormous threat to the convoys bringing essential food and materials from across the Atlantic. Without this lifeline from America and Canada, Britain would have quickly been strangled.

Left: On the deck of the mighty *Bismarck.* *Below:* The battleship *Bismarck* undergoing sea trials.

Then suddenly there came a more pressing desire to see the Bismarck sunk. For on its maiden voyage it confronted HMS Hood, elegant queen of the Royal Navy, and sank it with the loss of almost all the crew. It was a devastating blow to navy pride and one which had to be avenged. The humblest sailor and the most powerful admiral in the British fleet felt to a man that Bismarck's maiden voyage must also be its last.

Bismarck was built in Hamburg long before the opening salvoes of World War II were fired. The vessel was launched amid great pomp and ceremony on 14 February 1939. Nazi top brass, including navy chief Raeder, Goring, Goebbels and Hess, joined Hitler on a lofty podium when the great hull rumbled down the slipway. There to christen the ship was Dorothea von Loewenfeld, granddaughter of the celebrated German chancellor Bismarck after whom the ship was named.

After World War I, the German navy had been stripped of virtually all its assets and the Treaty of Versailles had strictly forbidden the creation of military muscle like the Bismarck. Hitler had been rebuilding the fleet and Bismarck was the largest addition to date. It was officially

A powerful battleship like the Bismarck *posed an enormous threat to the convoys*

listed at 35,000 tons, some 7,000 tons lighter than it actually was.

When war came, Bismarck stayed in dock while having chunky plating affixed to its sides and decks, the 22 sealed chambers beneath its waterline made watertight and the latest technology installed on the bridge. It was being fitted out for conflict to become, as Germany's Admiral Tirpitz put it, 'an unsinkable gun platform'.

Its first taste of sea salt came when it left Hamburg on 15 September 1940 for trials in the shelter of Kiel Bay. There were teething troubles and Bismarck had to slink back to Hamburg for modifications. It wasn't until the following May that the ship was ready to set forth.

■ AIRCRAFT COVER ■

Hitler arrived at Gotenhafen (now Gdynia) for an inspection of his seaborne gem on 5 May, where Bismarck was patiently waiting to embark on its first trip. He was, it appears, kept unaware that its sailing date was imminent. The Führer, distrustful of his navy and its short-comings, was wary of losing his prize vessel to the enemy and admiralty chiefs feared he would scupper their chances of getting underway at last.

Grand Admiral Erich Raeder believed it was vital to get Bismarck to sea. Germany now had the advantage of Atlantic ports in occupied France to provide bolt holes for its

---

◆ EYE WITNESS ◆

Frank Hewlett joined the Royal Marines in 1939 when he was 20 years old.

❛ I was on HMS *Aurora*, an escort to the *Hood*. We followed her a day after she left Scapa Flow. When *Hood* was sunk we were 40 miles away. We saw a big flash on the horizon. When we heard the news, nobody believed it.

Then the *Prince of Wales* came within our sights. She was damaged and we escorted her back to Iceland. There was an unexploded shell inside her bows. If it had gone off it would have destroyed the ship. When the shell was removed, it was full of sand. It must have been sabotaged in Germany.

Afterwards, we went to Newfoundland and sank the supply ship *Max Albrecht*, sister ship to the *Altmark*. She went down with a U-boat still attached to her. ❜

In one sense, the Bismarck was out of date even before setting sail

---

ships. Likewise, there was now extended aircraft cover from the Luftwaffe operating out of France. With summer drawing near, the lighter nights would significantly reduce the cover which was needed to spirit the ship into the Atlantic through the British sea blockade. Also, there was the increasing threat of America joining the war on the side of the Allies. The United States' naval power would dwarf that of Nazi Germany.

Fleet commander Gunther Lutjens was as confident in the strength of his new ship as the rest of Germany. But he had one nagging doubt that was shared by many senior officers in the Germany navy. It was the wisdom of going to sea without round-the-clock aircraft cover. In one sense, the Bismarck was out of date even before setting sail. The days of superships dominating the sea were rapidly diminishing. The sun was rising on the fleet air arms which

Below: HMS *Hood*, like the *Bismarck*, was thought by admirals to be invincible.

On 22 May, just a day after news of the Bismarck arrived in London, Hood, the Prince of Wales and six other vessels set off from Scapa Flow. The following day two of the fleet, the Norfolk and the Suffolk, encountered the Bismarck in the Denmark Strait, between Iceland and Greenland. As they dashed for cover in the icy fog, the Bismarck registered their presence and fired off a warning shot.

■ DEADLY BLOW ■

The mood was tense among officers and men on the Hood and the Prince of Wales as the hunt for their fearsome quarry continued. All the crew were poised to strike but lost their chance when their ships slipped past the giant battleship in the darkness as it skirted the Greenland ice pack.

Bismarck continued altering its course, not greatly but enough to put the ships commanded by Vice-Admiral Lancelot Holland in a

could offer so much more by way of flexibility and accuracy. While both Japan and America were gearing up their navies for the new age, Germany and Britain were lagging behind, both caught unawares by the outbreak of war. The Bismarck had the capacity to hold just four floatplanes, which were used primarily for reconnaissance missions.

Lutjens himself was the son of a retailer who shone at naval college in

> **It was only a matter of time before sighting of this monster was confirmed to London**

Kiel after making an early resolution to combat any hurdle placed in front of him. A veteran of the sea assaults in World War I, he had already earned the distinction of a Knight's Cross during World War II through his courage in the Norwegian campaign of 1940.

Loyal to his country, 51-year-old Lutjens was nevertheless not a Nazi and refused to offer the party salute. Instead he preferred the time-honoured navy salute and wore the old fashioned insignia of the Kaiser's navy instead of a swastika.

On 19 May the Bismarck sailed under cover of darkness to begin 'Operation Rheinubung'. In the company of the 17,000-ton heavy cruiser Prinz Eugen, itself a formidable ship, the Bismarck purred off into the Baltic to be joined by other German navy vessels for its historic voyage. Its aim was to sink the battleships protecting convoys while the smaller Prinz Eugen picked off the merchantmen.

■ VULNERABILITY ■

Slipping down the Danish waterways and shadowing the Swedish coastline, it was only a matter of time before the sighting of this magnificent monster was confirmed to London. It was enough to spark Sir John Tovey, commander in chief of the Home Fleet, into action. At the pinnacle of his plan would be HMS Hood, 20 years old but still an inspiring sight. It was a match for the Bismarck in size and gunnery but its weakness lay in the relatively thin armour plating which covered its body and decks. It was this vulnerability that Bismarck exploited to the full.

Above: Following his encounter with *Hood*, Admiral Lutjens bolted for France.

◆ HUNTING THE *BISMARCK*

On 19 May the *Bismarck* sailed under cover of darkness to begin Operation Rheinubung. In the company of the heavy cruiser *Prinz Eugen*, *Bismarck* headed through the Skagerrak to the Norwegian coast. Passing so close to the Danish and Swedish coasts, it was only a matter of time before the two warships were sighted by British agents, and the news transmitted to London. Sir John Tovey was ordered to get the *Bismarck*.

On 22 May, just a day after news of the *Bismarck* arrived in London, the largest ship in the Royal Navy, HMS *Hood*, and the brand-new battleship HMS *Prince of Wales* set off from Scapa Flow in the Orkneys, accompanied by six other vessels.

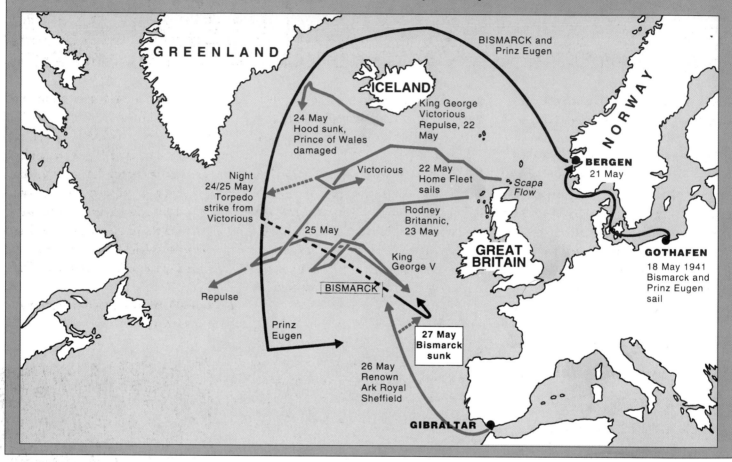

quandary. The initial plan had been to creep up on the *Bismarck* under cover of darkness in a short range strike. Now the *Hood* was forced to make a broad sweep at the enemy and would be exposed to the brunt of its firepower.

When they sighted *Bismarck*, the *Hood* and *Prince of Wales*, travelling in close formation, were about 17 miles distant. At Admiral Holland's command, both ships began a charge at the enemy.

Lutjens was under orders to engage only the escorts of convoys. He wasn't looking for a duel and had hoped to avoid one. But now he had no choice. When the *Hood* and *Prince of Wales*

The initial plan had been to creep up on the Bismarck *under cover of darkness*

---

closed the gap to 13 miles, they fired. Seconds later, the *Bismarck* and the *Prinz Eugen* replied in kind. And while the British ships failed to find their targets, the Germans had them well and truly in range.

The second salvo from *Prinz Eugen*'s guns struck the *Hood*, igniting anti-aircraft ammunition. Another hit and then a third slaughtered many of the gun crews taking shelter. Still the guns from both sides continued firing.

It was during a manouevre by the *Hood* trying for a better angle that the deadly blow was delivered by the *Bismarck*. A shell plunged down into the heart of the ship, penetrating the

Above: Prinz Eugen **was released from escort duty to escape the Royal Navy.**

deck with apparent ease. Somewhere in the bowels, it silently sparked an ammunition store, maybe two. The effect was catastrophic. Observers from both sides were astonished to see a massive plume of fire and smoke burst from the middle of the ship when there had been no explosion. The Hood, the most prestigious

> ## *The* Hood *folded in two and plunged to the bottom of the sea*

ship in old England, folded in two and plunged to the bottom of the sea.

With it went the vast majority of the 1,400 crew, trapped in the wreckage. It was several hours before a British cruiser came hunting for survivors. It found only three, cold and near death, clinging to small rafts in the middle of an oil slick.

The Prince of Wales was soon reeling from the effect of shells. It had been hit seven times, lost two officers and 11 men and was plagued with difficulties in its gunnery, making its own attack ineffective. Moments after

its stunned crew saw the Hood ditching into the sea, it was decided to withdraw. The showdown had lasted just 21 minutes.

Britain was devastated by the loss of the Hood and its men. After the shock, the public were baying for revenge – or feared the Bismarck really was indestructible. There was no time for sentimentality among the naval officers now in hot pursuit of the Bismarck.

The battleship Prince of Wales, plus the cruisers Norfolk and Suffolk shadowed the Bismarck as it moved south. Admiral Tovey, aboard King George V, was in command of Victorious, Repulse, four cruisers and nine destroyers hoping to intercept Bismarck from the south.

Visibility was poor, however, and the radar used by Suffolk to track its movements was patchy. Bismarck had, in fact, not escaped unscathed. It was holed twice by British shells which forced it to reduce speed and lost the vessel valuable fuel.

■ BISMARCK HURT ■

Lutjens felt he had no choice but to head for France for repairs. He released the Prinz Eugen to make a clean getaway, firing lazily at the Prince of Wales by way of distraction. Then he set a course which he hoped would take him to friendly

France or within the torpedo range of a protective U-boat.

It was with some degree of surprise that he and his crew looked up to the skies some hours later and saw a group of circus-style planes buzzing towards them. These were the Swordfish planes which had set off from the Victorious in order to wreak havoc on the Bismarck. With

Below: **Hitler failed to share the nation's pride in the navy.**

◆ EYE WITNESS ◆

Able Seaman Robert Kilburn was one of the three who survived the sinking of the *Hood*.

❛ I was a member of the anti-aircraft gun crew but, of course, we weren't needed. There were only two other people with me at the time. The others were in a shelter deck – a shell had gone in there and killed all of them, about 200 men – but I didn't know that at the time.

One of the shells hit one of the ready-fuse lockers for the four inch guns and there was a fire on board the upper deck and the ammunition was exploding. We were laid on the deck and then there was this terrific explosion. It was most peculiar, the dead silence that followed it – I don't know if we were deaf.

One of the other men was dead and the other one had his sides cut open and all his innards were tumbling out. I went to the ship's side to be sick. I noticed that the ship was rolling over and the bows were coming out of the water so I started taking off my tin hat, gas mask, anti-flash gear, overcoat, oilskin, so that I would have a chance to swim. With the ship rolling over, I just went into the water and the water came up to me.

I was terrified. I had a small rubber life belt on which you blew up – it was partially blown up. I started swimming away from the ship. I had a right belt on so I took my knife off and cut the belt off to breathe better. The ship rolled over and the yard arms which had been broken during the action hit me across the legs and the wireless aerials tangled around my legs, pulling me down with the ship. I cut my seaboots off with the knife and shot up, like a cork out of a bottle. I must have been about 10 ft down by then. The ship was around 10 yards away from me with her bows straight up in the air – and she just sank. ❜

In 1989 a team led by Dr Robert Ballard located the crusted hulk of the *Bismarck* (above) nestling on the ocean floor. Dr Ballard, the man who found and photographed the wreck of the *Titanic*, was aboard the *Star Hercules* when he discovered the *Bismarck* three miles beneath the ocean during a 10-day expedition. Among the photographs he took with a remote controlled underwater camera were those of discarded boots, the teak deck which was still intact and a 14-inch gun with a sea anenome bursting from its barrel.

survived the hair-raising attack and landed safely back on Victorious in the dark with next to no fuel.

The damage sustained by Bismarck was enough to make Lutjens review his course. With masterly intuition he turned suddenly westwards and, in doing so, shook off the Royal Navy shadow. It took 31 hours for the British to locate the Bismarck again.

By now most of the British ships in reach had been called in to help. Yet due to a series of mishaps and misunderstandings, they were unable to find the roaming battleship, having turned

On 26 May intrepid Swordfish planes found Bismarck *again and attacked*

in the wrong direction. In addition, many were running short of fuel and had to splinter from the body of the fleet to find more. Navy top brass was becoming increasingly nervous. Unaware that the Bismarck had been wounded, they knew its path must be taking it towards the 11 Allied convoys presently crossing the Atlantic.

On 26 May intrepid Swordfish, this time from the Ark Royal, found Bismarck again and attacked. Two torpedoes struck the big ship, wrecking the steering gear and ruining a propeller. It meant that Bismarck not only had to slow down further but also became locked on to a course which brought it directly into the path of the opposition, thanks to the jammed rudder.

The following day Bismarck came within range of the battleships Rodney and King George V. They weren't alone and soon the Bismarck was surrounded by British ships

their single propellers and stacked wings they look like something from a different age. Nevertheless, the torpedo they carried beneath their fuselage was powerful enough to

reckon with. The brave pilots of the Swordfish planes flew in low despite the barrage of anti-aircraft fire. Just one torpedo hit the mark. Yet all the eight attacking Swordfish planes

Above: The *Prince of Wales* was one of many ships to hunt the *Bismarck*.

firing when they could. Bismarck took punch after punch, losing men and guns with every minute of the merciless onslaught. Fires raged fore and aft while ammunition exploded all around. Yet still it stayed afloat.

. Afterwards, British sailors admitted they felt little elation at seeing the enemy ship battered so badly. However, they had no option but to continue the barrage while the Bismarck still fired back.

■ HITLER'S OUTRAGE ■

When streams of German sailors plunged into the sea, the shelling stopped. Tovey was not only mindful of their safety but also that of his own men. Fuel and ammunition were running desperately low in his fleet. It would not be long before the lurking U-boats would turn up looking for easy pickings.

Satisfied the Bismarck would no longer menace the shipping lanes of the Atlantic, he gave orders for the British ships to withdraw. The only ship left with torpedoes, the Dorsetshire, remained to finish off the job. Controversy raged afterwards

whether it was a British torpedo or a German sailor who sank the Bismarck by opening the sea-cocks.

The situation for the men floundering in the water after leaping from the Bismarck was bleak. At first the Dorsetshire and the destroyer Maori hauled up survivors. But their goodwill came to an abrupt end following the reported sighting of a U-boat. The ships revved up and pulled away from the bobbing survivors, ignoring their cries for help and leaving them to suffer a lingering death in the waves. Two other vessels

rescued a handful of survivors between them. Only 115 of the crew escaped with their lives out of a total of 2,206.

When news of the sinking reached Hitler he was outraged. Never mind that a fleet of five battleships, three battle cruisers, two aircraft carriers, 13 cruisers, 33 destroyers and eight submarines had been involved in the execution. He bitterly regretted ever putting his classic ship to sea.

Below: How the incredible story of pursuit was told to the British public.

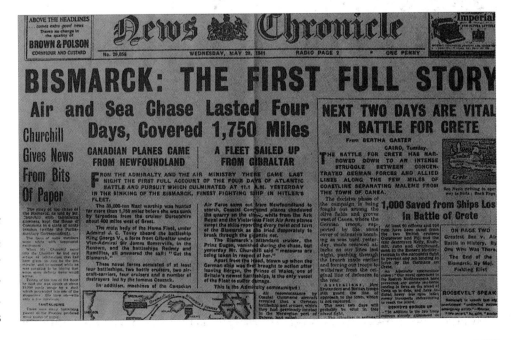

CORAL SEA AND MIDWAY

Pearl Harbor may have been the most spectacular action undertaken by the Japanese navy but it wasn't the last.

Here was the world's third most powerful navy staffed by efficient, skilled commanders and loyal sailors. It was their brief to roam the seas around Japan's newly acquired territories, protecting land-based flanks by fending off attacks from air and sea.

The Japanese navy played a major role in the domino fall of Asian and Pacific lands and islands, including that of Thailand, Hong Kong, the Philippines and Burma. Indeed, the noose put around Singapore by the Japanese navy during February 1942 ensured that none of the defending British or Australian troops could escape by sea and all those who survived the fighting were consequently taken prisoner.

When the Japanese cast their eyes in the direction of Java, the jewel they wanted in their crown, an allied naval force squared up to the challenge. Under Dutch officer Admiral Karel Doorman, a fleet of heavy and light cruisers and destroyers gathered from the Dutch, American, British and Australian navies determined to keep the Japanese out of the oil-rich colony.

■ BATTLE OF JAVA ■

The Battle of the Java Sea began on 27 February and was one of the largest naval confrontations the world had seen since World War I.

Both sides seemed equally matched when they began a mutual bombardment with guns. But the Japanese wreaked havoc when they edged closer to the Allied fleet and opened up with torpedoes.

Hostilities ceased while the Allied ships refuelled only to resume within hours beneath the moonlight. Doorman was delighted when he once again encountered the Japanese and sought to end their plans to invade Java once and for all. Little did he realise that he was being snapped up in a tactical pincer. When

The Japanese wreaked havoc when they edged closer to the Allied fleet

Left: Crews from USS *Lexington* go into action in the Coral Sea in May 1942. *Below:* Carrying the wounded off USS *Marblehead* in Netherlands East docks after the Battle of Java in February 1942.

In March US planes took off from the carriers Yorktown and Lexington to attack two ports on Papua New Guinea which had just been overrun by the Japanese. Again, the results were negligible.

America determinedly began to gather its strength. US troops were sent to Darwin in Australia and were

> ## The US felt confident enough only to take pot shots at the Japanese

by February under the command of General Douglas MacArthur. In fact, almost four times as many troops were sent from America to the Pacific at the time than took the shorter hop across the Atlantic to reinforce the Allied armies aiming to defeat Hitler.

Australian divisions, too, were recalled from the Middle East to help defend their homeland.

And the tide of Japanese successes was set to ebb as early as May 1942 with two historic seaborne clashes between Japan and America, one in

more torpedoes blasted his force in a surprise attack from a second angle there was chaos. In just seven hours, five Allied warships were sunk, while only one Japanese destroyer sustained damage. Doorman himself was lost when his cruiser De Ruyter went down.

■ BATTLE OF MIDWAY ■

So far the Emperor's fleet remained virtually unscathed by the ravages of war. During all its activities in the sea-borne invasions of Pacific and South East Asian islands only a total of four destroyers had been put out of action. Meanwhile, only four US destroyers had escaped to Australia from the treacherous waters around the Dutch East Indies. It seemed as if the Japanese navy was invincible.

Above, right, far right: The triumphant Doolittle raid on Tokyo. A B-25 comes under starter's orders on its way to Japan. Doolittle is pictured later by his crashed aircraft in China.

At the time the US felt confident enough only to take pot shots at the Japanese. The first skirmish took place in January when two US task forces bombed Japanese bases on the Marshalls and Gilberts. It was a tame event but nevertheless proved a small boost for American morale, being the first strike back at the enemy.

◆ BATTLE OF MIDWAY

Japan wanted a base within striking range of Hawaii. It also wanted the US fleet destroyed. Yamamoto hatched a plan to secure such a base and lure the US Navy to its downfall in the process. He launched a diversionary attack on the Aleutians while he struck at Midway Island. Unfortunately for him the Americans knew he was coming and had put to sea. The first wave of Japanese bombers caught many US aircraft on the ground at Midway. Nevertheless, enough got airborne to make a second Japanese strike necessary. It was while the Japanese were rearming that US Admiral Spruance struck. Aircraft from *Yorktown* and *Enterprise* destroyed four Japanese carriers; on the US side, *Yorktown* was sunk.

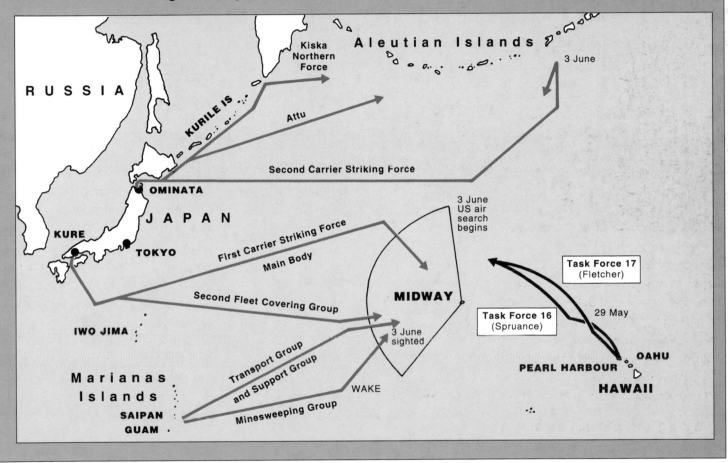

the Coral Sea and the other around the island of Midway.

The Battle of the Coral Sea was not notable for its end result as the outcome was so murky it was difficult to distinguish a winner. Japan certainly wasn't defeated but its navy was for the first time halted. However, it was the first ever confrontation at sea to take place with the enemy ships placed hundreds of miles apart.

The firepower was carried to the opposition entirely by the planes stationed on the mighty carriers ranged against each other, capable of causing wholesale devastation.

Meanwhile, the Battle of Midway proved to be a turning point in the fortunes of war and gave America the opportunity once more to assert naval superiority.

By May, Japan had control of New Britain, parts of Papua New Guinea and the majority of the Solomon Islands. It formed the outer edge of a

The island of Midway was a glaring hole in Japan's line of defence

Pacific empire which was fanning out towards Australia. The country's remaining aim was to secure the line of defence by conquering the remainder of Papua New Guinea.

Japanese priorities changed, however, with the most effective nuisance raid mounted by the Americans to date. It came with Lieutenant

Colonel J. Doolittle's bombing raid over Tokyo in April mounted through an open door from Midway. The island of Midway was held by a small garrison of American marines and was a glaring hole in Japan's line of defence. Although the damage caused during the 16-plane raid was light, it gave the Japanese hierarchy a shake up and compelled them to look again at domestic security.

■ FIRST BLOOD ■

Admiral Yamamoto, confident in the continuing might of his navy, was appalled at the Tokyo air raid. He felt sure the best way ahead was to knock the heart out of the American navy once again. To do it he wanted to put Midway Island under threat.

Yamamoto knew America valued the island because of its proximity to Pearl Harbor and would defend it in force with its navy, so he planned to lure the remaining big ships into action and then destroy them.

Below: **The last gasp of the Japanese carrier *Shoho* before it sinks.**

Meanwhile, the Japanese navy would also support a new thrust into Papua New Guinea where vital new forward bases could be installed.

Intelligence experts quickly grasped details of the preparations which would lead to the attack on Port Moresby, Papua New Guinea, after decoding Japanese communications. Tempted by the presence of some of Japan's finest ships, America's Admiral Chester Nimitz hastily drew together as many ships as he could for a surprise rendezvous with the Japanese in the Coral Sea.

Australian cruisers which had gone ahead to secure a vital seaway for the heavier ships came under attack from Japanese planes but miraculously escaped damage. So first blood in the four day battle went to the Ameri-

cans when a wave of planes located the light carrier Shoho and blasted it out of the water. It left the Japanese in a quandary as they had no idea where the attacking aircraft had come from.

The US tally included three direct hits on the aircraft carrier Shokaku

As night fell, Japanese planes were launched to locate their hidden enemy but, hampered by low cloud, were forced to ditch their bombs and head back to base. En route, they happened across the USS Yorktown

Above: **USS *Lexington* sustains critical damage at the Battle of the Coral Sea.**

which sent up aircraft for a confrontation. In total 17 Japanese planes were lost that night against only three American casualties. In fact, for a while both sides suffered from the main disadvantage that this new, long-distance warfare offered. Neither could locate the enemy ships.

■ TACTICAL VICTORY ■

The next day both sides sent waves of aircraft in pursuit of the other. The US tally included three direct hits on the aircraft carrier Shokaku which was forced to limp back to its home port for major repairs.

Meanwhile, the Japanese struck the carriers Yorktown and

Lexington. The Yorktown escaped with comparatively minor damage while the Lexington was crippled by three bombs and two torpedoes. It was to sink days later following an internal explosion. Both admirals decided against continuing the battle

---

The Lexington *was to sink days later following an internal explosion*

---

and pulled away from their respective battle lines.

Japan appeared to have inflicted the most damage on the opposition. In reality, however, the tactical victory belonged to the Americans. The Japanese had been contained and were forced to call off their strike at Port Moresby due to the large losses of essential aircraft.

◆ EYE WITNESS ◆

Mitsuo Fuchida, who led the air strike against Pearl Harbor, was aboard the aircraft carrier *Akagi* during the Battle of Midway.

❝ For Japan, the Battle of Midway was indeed a tragic defeat. The Japanese Combined Fleet, placing its faith in "quality rather than quantity" had long trained and prepared to defeat a numerically superior enemy. Yet at Midway a stronger Japanese force went down to defeat before a weaker enemy.

Not only were our participating surface forces far superior in number to those of the enemy but the initiative was in our hands. Nor were we inferior qualitatively in the crucial element of air strength which played a major role throughout the Pacific War. In spite of this we suffered a decisive defeat such as the modern Japanese navy had never before experienced or even dreamed possible.

With Midway as the turning point, the fortunes of war appeared definitely to shift from our own to the Allied side. The defeat taught us many lessons and impelled our navy, for the first time since the outbreak of war, to indulge in critical self examination.

The Japanese public, of course, was not told the truth about the battle. Instead, Imperial General Headquarters announcements tried to make it appear that both sides had suffered equal losses. The United States, however, promptly announced to the whole world the damaged inflicted on the Japanese acccurately naming the ships damaged and sunk. Thus it was clear that our efforts to conceal the truth were aimed at maintaining morale at home rather than keeping valuable knowledge from the enemy.

I myself had a rather painful taste of the extreme measures taken to preseve secrecy. During the battle I had been wounded on board *Akagi* and then transferred to hospital ship *Hikawa Maru* which brought me to Yokosuka Naval Base. I was not moved ashore until after dark when the streets of the base were deserted. Then I was taken to the hospital on a covered stretcher and carried in through the rear entrance. My room was placed in complete isolation. No nurses or corpsmen were allowed entry and I could not communicate with the outside.

In such a manner were those wounded at Midway cut off from the rest of the world. It was really confinement in the guise of medical treatment and I sometimes had the feeling of being a prisoner of war. ❞

Above: *Shokaku* pulled back to Japan following the Coral Sea battle.

The Japanese High Command decided to abandon that first objective in favour of the capture of Midway, a far more ambitious undertaking. While the commanders had sought outright victory in the Coral Sea, they were convinced by their own glowing track record that the US navy could still be annhilated.

Once again intelligence reports gave the United States fair warning of the Japanese plans which they had tagged Operation MI. And again Admiral Nimitz called in as much support as he could from ships and submarines in the region. Aircraft carriers Enterprise and Hornet were

Japanese commanders were convinced that the US Navy could be annihilated

summoned along with the damaged Yorktown which had been hurriedly repaired so it could rejoin the action.

They sailed with six cruisers, 14 destroyers and 19 submarines to the north of Midway to await the attackers. On the island itself the garrison had been strengthened and increased numbers of aircraft brought in.

The Japanese strike force, including half the navy's aircraft carriers, came from several directions, one arm to land troops, another to tackle the American naval presence.

At dawn on 4 June, bombers took off from Japanese aircraft carriers and

■ SURPRISE RAID ■

blasted the land-based defenders of Midway. Aircraft from the island attempting to deflect the invaders suffered huge losses and made little impact. It seemed the Japanese navy was to escape once more intact.

But before a second wave of bombers could be launched, Japan's Vice-Admiral Chuichi Nagumo was told of the presence of enemy ships signalled by the first attack by their planes. Instead of the continuing bombardment of the already shattered small island, he decided to swing north and pursue the US Navy prey.

By now torpedo bombers from all the aircraft carriers had been

launched and began a comprehensive strike lasting 55 minutes on three of Japan's aircraft carriers. Japanese pilots supported by anti-aircraft fire defended the ships fiercely. Of the 41 US planes which set out on that

Of the 41 US planes which set out on that mission, only six returned

mission, only six returned. It seemed victory was in the grasp of the Japanese. Yet they barely had time to congratulate themselves on their luck and judgement when the subsequent wave of dive-bombers sent by the Americans arrived on the scene.

As the Japanese sailors and airmen struggled to rearm in the disarray,

Above: *Akagi*, another Japanese navy gem, weaves its way out of fire at Midway.

bombs rained down on them and exploded on the decks crowded with aircraft. Afterwards, Japanese sailors told how the raid took them by surprise – which is why the prized planes were crowded on deck. It took a matter of minutes to reduce the

It took a matter of minutes to reduce the carriers to smoking crates

carriers to smoking crates. Two of the Japanese carriers, the Kaga and Soryu, sank within hours. The Akagi drifted hopelessly and helplessly until a Japanese submarine punctured it for the last time the following day.

Below: **US giant USS *Yorktown* lists helplessly following Midway.**

Half an hour afterwards, bombers from an unscarred Japanese carrier, the Hiryu, went looking for revenge. Their target was the Yorktown on which the battle commander Rear-Admiral Frank Fletcher was based. A volley of hits during two onslaughts finally put paid to the veteran carrier which was abandoned by its crew later the same day. A Japanese submarine sent its skeleton to the bottom two days later.

It was not the end of the bloody battle, however. At 5pm, less than 12 hours after the conflict began, USS Enterprise – nicknamed the 'Big E' – launched bombers in pursuit of the Hiryu. They caught up with their target and sparked a catastrophic blaze on board. The Hiryu, Japan's fourth and final aircraft carrier in the offensive, was finally laid to rest by a Japanese cruiser.

Admiral Yamamoto continued his assault on Midway from the heavy cruisers that remained. But when two of them collided trying to evade an American submarine, he was finally convinced of its folly.

The American navy's Rear-Admiral Raymond Spruance risked one final

■ HUGE VICTORY ■

foray against the Japanese, holing one of the already damaged cruisers and sinking the other. Even then Admiral Yamamoto was ready to spring a trap on the American fleet by luring them into combat with a light force and then pounce with much bigger guns.

Admiral Spruance was not to be drawn. Content with his enormous victory, he headed for home, leaving Yamamoto helpless in his wake. A Japanese submarine managed to claim one destroyer before Spruance pulled out of the region.

The decisive result was trumpeted around the Allied world. From Pearl

Harbor Admiral Nimitz announced: '. . . the enemy's damage is very heavy indeed, involving several ships in each of the carrier, battleship, cruiser and transport classes. This damage is far out of proportion to

Left: Admiral Raymond Spruance, an engineer of the Midway victory.

that which we have received.

'The brunt of the defence to date has fallen upon our aviation personnel, in which the Army, Navy and Marine Corps are all represented. They have added another shining page to their record of achievements.'

From a position of seemingly indomitable strength, the Japanese navy had within a few short days been for the first time mauled and gored. The defeat was so terrible that it was cloaked in secrecy in Japan for the duration of the war. While scores of heroic American pilots lost their lives in the battle, they inflicted devastation on their hitherto unbroken enemy and it was their courage alone that turned the tables. Four aircraft carriers, together with more than 300 aircraft and the cream of the Japanese naval pilots were at the

The steamroller successes of the Japanese forces had been stopped

bottom of the ocean. The steamroller successes of the Japanese forces had been stopped, Midway was saved and further plans by the Japanese to occupy other Pacific islands were shelved.

Below: Admiral Nimitz considers his next move from the bridge of a destroyer.

JAPAN'S LAST GASP

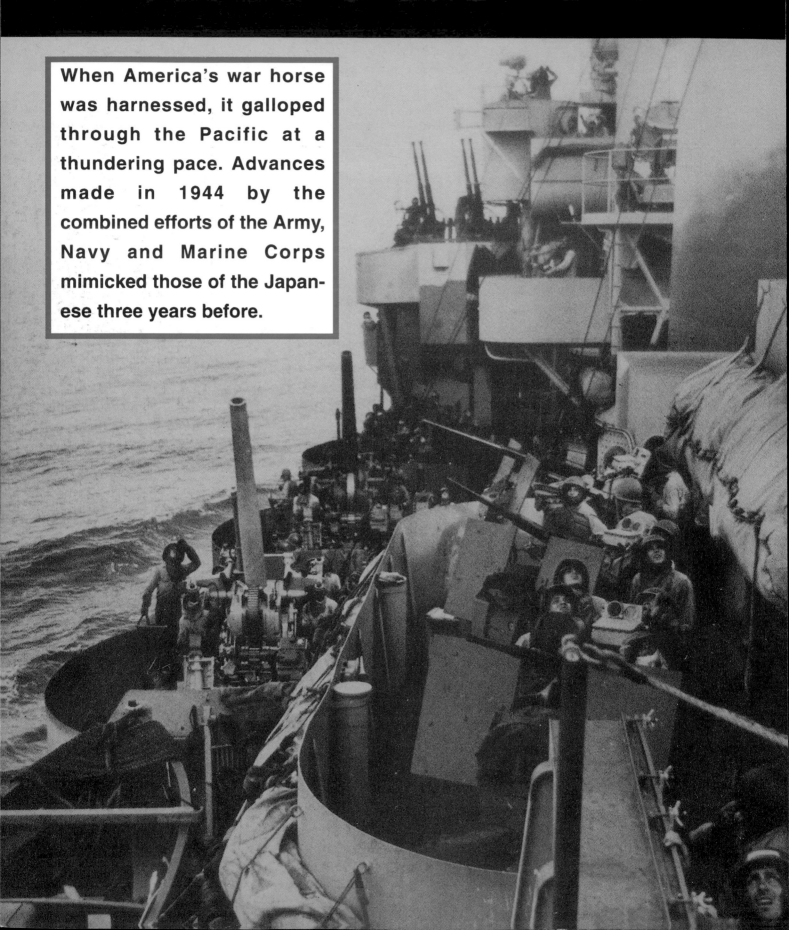

When America's war horse was harnessed, it galloped through the Pacific at a thundering pace. Advances made in 1944 by the combined efforts of the Army, Navy and Marine Corps mimicked those of the Japanese three years before.

By now the US strength at sea was awesome. Since the outbreak of the war with Japan a further 21 aircraft carriers had come into service capable of holding a total of about 3,000 planes.

That was in addition to a splendid array of new battleships, transports, cruisers, destroyers and landing craft newly arrived and ready for action.

On the other hand, the Japanese had suffered severe losses at sea and were continuing to do so. Apart from naval conflicts, the Japanese ships had to contend with the numerous American submarines now patrolling the Pacific in force.

Tiny Japan, so dependent on the resources it imported from overseas, was unable to replenish the fleet, with much of its merchant fleet being sunk bringing home vital war production materials. By 1944 two thirds of the tanker fleet bringing oil to Japan from the South Pacific fields had been wrecked by the Allies.

While 40 per cent of the oil produced in those fields reached Japan in 1942, only 13.5 per cent was unloaded at Japanese ports in 1944 thanks to the efficiency of the submarines and fleet ships. Oil reserves were dwindling fast, threatening to grind the war effort to a halt. Hopelessly outnumbered, it seemed on paper that Japan's navy was all but finished.

When it became clear that the US was preparing to attack the Philippines in the autumn of 1944,

In the autumn of 1944 Japan drew up plans for one final sea battle

however, Japan drew up the plans for one final sea battle which could have tipped the balance in its favour. It was a simple manoeuvre by what remained of the Japanese navy but might have been enough to defend

Left: All eyes turn skywards when a Kamikaze aircraft is spotted in the vicinity.
Below: Vice Admiral Jisaburo Ozawa was defeated by superior US tactics.
Bottom: The scale of the US seapower is illustrated in this picture of Task Force 58 in the Pacific.

Above: **Vice-Admiral William Halsey looks out to sea and draws up a winning strategy for the American fleet.**

shipping lane to the south would be completely cut off so that the fleet, if it should come back to Japanese waters, could not obtain its fuel supply. There would be no sense in saving the fleet at the expense of the the loss of the Philippines.'

In essence, Japan's ploy was to use what was left of the carrier fleet as a decoy to lure the main thrust of the American navy away from the Philippines. Once the large ships were out of the way, a two-pronged attack from the sea was planned on Leyte, the small island in the centre of the Philippines on which the Americans had already began an assault.

■ AMERICAN ATTACK ■

The operation began badly for the Japanese. One arm of the fleet earmarked to blast Leyte was itself fired on by American submarines on 23 October, well before it reached its destination. Three cruisers were

badly damaged. There was a two-fold result to this action. The strength of this attacking arm was depleted and all the American shipping for miles around became focused on this single Japanese force. Despite frantic efforts to announce his presence by uncoded radio messages, the arrival of Admiral Ozawa and his decoy carriers went unnoticed by the Americans.

Now American battleships joined the attack on the hapless Japanese detachment whose brief had been to slip unobtrusively into the Philippine Sea. Japanese land-based bombers as

the Philippines. And it was a gamble worth risking for the Japanese. If the Americans had installed themselves on the Philippines, it would have meant the end of oil supplies from

The arrival of Admiral Ozawa and his decoy carriers went unnoticed

the Dutch East Indies, now more crucial than ever before to the teetering Japanese.

After the war, Japan's Admiral S. Toyoda explained his country's actions: 'If the worst should happen there was a chance that we would lose the entire fleet; but I felt that chance had to be taken . . . should we lose in the Philippine operations, the well as those from the distant carriers rained bombs on the American fleet, crippling the carrier Princeton.

There was a high price for this success, however. The relentless onslaught by American fighter planes finally sank the majestic Musashi, one of the biggest battleships in the world. It had been hit by 19 torpedoes and 17 bombs. Japanese commander Admiral Kurita finally broke off from the action and appeared to retreat.

■ BATTLE OF LEYTE ■

The absence of Japan's aircraft carriers was spotted by the sharp-witted Vice-Admiral William 'Bull' Halsey, who was in control of the American fleet. When he sent out reconnaissance planes to assess the movements of the Japanese fleet, Ozawa was finally detected. It seemed a golden opportunity to Halsey who gathered up his entire force to pursue the

prized carriers, Japan's last surviving ship of the type in action.

Almost as soon as American backs were turned, Kurita reversed his course and began steaming towards his initial target once more, Leyte.

American sea defences were badly lacking after Halsey set off with his full complement of ships. Mostly it comprised a small force protecting the landing beaches at Leyte, just six

Japan's remaining battleships were no more than sitting ducks to the enemy

escort carriers and five destroyers. In charge, Vice-Admiral T. C. Kinkaid sent a series of urgent messages to Halsey, asking him to return at once. Halsey, however, was determined to snare the carriers once and for all. He refused to turn around until he delivered some decisive damage to the carrier force. Only time would tell if his instincts were the right ones.

Meanwhile, the destroyers were defending the vulnerable section of

Left: **The carrier USS *Princeton* is hosed after taking a direct hit from a bomber during the Battle of Leyte.**

Above: **Devastation among Japanese shipping in the run-up to the invasion of the Philippine island of Leyte.**

the US fleet as best they could. One escort carrier and three destroyers were lost, however, in its retreat.

Now Kurita was steaming towards the Leyte Gulf where a collection of US transports and men lay wide open to attack. Then he hesitated. As Kinkaid watched and waited with bated breath, Kurita finally pulled his forces to the north, away from the beach targets.

Thanks to confusion among the intercepted radio messages aboard Kurita's ship, he believed Halsey and his powerful ships were only 70 miles away when in fact there were hundreds of miles between them. He was also gravely concerned about the risk of attack by air when he himself had no air cover.

■ SITTING DUCKS ■

While the survivors of Kurita's force escaped, the fate of the carriers gave credence to Halsey's actions. All four – Chitose, Zuikaku, Zuiho and Chiyoda – were sunk, completing the effective destruction of the Japanese navy. With the long-range power of aircraft, Japan's remaining battleships were no more than sitting ducks to the enemy. There was little

EYE WITNESS

Yasuo Kuwahara was a skilled Japanese pilot who was in a Kamikaze squadron in the final year of the war.

It was New Year's Day 1945 at Hiro Air Base in western Honshu. Captain Yoshiro Tsubaki, commander of the Fourth Fighter Squadron, has just called a special meeting. A silence settled over us – only the patter of rain on the roof. The captain permitted us to sit while he stands, arms folded, eyes dark and unblinking – seemingly to spear us one by one.

After a long while, he spoke sonorously: "The time has at last arrived. We are faced with a great decision."

Again, he pauses but I feel it coming – the fear, greater than I have yet known. Death is there with us, enfolding each man, lingering, growing stronger. And the words from our captain flow so strangely.

"Any of you unwilling to give your lives as divine sons of the great Nippon empire will not be required to do so. Those incapable of accepting this honour will raise their hands – now."

Once more silence and death are almost palpable. The rain has subsided to a soft drizzle. Then hesitantly, timidly, a hand goes up, then another and another . . . six in all. The decision is mine; I can choose to live or die. Hasn't the captain just said so? But somehow… Of course, I want to live. But my hands – they remain at my sides trembling. I want to raise them but I can't. I want to raise my hands, even my soul would have me do it. Am I a coward? I cannot do it.

"Ah so," Captain Tsubaki fixes those who have responded in his stare. "It is good to know early exactly where we stand." They are summoned before us. "Here gentlemen," he points to the ashen faces, "are six men who have openly admitted their disloyalty. Since they are completely devoid of honour – without spirit – it becomes our duty to provide them with some. These men shall be Hiro's first attack group."

The breath, held so long within me, struggled out. I want to draw in more air, to expel it with relief, but something clenches inside. Six men from my squadron have just been picked for death. Hiro's first human bombs.

Above: **A Japanese destroyer is smashed in two at Ormoc, Leyte, by a US B-25.**

more they could contribute to Japan's war effort.

From first to last, the three-day Battle of Leyte Gulf was the largest in history. In total, 282 ships were engaged along with hundreds of aircraft. It took the title of largest battle from the World War I Battle of Jutland when 250 British and

---

Those who felt disgraced in some way would commit 'hari kiri'

German ships ships had met in combat, with only five seaplanes.

At the end of it, the Japanese had lost not only four carriers but also three battleships, six heavy cruisers, three light cruisers and eight destroyers. The triumph clearly belonged to the Americans whose casualties amounted to just one light carrier, two escort carriers and three destroyers.

Yet had the whim of the Japanese Admiral Kurita been different on the day and had he chosen to bombard the American beach positions, history might have had a different story to tell.

■ SUICIDE SQUADS ■

The Battle of Leyte Gulf is not only remembered as being the biggest naval battle ever. It was also the first to see the co-ordinated use of kamikazes – Japanese suicide squads.

Among the Japanese there was a strict code of honour. It had been instilled in them for centuries that death was better than dishonour or defeat. The first form of ritual suicide in Japan, called 'seppuku', was reserved by law for the samurai and was considered a privilege. Suicides could equally be carried out as a mark of respect.

Centuries later, those who felt disgraced in some way would commit 'hari kiri', literally translated to 'a cut to the stomach'. The aim for the person committing suicide was to disembowel themselves by using a ceremonial sword, an agonising process. As the years wore on, many made a symbolic cut in the stomach before turning a gun on themselves.

Surrender was abhorred by the Japanese, particularly among the troops, which explains the antipathy they displayed towards their own Japanese victim, the latter would devote his last burst of energy to pulling the pin from his final grenade, killing both men outright.

■ DESPERATE ACTS ■

Others would strap explosives to their bodies and hurl themselves at tanks or enemy positions to cause as much devastation as possible. Until now, these desperate acts were committed very much on an individual basis. But by 1944, staring into the jaws of defeat, the Japanese commanders decided to orchestrate suicide missions to cause the maximum hardship and loss of life to their enemies. Behind the enterprise

> *Japanese commanders orchestrated suicide missions to cause maximum loss of life*

was Vice-Admiral Takijiro Onishi who himself committed hari kiri at the end of the war.

Kamikaze pilots in small planes would target the deck of an enemy ship. While bombs dropped by planes often fell short of the mark, the kamikazes' aim was unerringly accurate. British ships which generally boasted more deck armoury than

Above: USS *St Lô* takes a direct hit from a kamikaze in the Battle of Leyte.
Right: USS *Suwanee* gets running repairs after sustaining damage from a kamikaze.

prisoners of war. Many Japanese servicemen readily chose suicide rather than shame. High ranking officers also used to inspire courage and commitment among their men by killing themselves.

This made the Japanese particularly difficult enemies in the field. They were reluctant to be rescued if their missions went awry. In the sea, mystified Allied sailors watched in disbelief as the survivors of a wrecked ship tried to drown themselves or cut their own throats if they were armed. For if any unfortunate Allied soldier stopped to help a wounded or dying their American counterparts were better defended against such attacks.

There were also plans for suicide motorboats to target major ships. Beneath the waves there were one-man midget submarines which would set themselves on a collision course with a much larger vessel. These were difficult tactics to counter.

kamikaze squads whether the men were willing to die or not.

Inevitably, it undermined the success of the squads. Those without the necessary iron nerve were just as likely to plunge themselves and their aircraft into the sea instead of a ship, representing a waste of valuable resources. In a panic, many chose the

After the war, Japan's Lieutenant-General Torashiro Kawabe explained the reasoning behind kamikaze attacks. 'We believed that our spiritual convictions and moral strength could balance your material and scientific advantages. We did not consider our attacks to be 'suicide'. The pilot did not start out on his

Above: **Wardroom of the carrier USS *Suwanee* becomes an emergency sick bay after the kamikaze attack during the Battle of Leyte Gulf.**

Those without the necessary iron nerve were just as likely to plunge into the sea

mission with the intention of committing suicide. He looked upon himself as a human bomb which would destroy a certain part of the enemy fleet... he died happy in the conviction that his death was a step towards the final victory.'

At the Battle of Leyte Gulf, six aircraft took off from Cebu in the Philippines on 25 October 1944. Two hours later when they arrived at Leyte the planes deliberately rammed the US carriers Santee and Suwanee, causing extensive damage. The next day one American ship, St Lô, was sunk by use of kamikaze.

■ BEST DEFENCE ■

In the next three months, 22 Allied naval vessels were sunk by kamikaze pilots against 12 holed in conventional air attack. A further 110 kamikaze strikes damaged shipping.

They were a hazard which was to plague the Americans, Australians and British for the rest of the war. The best defence against kamikaze was interception by fighter planes or a volley of anti-aircraft fire, but it was not guaranteed to work. A lone Japanese pilot could still bring about the deaths of many.

Stepping forward for these 'special' one-way missions were upright, traditional, fervent and deeply patriotic young men who thought little of laying down their lives for their country. They were, however, the elite. Despite the glory heaped on such pilots in domestic propaganda, the volunteers for the kamikaze ('divine wind') squads were drying up. Japanese commanders had no choice but to brand units as

first ships they saw to descend on. These were generally strategically less important than others in the fleet, once again wasting man and machine. Others would fly off in search of a specified target and return claiming the ship they were after could not be found. There were many accidents too, as the fuel-starved Japanese economised with all-important oil and stoked up the kamikaze aircraft with 50 per cent alcohol. If the aircraft engine failed, it was impossible to restart.

Commanders had no idea about the kamikaze success rate as there was no one left to report a result.

Battle for the Skies

BATTLE OF BRITAIN

When France was overrun, Führer Adolf Hitler cast his eyes across the English Channel and set his sights on Britain.

Although he never had an appetite for war with the island, he now saw it as the next jewel in his crown. He even believed its government and people would choose to make peace after the unstoppable power of the Reich had been so amply illustrated in France.

He was, of course, wrong. A peace offer made to Britain in July 1940 was rebuffed – even though the remnants of its army, hounded out of Europe via Dunkirk, were in disarray. Hitler made up his mind to invade and began gathering the necessary invasion forces in the newly acquired Channel ports of Holland, Belgium and France.

Yet while the Germans were veterans of waging attacking wars on

> ## *Göring pledged to the Führer that the Royal Air Force would be banished forever*

land, they had never tackled the sea before. Nor was Germany a great seafaring nation. Hitler believed the necessary arrangements for taking war across the water could be made in a matter of weeks. Given that 'Operation Overlord', carried out from Britain in 1944 to free France, took upwards of a year to plan, he was woefully shortsighted.

The effectiveness or otherwise of his plan was never revealed, however.

Left: Spitfires like this one proved the saviours of Britain.
Top right: Göring was confident his Luftwaffe aircraft could finish the RAF.
Right: Air crews were scrambled at a moment's notice when attacks came.

For it was clear even to the buoyant Hitler that an invasion could not go ahead until his air force had charge of the skies. It was one of the few issues that united his warring chiefs of staff, too.

'The British Air Force must be eliminated to such an extent that it will be incapable of putting up any substantial opposition to the invading troops,' Hitler told his generals. Göring, the supremo of German air power, was all ears. He blithely pledged to the Führer that the Royal Air Force would be banished forever.

■ IN EASY REACH ■

On paper, it seemed Göring had good reason to be confident. The Luftwaffe had a three-to-one numerical superiority against the RAF which had lost nearly half its strength during the Battle of France. German pilots were experienced, having flown missions throughout the Spanish Civil War as well as the more recent hostilities. Now they were installed in airfields in France, the Low Countries and Norway, within easy reach of Britain.

Göring believed his men would smash the Royal Air Force in much the same way as they had destroyed the Polish and French air forces before.

'Operation Sealion', Hitler's planned offensive against Britain which would bear him triumphantly to London, was set for 15 September 1940. The German navy chief Admiral Raeder had convinced Hitler his forces could not be prepared any sooner. Nor could it happen much later than that for fear of the invasion force falling foul of autumn storms.

Timing was crucial – but this did not unduly concern the Luftwaffe

Top: Formations of Messerschmitt 110s became a familiar sight in the skies.
Above: Britain and the Commonwealth countries were recruiting air crews.

chief, who was still smarting at the way the British Expeditionary Force had escaped from the French coast under his nose. When the Luftwaffe began its operations against Britain in July, Göring was sure he had time enough to fulfill his part of the bargain. Privately, he thought four

days would be sufficient to virtually annihilate his opposition. Events proved his optimism to be wildly misplaced.

For its part, Britain waited in anticipation during the summer of 1940 for the start of a battle for its very existence. Air reconnaissance teams spotted the gathering German forces. Hitler's intentions were clear.

Many of the men plucked from the beach at Dunkirk were redeployed on coastal defences. The Royal Navy played its part by attacking the collection of landing craft mushrooming at the occupied ports. Airmen joined the action and laid still more mines in the Channel to hamper a seaborne force destined for Britain.

There was a new evacuation among the children of London and the south east. As tension and expectation mounted on the home front, production doubled during June in factories working round-the-clock in a bid to help Britain's defenders meet the foe on equal terms. Lord Beaverbrook, minister of aircraft production, appealed to the public to

donate its metal scrap to build fighters. The result was mountains of old iron which could never be transformed into Spitfires or Hurricanes. But in terms of a morale-boosting exercise, it was a runaway success.

■ CONVOYS ATTACKED ■

As the German victory parades and celebrations died down in France there came the opening salvos of the Battle of Britain. They were quite tame affairs by comparison with what was to come, a bid to 'soften up' Britain. The targets were Britain's lifeline convoys as they reached home

---

Lord Beaverbrook appealed to the public to donate its metal scrap to build fighters

---

waters and the coastal ports, most notably Portsmouth and Dover. Both sides suffered losses in the air, with the English pilots, ground controllers and radar operators learning some valuable lessons.

Germany had begun with about 2,600 aircraft ready for action. They were in the main Messerschmitt fighters and Dornier, Heinkel, and Junkers bombers. They were well-organised into groups – Luftflotte 2 flew from Belgium, Luftflotte 3 from northern France, and Luftflotte 5 was based in either Norway or Denmark.

■ FIGHTER COMMAND ■

Lining up against them were fewer than 700 operational aircraft for the Royal Air Force. There were the legendary Spitfires and Hurricanes and some outdated Blenheim bombers.

Britain's aerial defences were divided into four groups. Fighter Command 10 Group covered south west England, Fighter Command 11 Group oversaw the south east including London, Fighter Command 12

FINEST HOUR

'Let us brace ourselves to our duty and so bear ourselves that if the British Commonwealth and Empire lasts a thousand years men will still say, "This was their finest hour".'

(Winston Churchill after the fall of France.)

In the middle of August Göring opened phase two of the Battle of Britain

Irish, seven Americans, two Rhodesians, one Jamaican and a Palestinian.

Now Germany was down by some 217 planes. The losses by Fighter Command were fewer than 100 but its outlook was bleaker than that of the enemy. British aircraft reserves were tiny. Yet it was the loss of experienced pilots either by death or injury that began to concern Air Chief Marshal Sir Hugh Dowding most. Despite the acute pressure of his position, Dowding, a master tactician, did a first-class job of keeping the marauding German planes at bay during those hectic months of summer and autumn 1940. Yet Churchill unceremoniously replaced him once the threat of 'Operation Sealion' had passed.

Aboye: Göring and his staff officers survey England across the Channel, convinced the island would easily fall.

Group patrolled the airspace over the Midlands, while Fighter Command 13 Group was based in northern England and Scotland.

Britain was not standing entirely alone, as the line-up for the ensuing battle proved. Although more than 2,500 of the men who took part were British, there were also 147 Poles, 101 New Zealanders, 94 Canadians, 87 Czechs, 29 Belgians, 22 South Africans, 22 Australians, 14 Free French, ten

In the middle of August, Göring opened phase two of the Battle of Britain. His target now was RAF Fighter Command itself. Daily attacks were made on the airfields of southern England. Unlike the unfortunate air forces of crushed Allies Poland and France, the British planes position to carry out attacks on the German formations as they crossed into Britain. Not wishing to waste vital manpower and resources, ground control never scrambled pilots until the last moment when they were sure a raid was imminent. It gave them little time to plan the most effective attack.

Both sides fell victim to erroneous propaganda. The RAF airmen were buoyed to hear that German air force losses were running at three or four times their own. In fact, vastly

Left: **Air crews at Biggin Hill, Kent, enjoy a few moments' respite.**
Below: **Despite the dangers, pilots and crews always appeared relaxed.**

were not caught on the ground. Britain's radar system, the most advanced in the world, gave early warning after seeing incoming formations of enemy bombers. There was just enough time to scramble the pilots and bring the valuable men and planes into the air.

Smoke from planes embroiled in dog-fights was scrawled across the sky

For now the heroes of the battle were the ground crews. It was their job to patch up not only the planes which were battered during aerial spats but also the hangars and runways damaged by bombs, to keep the Royal Air Force working.

Göring earmarked 13 August as 'Eagle Day' when a preponderance of German planes would swarm over the British skies and finally subjugate the stubborn RAF. Despite wave upon wave of Luftwaffe planes, his

plan failed. Smoke from planes embroiled in dog-fights was scrawled across the sky. The British fighters held their own.

■ NIMBLE SPITFIRES ■

German bombers were at a disadvantage against the nimble Spitfires. Laden with bombs, they were no match for the British planes. But the RAF fighters were constantly struggling to achieve the best height and

inflated German casualty figures were broadcast, some of which were not rectified until after the war. Göring, meanwhile, was happily convinced during the early stages of the Battle of Britain that many airfields were out of action and scores of British planes were destroyed, estimates which were grossly exaggerated.

On 15 August nearly 1,800 sorties were flown by the German airmen,

◆ BATTLE OF BRITAIN

In the Battle of Britain, RAF Fighter Command was divided into groups distributed throughout the country. The south west of England was the responsibility of 10 Group, London and the south east was covered by 11 Group, the Midlands region was patrolled by 12 Group, northern England and Scotland was the beat of 13 Group. Against these forces were three Luftwaffe formations – Luftflotte 2, Luftflotte 3 and Luftflotte 5.

attacking targets from Newcastle to Hampshire. Britain was forewarned by radar, and each flight was attacked from the ground and the air and there were 75 German losses against Britain's 34.

The following day 1,700 sorties were made over Britain, with Göring confident the RAF would be left in tatters. Yet on that day and on many days to come, the German pilots found themselves confronted with healthy numbers of British planes and pilots.

Göring was left fuming at the apparent inability of his men to finish off the RAF. In addition, he was counting the cost of 363 lost aircraft and crew.

Above: A Heinkel 111 over the Thames, taken from another German plane.

Of course, the incessant demands on each and every British squadron were causing immense difficulties by mid-August. Britain had lost 181 fighters in the air and 30 more on the ground. Only 170 replacement aircraft had thus far been manufactured, while just 63 new pilots had been brought up to replace the 154

Left: **Temple Underground station doubled as an air-raid shelter during the Blitz.**

Now it was Hitler's turn to be furious. He pledged in turn to annihilate London, abandoning his deeply held wish to occupy the city unscarred by bomb damage. With the German campaign to obliterate the RAF clearly failing, he thought it was time for a new and different tactic. The wholesale bombing of London would not only hit at the heart of the British government but would demoralise its people. 'Sealion', he believed, would still go ahead as planned. The gloves were now off. It was the start of an arduous period of bombing raids which would test the strength of the RAF and also the people of Britain to the very limit.

lost in battle. The raiders had succeeded in knocking out a radar station at Ventnor on the Isle of Wight, which was a serious blow, although their main aim of wrecking airfields had been frustrated. How long could the casual, seemingly cheery young men in silk scarves and leather jackets who laid their lives on the line several times a day without an outward trace of anxiety hold out?

· Dowding, by skilful management, contained the mounting problems. Yet he was wearied by the effort and

certain in the knowledge that Fighter Command could not cope with many more all-out raids. Another change in German tack saved the force from certain defeat.

Stage three of the Battle of Britain was sparked in part by accident. On 23 August a German pilot ditched his bombs over London, not to cause mayhem in the capital but rather to speed his flight home. Churchill was outraged. In retaliation, he ordered the bombing of the German capital, Berlin.

Below: **The unmistakeable shape of St Paul's cathedral stands firm among the bomb damage in the City of London.**

Now the German forces were throwing their entire weight at Britain. With their losses amounting to 60 planes on 15 September, the decision to undertake mostly night bombing raids was made.

Searchlights in London were unable to track the fast-moving attackers. Night fighters in the RAF squadrons badly needed airborne interception radar to hit back, which took valuable time to provide. The demands on the men of the RAF, already weary from their exertions, were enormous, and their ability to strike back under cover of darkness was limited. They were sleeping for just a few hours in every 24 before being scrambled once more. The casualties among them continued to mount and, for the first time, their losses exceeded those of the enemy.

It took hours, sometimes days, to find bodies trapped in their wrecked homes

Meanwhile, on the ground, the conditions for residents of London and, eventually, other main British cities were appalling.

The London docks were among the first targets in a daring daylight attack on 7 September. Nearby residents watched in horror as scores of German bombers sparked a ferocious blaze. It took just an hour for the Luftwaffe to drop 300 tons of high explosives and countless numbers of incendiaries. Hours later several hundred more bombers returned.

At night the raging fires burned like beacons, guiding Luftwaffe pilots to their target.

Before very long, London Underground stations became shelters for

Fred Graves, of Swindon, Wiltshire, served in the RAF ground crews which worked on Hurricanes and Spitfires during the Battle of Britain. Later in the war he serviced Lancasters of Bomber Command and was based near Newmarket.

I remember the Battle of Britain as a non-stop series of dog-fights in the skies above us. Our pilots knew they had a very low life expectancy. I lost an awful lot of friends.

I was particularly impressed by the Polish airmen serving with us. Every time there was a scramble alert they would race out, usually still in their shirt sleeves, jump into a plane and take off. They were very highly motivated to hit back at Germany.

Airmen rarely if ever showed they were scared. Even the Lancaster bomber crews assigned to missions over the Ruhr somehow coped with the pressure. You could detect a reluctance among them – simply because the Ruhr industrial region was so heavily defended – but they did their duty.

I think teamwork helped beat the fear. Bomber air crews were teams. If one of them wasn't fit or well then the whole crew was grounded until he was. They also had to have faith in their aircraft and in us as ground crew. We were the last friendly faces they saw before they flew east.

Looking back it is a miracle some of these men ever made it home. Their aircraft were so shot up they were almost unrecognisable.

frightened city folk despite an immediate ban on such a use. People slept end to end in close proximity to friends, neighbours and complete strangers. Those lucky enough to have gardens and shelters in their gardens became accustomed to retiring to them in time for tea and staying put until daybreak. It was soon clear that the option of sheltering under a sturdy wooden table was not an inspired choice as house after house was reduced to rubble by the bombs.

It took hours, sometimes days, to find bodies trapped in their wrecked homes. There was trial by fire as intense blazes raged. If bombs had failed to explode, there was continuing danger for the residents and workers of London even after the planes were long gone.

On the ground fire-watchers, full-time firefighters and auxiliaries, air raid precaution wardens and the Home Guard did their best to combat the terrible ravages of the raids.

Above: **Coventry was blitzed in a raid code-named 'Moonlight Sonata'. The raid claimed 568 lives.**

Despite all this, the mood in London was far from one of defeatism. The spin-off planned by Hitler of grinding the British public into the ground with the incessant bombing raids was failing miserably. In the tube stations there was impromptu entertainment from singers and musicians. Cups of tea were passed around and soon people learned to pay little heed to the sound of pounding bombs above.

■ BUSINESS AS USUAL ■

Instead of people weeping and wailing on the streets when the harsh light of day revealed the full extent of the night raids, there was a camaraderie which no one could have foreseen. Business went on as usual in daylight hours, despite shattered windows, fractured gas and water pipes and the unnerving sight of double-decker buses upturned in bomb craters. The spirit of the people of London was ultimately symbolised in the great cathedral of St Pauls, which stood intact overlooking the battered city while smoke from incendiary fires plumed around its dome.

If anyone was demoralised by the successive and apparently fruitless attacks it was the German pilots who were patently failing in their task of bringing Britain to its knees.

The attacks came in earnest from 15 September as Göring tried to

Hitler had no option but to call off 'Sealion' indefinitely

ground the British air force in time for 'Sealion'. That day a record 56 Luftwaffe planes were brought down. Hitler twice postponed making a final decision on whether or not to go ahead before making his decision day 17 September. As the day dawned, London was smoking. But the Luftwaffe had paid a heavy price for the privilege of setting alight this

THE FEW

'Never in the field of human conflict was so much owed by so many to so few.'

(Winston Churchill after the Battle of Britain.)

historic capital, and the planes of the Royal Air Force were not only still challenging their fighters but also found time to bombard the Channel ports where the German invasion fleet was based.

Hitler had no option but to call off 'Sealion' indefinitely. The Battle of Britain was won and the stout little island was safe from invasion. That meant renewed hope for occupied Europe, for without Britain from which to mount an attack on Hitler's Nazi empire there would have been barely a flicker of opportunity for liberation. Churchill's words of praise and thanks for the gallant RAF, spoken back in August, echoed through the free world. 'Never in the field of human conflict was so much owed by so many to so few.'

Yet the ordeal went on for both the men of the RAF and the people of Britain. Luftwaffe attacks continued unabated. London was attacked for 76 nights in succession and failed to enjoy much more than a few hours of eerie peace until the middle of 1941.

Anti-aircraft guns boomed in answer to the rain of bombs. There was little chance of them hitting their target. Only 75 aircraft were brought down by anti-aircraft shells – when the Luftwaffe flew about 12,000

RUDOLPH HESS

The Führer flew into a three-day rage when his deputy, Rudolph Walter Richard Hess, flew to Britain to make peace. A full day after the flight from Germany in a Messerschmitt 110 fighter aircraft, German radio explained away the demoralising desertion by claiming Hess was suffering from hallucinations.

British intelligence chiefs, meanwhile, were similarly at a loss to know what to make of the ace pilot who had been a loyal member of the Nazi party since 1920. On 10 May 1941, when he came down to earth at the end of a parachute and suffered a broken ankle, he claimed he had an important message for the Duke of Hamilton. This message was, apparently, a peace formula which would end the conflict between Britain and Germany.

High-ranking British officers and Churchill himself would not hear of making peace by the back door. Nevertheless, they were reluctant to trumpet the capture of such a key Nazi. Were they being duped by Hitler? Was there a further dimension to this unexpected prize which had fallen into their laps?

Even today, no one can tell whether Hess was demented at the scale of the bloodshed and hatched his plan to end the war accordingly; whether he discussed the plan with Hitler who wished to secure peace with Britain before invading Russia; or whether it was in fact the real Hess who carried out the madcap caper. Years later there were claims that the man held by the Allies was in fact an imposter, dispatched by Himmler or Göring after the murder of Hess.

What remains certain is that the man who fell to earth that night in 1941 was tried as a war criminal at Nuremberg, sentenced to life imprisonment and incarcerated at Spandau prison in Germany for 46 years until his death, apparently by suicide.

sorties over Britain. Post-war investigation proved that for every bomber shot down by an anti-aircraft gun in September 1940 the gun had to expend an enormous 20,000 rounds. Results did improve and by February 1941 the figure was down to 3,000. Still, the knowledge that something was being done was at least a small comfort to the population.

Göring also turned his attention to other British cities. Perhaps his aim was to eliminate great industrial centres and not simply to mete out punishment to British civilians. In fact, the lack of accuracy among bombers of the age ensured that civilians were foremost among the casualties.

In Coventry, 568 people were killed on 14 November 1940 when German bombers opened their doors and let 450 tons of bombs drop on the city. Its historic cathedral was ruined. Birmingham, Manchester, Exeter, Sheffield, Liverpool, Cardiff, Swansea, Bath, Plymouth, Ipswich, Norwich, Southampton, Sunderland, Hull, Middlesborough and Canterbury all also received a battering.

■ BITTER TRUTH ■

Countless thousands of people were made homeless by these air raids, being left only with the clothes they stood up in. During the worst of them which occurred in December 1940 and May 1941 in London, the firefighters ran out of water as they fought hundreds of blazes and were left with little option but to let them rage on. On 10 May 1941 550 German bombers unleashed 700 tons of high explosives and thousands of incendiaries, killing 1,436 people and destroying 700 acres of city. Just 14 of the attackers were brought down.

From August 1940 to May 1941, 44,000 civilians died and 103,000 were injured. The bitter truth was that the destruction and misery was no precursor to an invasion of

From August 1940 to May 1941, 44,000 civilians died

Britain. It was merely a camouflage for Hitler's real intentions, to expand eastwards across the Russian borders, to Moscow and beyond. Only when Luftwaffe planes were pulled out of France to concentrate on the Russian front did the attacks on Britain subside.

Left: **As dawn breaks, the destruction of the previous night's raid on London's docklands is revealed.**

AIR BATTLE – BALKANS

Both Axis and Allied powers saw benefit in opening a battle-front in the Balkans.

For Hitler, there was a chance of mopping up a potentially troublesome southern flank before mounting 'Operation Barbarossa', the invasion of Russia.

Churchill and his top brass saw a successful campaign in Greece or Yugoslavia offering a possible backdoor entry into Germany when no access seemed available at the front.

In the event, the short and bloody campaign in the region left both sides as losers when it illustrated both the advantages – and drawbacks – of an airborne campaign.

Mussolini had opened hostilities when he invaded Greece on 28 October 1940. It was an impetuous decision which he lived to regret. Not only did it infuriate his ally Hitler, who had fostered an amenable relationship with Greece's ruler General Metaxas and considered the country in the bag. But it served to further humiliate Mussolini and his troops in addition to their inept showing in North and East Africa.

For the Greeks, although poorly equipped for modern warfare, were imbued with fighting spirit and managed to see off the Italians, pushing them back behind their lines in occupied Albania.

Britain was determined to stand by pledges of aid made to Greece – even though it had been unable to honour promises made to Romania, which was occupied by German troops at the start of October 1940.

■ ALLIES IN GREECE ■

Hitler had no option but to intervene in the action. However, for a few months he bided his time.

Having dispatched several thousand men, the British were keen to send even more of their contingent presently in North Africa to the aid of the Greeks. Metaxas was unsure. Although the presence of air support was welcomed, his own men were putting up an adequate performance and the presence of Allied ground troops would only succeed in drawing the awesome firepower of an irate Hitler. Instead of men, he said, he would rather have their boots. His own soldiers were suffering greatly due to the inadequacies of their footwear.

By the end of November 1940 three squadrons of Blenheim bombers and fighters had been stationed in Greece and the numbers continued to increase. Their brief, to defend Athens.

The political outlook changed at the end of January 1941 when Metaxas died suddenly and was replaced by Emmanuel Tsouderos who was well-disposed towards the Allies.

At a meeting in February, it was agreed the 1st Armoured Brigade, the 6th Australian Division and the 2nd New Zealand Division would be stationed in Greece to repel possible German aggression. With Bulgaria to the east rapidly falling under the influence of Germany, and with Italy in the west, the fresh troops could plug defensive gaps left open by the Greeks fighting in Albania. Churchill enjoyed the idea of rescuing the

> **The Greeks were imbued with fighting spirit and managed to see off the Italians**

'cradle of civilisation', as Greece is known, from the clutches of Nazism.

Also feeling the weight of the Nazi jackboot was neighbouring Yugoslavia, a country Britain failed to support. The government, under Prince Regent Paul and Prime Minister Dragisa Cvetkovic, were given an invitation-ultimatum in March 1941. Yugoslavia was to join the Axis powers. Prince Regent Paul was unable to secure aid from the British. With a heavy heart he finally gave his

Far left: A ship unloading supplies for the Allies in Suda Bay comes to grief.
Left: Italian soldiers were held at bay when they tried to invade Greece.

◆ EYE WITNESS ◆

Howard Ganly was in the US 82nd Airborne Division. He was dropped behind enemy lines before D-Day to act as a pathfinder.

❝ I was a little bit lost. They gave us the wrong maps. I made a few mistakes. I was shot at by my own men. They had got hold of some farmers' clothes and put them on, thinking they would be good disguises in German territory. Some of them were from my own company. I could have had them court martialled but I didn't. They stuck to me close for the rest of the war.

I was looking for open fields that weren't mined and didn't have big stumps stuck in the ground so they would be suitable for landing gliders. I would signal the gliders if it was OK to come in, with special lights and flares. We didn't dare use radios too much. I was very scared, I was just 19 years old. I came into the service when I was 17. The army kept pushing me around from one place to another. I didn't have any family, I spent most of my childhood in orphan asylums. I joined up to get a job and the money was good.

I survived D-Day but ran into trouble later on in Europe. I baled out in Holland behind enemy lines. A young Dutch girl put me in a barge and hid me from the Germans. She probably saved my life. I looked for her a few times after the war but never found her. I broke my leg and back in the fall. I have been disabled ever since. I was hospitalised for two years. I worked on and off but most of the time I have been crippled up. ❞

Luftwaffe wreaked havoc on Piraeus, the harbour of the Greek capital, which was crowded with ships from an incoming convoy. As the German bombs rained down destruction, one ship at anchor, SS Glen Fraser, had its 250-ton cargo of explosives ignited by a direct hit. The roaring explosion that followed flattened much of the harbour, sank yet more

'It is especially important that the blow against Yugoslavia is carried out with pitiless harshness'

consent and the Tripartite Pact was signed on 25 March.

Fury against the agreement among the Yugoslav people erupted immediately. There was an internal revolt which unseated the prince regent and put 17-year-old King Peter II in his place. On 27 March the pact signed with Hitler was ripped into pieces. The sombre mood which had descended on Belgrade and beyond was suddenly lifted, to be replaced with rejoicing.

■ HITLER OUTRAGED ■

The outbreak of anti-Nazism outraged Hitler. He resolved to teach the people of Yugoslavia a lesson. German commanders were told: 'Politically it is especially important that the blow against Yugoslavia is carried out with pitiless harshness.' It made sense to combat the Greek problem at the same time so 'Operation Strafgericht' (punishment) against Yugoslavia and 'Operation Marita' against Greece were co-ordinated to begin on 6 April.

Hitler's campaign to pummel Yugoslavia into submission started with a dawn raid by the Luftwaffe. The sole declaration of war was the shower of bombs which hit Belgrade at 6am. The day-long assault claimed 17,000 lives and the grand buildings of the capital crumbled.

The day closed with another disaster, this time for Greece. The

vessels and even shattered windows in Athens some seven miles distant.

German armies began driving into both countries at the usual alarming Panzer pace. Yugoslavia, which had a small army, held out for just 11 days. Much of its air force was knocked out on the ground by Luftwaffe attacks. The inglorious fortnight was compounded when Royal Yugoslav Air Force Hurricanes became

Right: Germany soon won command of the skies over Greece, and this tipped the balance of the battle in their favour.

embroiled in a dog-fight over Belgrade with some BF-109s which unfortunately belonged to the very same air force.

■ RETREAT TO CRETE ■

The Greek army, too, was having difficulty fending off the advance. The fighting was gruelling. British commander General Sir Henry 'Jumbo' Maitland Wilson soon saw the hopelessness of the situation and ordered an evacuation to the south. On 22 April Greece capitulated also. The initial destination of the fleeing Allied troops was the Peloponnese islands linked to mainland Greece by a bridge at Corinth. Then it was onwards to the island of Crete.

Under fire from the Luftwaffe above, the Royal Navy came in to the southerly beaches on 26 and 27 April to hoist 26,000 men to safety. Left behind were 900 dead, 1,200 wounded and something in the order of 10,000 men who had fallen prisoner to the Germans. Then there was the abandoned weaponry, amounting to more than 100 tanks, 400 guns, 1,800 machine guns and 8,000 vehicles. The RAF had lost more than 200 aircraft in total while

> ## On Crete there was chaos with hundreds of leaderless men awaiting an uncertain future

the Royal Navy had had two destroyers and about 25 other ships sunk.

On Crete there was chaos with hundreds of leaderless men awaiting an uncertain future. The only thing

Above: **Serbs in Yugoslavia were no friends of the Germans. Many fought as guerrillas against the invaders.**

of which they could be sure was that Hitler's men would not rest until Crete too fell into their grasp.

In command was Major-General Bernard Freyberg, a pugnacious New Zealander who was ready to refuse the mantle of leadership until he discovered there was a sizeable number of his own men on the island – troops he believed had been taken back to Egypt.

His force amounted to two New Zealand brigades, about 7,750 men, plus an Australian brigade, two further battalions of Australians and a field regiment of artillery, with a combined total of 6,500. There were 15,000 British troops, too, comprising a brigade of infantrymen and part

Above: A Panzer division parades its might before the centuries-old Acropolis in Athens, after the city was overrun.

of the 1st Armoured Brigade, complete with two light tanks. Also at his disposal were about 10,000 Greeks. The Allies also had the support of the local population, many of whom would take up arms against the incoming Germans.

Freyberg, who won the VC in World War I, set about defending the island as best he could. He focused his forces at the three airfields, Maleme, Retimo and Heraklion, and the easily accessible Suda Bay.

From North Africa he received some tanks – less than two dozen but welcome nonetheless – and some rather war-worn artillery. There was

a further injection of men, the 2nd Leicesters, who arrived on 16 May.

Crete – 136 miles long and an uneven 40 miles wide, and full of mountainous terrain – could hardly be adequately defended given the small number of men. Yet Freyberg

From North Africa Freyberg received some tanks – less than two dozen but welcome

was determined his men would give it their best shot.

For Germany, the invasion of Crete posed some difficulties, not least in how to transport troops to the island. The Royal Navy had

established a command of the seas. Already the shortcomings of the Italian navy had been shown up and the German command did not trust its ally's sailors with the lives of crack soldiers of the Third Reich. So an all-out amphibious assault was deemed too dangerous.

Yet in the air the Luftwaffe was unrivalled. By 18 May only seven RAF aircraft were left on Crete, and these were promptly withdrawn to Egypt. An airborne assault might work. Airborne forces had been in existence since 1927 when the first was formed by Italy. The Soviet Union soon followed suit and the value of these sky-fliers was clear. They could be dropped into enemy territory either in small numbers for the purpose of sabotage or in large numbers to begin an invasion.

There were, of course, numerous hazards inherent in airborne operations, but until now the Germans had known only successes. Their use of paratroopers in Norway, Belgium and Holland during 1940 had brought striking results. The 55 men

---

The use of paratroopers in Norway, Belgium and Holland during 1940 had brought striking results

---

from the 'Granite' assault team who parachuted into Eben Emael, the strongest fortress in the world, on the Belgian-Dutch border, in May of that year, defeated 700 defenders in less than a day.

The Luftwaffe's airborne supremo was Kurt Student, a World War I fighter pilot and squadron leader. He had keenly studied the potential of airborne techniques in Russia during the 1930s and saw 'Blitzkreig' as an excellent opportunity to put theory into practice.

Not only did he have troops leaping from flying aircraft but also equipment-bearing soldiers carried in gliders, and 'air mobile' forces, men trained in the art of going into action straight from the door of a landed plane. He sought to use all types in the invasion of Crete.

■ 'MERKUR' ■

'Operation Merkur', the German attack on Crete, was to be launched following days of heavy aerial bombardment, with the landing of 36 gliders whose elite troops would knock out anti-aircraft guns and capture key locations.

The men of XI Air Corps' 1st Assault Regiment were the next penned in to see action, capturing an airfield and other key locations. At the same time, men of the 3rd Parachute Regiment would drop further up the coast and the aim was for both prongs to battle to a reunion.

Then a second wave was planned in which the 1st and 2nd Parachute Regiments were introduced with heavier arms, while two further battalions arrived by sea in fast motor-

cutters. More amphibious activity was planned when the island was in German control. First hitch for the Germans came when too few planes were provided, forcing the commanders to cut the size of the airborne assault.

Student and his men believed only a few thousand men would be there to meet them when the attack on 20 May got underway. It was a catastrophic miscalculation.

As a swarm of aircraft receded into the distance, hundreds of parachutes billowed in the breeze. The troops on the ground had plenty of time to take aim and fire, relishing a chance to get revenge on the men who had so recently chased them out of Greece. The helpless paras were picked off one by one as they all fell

Right: **General Kurt Student was the mastermind behind German paratroopers' triumphs – and their failures, like the ill-fated assault on Crete.**

Above: German paratroopers were confident as they embarked for Crete, with good reason. Until then, they had only known success.

Communications were poor on both sides. With telephone lines down and radios suffering patchy reception, the Allied groups felt equally isolated from assistance and exposed to the enemy. It caused one New Zealand commander to withdraw his men from a commanding position in the heights above an airfield, leaving a vital foothold open to the attackers.

Groves and escarpments were littered with bodies, many still strapped into their 'chutes

There followed more of the bitter fighting, often at close quarters, with many Allied soldiers claiming victims at the point of a bayonet. Both sides vied for the airfields. There was an uncomfortable stalemate as both Allied and German commanders tried to land reinforcements. The Royal Navy sank the German transports while the Luftwaffe holed the British ships.

■ GERMAN VICTORY ■

At Maleme airfield under a barrage of crossfire, brave German pilots began to land their transport planes, some coming to grief on the runway, others colliding with planes that had preceded them. Inside were well-trained, well-armed soldiers fresh and ready for the fight.

The New Zealanders at Maleme were finally overwhelmed. Germany had scored the first victory in the battle for Crete.

And it was a key triumph, for now that the attacking troops had control of Maleme airfield, the gateway was open for supplies and still more troops to be transported in.

virtually on top of the defending Anzac and British forces. Olive groves and rocky escarpments were littered with bodies, many still strapped into 'chutes.

Some parachutists didn't even make it out of their planes. Ground fire penetrated the hulls of the low-flying aircraft, killing or wounding men while they were still inside.

The few that survived were compelled to seek cover and join up with their comrades as soon as they could. Only those who dropped away from their targets – and thus away from defensive fire – escaped being cut down. It was for them to fight their way across the rocky landscape and unite with other groups.

OTTO SKORZENY

A scar-faced German captain called Otto Skorzeny was the action-man asked by Hitler to rescue Mussolini from imprisonment in September 1943. Skorzeny, who was frustrated in earlier plans to snatch the Duce to safety by the diligence of the Italian authorities who kept their prized prisoner on the move, planned for a German plane to land on a precarious mountain plateau while he in the company of other troops parachuted into the hotel hideaway where Mussolini was held. Italian guards at the mountain village of Assergi abided by his requests not to resist the bold German move. Mussolini was flown off in the tiny plane which battled to ascend from the plateau. On reaching Rome he was transferred to a Heinkel 111 for a flight to the safety of Vienna.

In less than a week, Freyberg assessed the situation as hopeless. He ordered the Allied troops, by now mentally and physically exhausted, to withdraw to the south where an evacuation was being launched by the Royal Navy.

Between 27 May and 31 May, about 16,500 Allied men were taken off Crete. Germany had sealed its Balkan front.

■ BALANCE SHEET ■

Both sides were left counting the cost, however. Left on Crete were 1,750 Allied soldiers killed in action, two thirds of them Anzacs, and 13,500 men now held as prisoners of war. The Royal Navy lost three cruisers and six destroyers in the rescue bid, along with about 2,000 sailors killed or taken prisoner. Also left behind were Greek, British and Anzac soldiers who turned guerrilla to fight a cloaked campaign against the occupiers. It was another inglorious rout for the Allies.

As for the Germans, nearly half the initial force were killed on Crete, amounting to some 3,700 men. Among them were high-ranking officers including a divisional commander, and a colonel. The number of aircraft shot to smithereens by the Allies or junked on the island airstrips was also immense.

Hitler surveyed the results – and decided the price was unacceptably high. Matter-of-factly, he told Student afterwards: 'Of course you know, General, that we shall never do another airborne operation. Crete proved that the days of parachute troops are over.'

It was a gross over-exaggeration. Germany continued to employ parachute troops although never again in such vast numbers. Nevertheless, Hitler did decide to abandon plans to parachute men into Malta, the stepping-stone island in the Mediterranean. Had he won Malta, Hitler might have found victory in the North African campaign, and pushed into the Middle East and India to join hands with Germany's ally Japan.

The Allies observed the German experience on Crete but also decided in favour of using airborne troops in future engagements. Paratroopers played a pivotal role in the success of the D-Day operations in 1944. Theirs was a precarious job, dropping behind enemy lines in darkness to act as pathfinders for the incoming gliders. Men of the US 82nd and 101st Airborne Divisions were also

> ## 'Of course you know, General, that we shall never do another airborne operation'

charged with hindering the enemy advance towards to the coast. But the landings did not go as planned.

A combination of inexperienced piloting and mistakes in navigation had the men dispersed over a huge

Right: Captured Australian servicemen are a source of curiosity for their German guards.

Left: 'Pathfinder' parachutists are briefed before dropping into France, their task to direct airborne forces to landing points.

were thrown into confusion by the unexpected and unseen troops. One regiment in the 82nd Airborne Division managed to capture the town of Ste Mère Eglise.

British airborne troops were also seeing action as they seized vital bridges and knocked out a battery of guns aimed at the coast. For the British paratroopers, the ultimate test of endurance was to come later in the year at Arnhem in 'Operation Market Garden'.

Montgomery was eager to persuade Eisenhower of the wisdom

area instead of being in a concentrated group. Parachutists found themselves landing in some of the many engorged rivers in the region. Weighed down by their equipment they floundered for hours trying to get out. Others drowned in the struggle. It meant both Divisions were literally thousands of men short

Weighed down by their equipment they floundered for hours trying to get out

when they went into action. All the hazards of airborne operations, particularly those carried out at night, appeared to be coming in at the Americans.

Yet success bred out of disaster. Undoubtedly, the German defenders

Right: Horsa gliders lie in pieces after landing men in northern France in 1944. On these gliders the fuselage is split from the wings to unload.

ALLIED SUCCESS

Air superiority during D-Day became the key to Allied success. While it was thought that the Luftwaffe would sent up some 900 aircraft to make 1,200 sorties on D-Day, in fact only 100 were made in daylight and a further 175 after dark. By contrast the RAF alone flew 5,656 sorties on D-Day, about 40 per cent of the total made by the Allies.

Allied aircraft dropped a total of 4,310 paratroops and towed gliders containing 493 men, 17 guns, 44 Jeeps and 55 motorcycles without suffering harassment from enemy bombers.

As well as protecting troops and ships, Allied aircraft dropped 5,267 bombs against the coastal gun batteries.

The first German plane to fall victim on D-Day was a Ju 88, brought down by New Zealand Flying Officer Johnnie Houlton, one of 2,000 pilots in the Second Tactical Air Force who was in a Spitfire.

In the months which followed, three times as many bombs were dropped on Germany than in all the previous years.

of committing the ground troops to one hammer-blow into northern Germany. Eisenhower favoured a fan-shaped attack instead.

■ 'MARKET GARDEN' ■

'Operation Market Garden' was designed to capture key bridges in Holland through which Allied troops could be funnelled into Germany. The US 101st Airborne Division was charged with gaining land north of Eindhoven, the US 82nd Airborne Division was allocated two big bridges over the Meuse and the Wall rivers, while the British 1st Airborne Division had to seize bridges over the lower Rhine at Arnhem.

The men were carried to their targets in a total of 1,068 aircraft and 478 gliders. While the Americans experienced considerable success on their fronts, the British met enormous German resistance en route to their target. Just one battalion, the 2nd, reached the bridge at Arnhem. Soon after, they were cut off.

Right: Troops taken by gliders into Arnhem in a bid to short-circuit the route to Berlin. The Britons had a grim fate in store.

Unfortunately for the British paratroopers, the Germans picked Arnhem as a focal point of defence and reinforced their lines with troops, including an SS Panzer corps containing two armoured divisions. All efforts by the British to reach the men isolated at Arnhem were repelled after fierce clashes.

At the bridge, the paratroopers were pushed back into a defensive

---

It took nine days for the men to establish an escape route across the Rhine

---

margin. It took nine days for the men to establish an escape route across the Rhine. Just 2,200 men got out from a force which began with a strength of 10,000. Montgomery's plan to by-pass Germany's defensive Siegfried line had failed. The thrust continued as before.

WINGS OVER THE DESERT

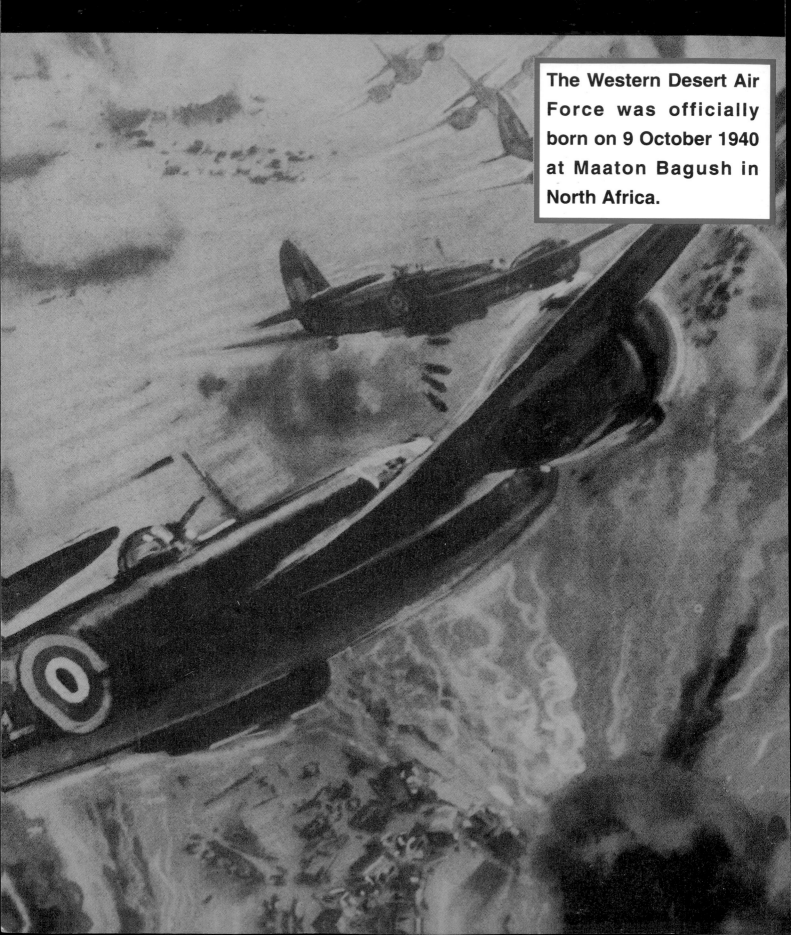

The Western Desert Air Force was officially born on 9 October 1940 at Maaton Bagush in North Africa.

Here in the African desert, the theories of modern air warfare were established. For it was in North Africa that the principles of 'partnership' between air, sea and land forces were tried and tested for the first time, helping to put an end to decades of overt inter-service rivalry.

Co-operation of the kind enjoyed by air, sea and naval personnel among the Allies was unthinkable for their German and Italian counterparts, who not only fought a common enemy but were constantly embroiled in sniping against different factions on their own side. Indeed, there were plenty of hiccoughs along the way among the Allies with soldiers convinced the only worthwhile aeroplane was the one that flew protectively above their heads, regardless of the risk to the pilot and his inability to achieve results from that vulnerable spot.

The initial trials of tactical airborne operations were honed by the men of the Desert Air Force until they finally became adopted everywhere.

Unfortunately for the Italians, early promise was soon done down by the Desert Air Force

Lessons learned in the Desert Air Force now seem rudimentary and even naive. Yet aerial combat was still in its infancy when the war commenced. Fliers in World War I had the opportunity to make only elementary trials and errors. Little was done to advance the theory of warfare in the air after 1918 as most nations were concentrating on peace.

And until the conflict in the desert got underway, the Royal Air Force was from necessity concentrating primarily on defence.

To call it simply a Desert Air Force is to vastly over-simplify the case. The men who worked under its umbrella saw action in the skies above Egypt, Libya, East and West Africa, Greece, Yugoslavia, Palestine, Italy and other hot spots in the region.

This tremendous fighting force grew from an original nucleus of some 29 squadrons – a total of 600 aircraft. These were all that were available to Middle East commander Air Chief Marshal Sir Arthur Longmore when hostilities with Italy commenced in 1940. Included in this total were a goodly number of outdated biplanes and obsolete Blenheim bombers. That summer on the home front saw the Battle of Britain reach its momentous heights. So the chances of getting top-notch replacements were slim.

In addition, the airmen faced the same shortages that cursed the soldiers on the ground, those of water, fuel and spare parts to replace those worn by the inhospitable terrain.

Above: **Mussolini believed his air force could win the skies over Africa.** *Left:* **Stalwart Beaufighters played a key role in the North African campaign.**

Against them was the might of the Regia Aeronautica, the Italian air force, which had proved itself already in the Spanish Civil War and Mussolini's Ethiopian campaign in the mid-1930s. The Italians were flying home-produced planes like Capronis and Fiats. Unfortunately for the Italians, their early promise was soon done down by the Desert Air Force.

■ MALTA ATTACKED ■

The Regia Aeronautica went into action for the first time on 11 June 1940, with 35 Savoia-Marchetti bombers attacking Malta. Pitted against them were four Gloster Sea Gladiators, constituting the island's only fighter defence force. By the end of the day, the Italians had launched seven attacks for no loss.

By way of response, 26 RAF Bristol Blenheims launched an attack against an Italian airfield in North Africa, eventually destroying 18 enemy aircraft on the ground.

Above: **Despite their years of experience, Italian aircraft and pilots proved no match for the Desert Air Force.**

There followed a number of skirmishes. Prime targets for the Italians were Malta, Gibraltar, the British base at Alexandria in Egypt and the British Mediterranean Fleet.

The action in Africa then forked, with General Graziani leading his contingent of Italians in the Western Desert against Wavell, while the Duke of Aosta led some 215,000 troops out of Italian East Africa and into a British dominion. To meet Graziani's men were the British 7th Armoured Division, soon to be joined by the 6th Australian Division. Meanwhile, the 4th Indian Division was dispatched to meet the threat in East Africa.

It was in the East African campaign that vital steps towards an orchestrated plan for close air support were made. At the outset in October 1940, the Italians in East Africa were a formidable enemy. Their spirits were high, their maturity in desert warfare a major advantage. But much of their buoyancy could be put down to the fact that they enjoyed air superiority. Italy had 14 bomber squadrons or gruppi in East Africa, and five supporting fighter gruppi. The over-stretched British forces, comprising nine squadrons, were happily reinforced by a further eight squadrons from South Africa, flying Hurricane aircraft.

Soon the battle to win supremacy of the skies began to swing in favour of the Allies

---

Soon, the battle to win supremacy in the skies began to swing in favour of the Allies. Both sides fought bitterly, both on land and in the air, for command of Keren, a fortified hill top in Eritrea. At the end of eight weeks, however, the Italians were turfed out of their stronghold and, by April 1941, a corner in the war of East Africa had been turned. As the campaign toiled on, the South African Air Force formed a first Close Support Flight to co-operate with ground troops, achieving a good measure of success.

■ FIVE LESSONS ■

After the battle of Keren, one British observer noted five lessons to be learned. They were: the need for transport planes; the need for supplies to be dropped by air (which was to prove crucial in the jungle wars of Burma and the Pacific); the advantage lent by long-range fighters which could destroy the enemy's aircraft before they lifted off; the need for Red Cross air ambulances to evacuate the wounded; and the preference for dive bombers.

These were all points which would be brought home to subsequent

◆ **EYE WITNESS** ◆

Ern Stanton, from New South Wales, was 18 when he joined the Royal Australian Air Force and qualified as a flier on the Empire Air Training Scheme.

❛ Of our EATS course in Canada, about 40 per cent were later killed. It was very sad and disheartening to hear about your mates dying in action but I was really too young and conditioned too much to death to realise the more serious aspects of war

I do particularly remember one little bloke in our squadron who would give away all his personal effects before he went on a mission because he was convinced he wasn't going to come back. When he did return safely, he would go around and get them all back. But he did finally get killed. ❜

Below: Hurricane pilots of 73 Squadron line up before a desert-worn aircraft in North Africa during 1941. The Hurricane was the RAF's first monoplane fighter.

senior air force officers. For now, only the immediate achievement of winning an important initial victory was noted. As the Allies took greater command of the action, Italian commanders found themselves battling not only against the Allies but also against a sapped will among their own men. A proportion of their troops were native Africans whose loyalty was suspect.

The campaign in Eritrea was to end in a complete and resounding victory for the Allies by the middle of 1941. Yet short on success though the Allies were at this stage, there was little chance to celebrate. Much as the British commanders had feared, Hitler had sent German forces into the region to assist his floundering fascist soul-mate.

Early in 1941 it was clear the Luftwaffe were installing units of Fliegerkorps X in Sicily, a specialist branch of the air force which had cut its teeth in the Norwegian campaign

and specialised in picking off ships. The Mediterranean Fleet first felt its presence on 10 January 1941 when up to 40 aircraft attacked a convoy. In aerial warfare, the Luftwaffe quite simply outclassed the Italians.

At the same time, the conflict in Greece was intensifying. The only assistance actively required by the

Early in 1941 it was clear that the Luftwaffe were installing units of Fliegerkorps X in Sicily

Greeks at the start was an injection of air power. Here the expanding Allied air strength had little problem asserting its authority. In one battle which took place on 28 February 1941, 16 Hurricanes and 12 Gladiators were patrolling at 14,000 feet when they were attacked by 50

Above: **German aircraft and pilots suffered the same difficult conditions as their Allied enemies.**

Italian Fiat planes. In the two-hour clash which followed, the Royal Air Force fighters claimed 27 enemy planes for just one Gladiator lost.

The string of successes were a tribute to the ground crews who faced appalling winter conditions in the most primitive of airfields in order to keep the planes airborne. Spring saw further aerial reinforcements sent in by the British but the leaders in the field were uneasy. It was surely only a matter of months before Hitler made that battleground his own as well.

■ LUFTWAFFE ARRIVES ■

In April those grim predictions became reality. The Royal Air Force found its forces and those of its Greek and Yugoslav allies suddenly dwarfed by the arrival of the Luftwaffe. Its ranks included 430 bombers, 180 fighters, 700 transport planes and 80 gliders.

By 19 April the four Hurricane squadrons in Greece could rally just 22 operational aircraft between them. All were pulled down to Athens to lend air support to the evacuation of troops from Greece to Crete and North Africa. In the end there were only seven Hurricanes left.

On Crete they were joined by four Sea Gladiators and three Fairey Fulmars of the Fleet Air Arm. The abysmally small fighting force was virtually wiped out on the ground by the marauding Germans.

Added to the boiling pot was the Iraqi uprising against the British in May 1941. The Desert Air Force was by now staffed with Australian, New Zealand, Rhodesian and Free French units, as well as British and South African. But the ceaseless demands took their toll of its strength. And the menace from the Third Reich in the

> **By 19 April the four Hurricane squadrons in Greece could rally just 22 operational aircraft**

region did nothing to recede during that period. In fact, it gained momentum. Hitler was dallying with the idea of invading Malta. The little island which had found some relief when attacking forces were diverted to assist in the invasion of Greece, was once again at the top of the agenda for the Luftwaffe.

■ MALTA REPLENISHED ■

Its defences amounted to just four fighter squadrons as well as bombers and Fleet Air Arm forces based off the island. The succession of raids both by the Italians and increasingly by the Germans pared down the number of fighters. But the ranks were replenished on 15 June 1941 when 47 flew from the deck of the

Below: **SS** *Talbot* **was one of scores of ships to fall foul of enemy planes in Malta's Grand Harbour.**

Ark Royal, and a further 64 were dispatched by similar means before the month had ended.

The hectic months ahead saw the Malta-based fliers toiling to keep the convoys safe, and so deprive Hitler and Mussolini of the toe-hold they both sought. In addition, they attempted to destroy enemy convoys and hit targets in Italy – particularly Naples where, on 16 December 1941, 16 Wellingtons showered a torpedo factory with 4000lb bombs, the largest used in the Mediterranean to that date.

Between June and October 1941, 220,000 tons of Axis shipping was sunk en route to Libya, of which 115,000 tons could be marked down

to the Desert Air Force, especially its Maltese division.

The fruits presented to Churchill by the frustrated Longmore were too few and far between to impress.

> ## On 16 October 1941, 16 Wellingtons showered a Naples torpedo factory with 4,000lb bombs

Friction between the ground and air forces was still very much in evidence, never more so than when a reconnaissance flight reported enemy troops approaching a vital petrol dump in

Above: On Malta, air strips like this one provided constant targets for Luftwaffe pilots. *Right:* Air Chief Marshal Sir Arthur Tedder.

◆ EYE WITNESS ◆

Post Office worker Arthur Helm was one of the first New Zealanders to sign up and fight for Britain following the outbreak of World War II.

 I had read a lot about the Germans and I knew how despicable they were. And I knew what I was letting myself in for.

I was a member of the First Echelon, the 6,607 men who first left New Zealand for Eygpt. Later I was in northern Greece as a member of 4th Brigade Signals. After the invasion of the Germans, we moved to fight a rearguard action at Thebes. I saw the Acropolis about four hours before the Swastika was raised over it. At Port Rafti we held a two-mile stretch of coastline and two miles inland during the evacuation. We had to throw everything overboard except for our rifles, the clothes we stood up in and a small haversack.

Author Laurence Durrell wrote that when everyone arrived in Crete they were dishevelled, dispirited and defeated – except the New Zealanders. They came up the beach with their rifles poised, their hats on and every one had a book under his arms. He was wrong – I had two books, a book of poetry and a Bible.

Spirits were high among the New Zealanders. We simply felt sorry for the Greek soldiers we left behind.

We expected the arrival of the Germans. I had just knocked off after 24 hours on duty and was having my breakfast when the first parachutes appeared.

There was a lot of deer-stalking and rabbit-shooting in New Zealand so most of us could shoot pretty straight. You knew when you had hit a parachutist coming down. He retracted his legs up as an automatic reaction.

Later I got involved at Galatas where we went in with bayonets after dark and drove out a bunch of Germans from the houses there. It was very nerve-racking but we got rid of them – even if we did have to retreat the next day.

I got out over the mountains to the harbour for evacuation. I met an English soldier at the side of the track and pointed out the way. He said: "I'm not going any further." I gave him some water and he told me he had been through Dunkirk but it wasn't a patch on this.

He just laid down on the hillside and died. He was done for, absolutely exhausted, and he had no will to live.

We lost Crete because the Germans had planes and we didn't. But we never lost heart. After being evacuated from Crete we went to Sidi Rezburgh. That was probably the worst campaign of the lot.

the North African desert. The dump was destroyed before it was discovered the troops in question were, in fact, British. Never mind that it was notoriously difficult to positively identify the nationality of soldiers from the air. The fighters on the ground had been deprived of valuable fuel for no reason. Longmore's repeated requests for more aircraft did little to endear him at home, either. Duly, Longmore was replaced by Arthur Tedder in May 1941.

■ AIR FLEET ENLARGED ■

The following month, Wavell was dispatched from North Africa by an irate Churchill. Happily, his replacement, General Sir Claude Auchinleck, struck an immediate harmonious note with Tedder which helped to end the bubbling army-air force discord.

Tedder, with support from the Air Ministry, helped to overhaul the repair and maintenance operations in the region which were proving so inefficient and therefore costly to the service.

Once he had enlarged the fleet of aircraft available to the Desert Air Force to beyond 1,000 in November 1941, Tedder turned his attention to the quest for new, well-trained recruits. There was a chronic shortage of training facilities in the Middle East.

Two operations to relieve Tobruk, 'Brevity' and "Battleaxe', had failed in the early summer of 1941

Tedder fell back on his usual standpoint, which was to employ an expert – in this case Air Commodore B. Embry – who could devote the best of his time and attention to the problem.

■ CO-ORDINATED ACTION■

Two operations to relieve Tobruk, 'Brevity' and 'Battleaxe', had failed in the early summer of 1941 and once again it seemed the relations between army and air force would be strained. It was in September 1941 that a satisfactory blueprint for co-ordinated action was finally drawn up to at last eliminate this problem. Drawing on the illustrations of the East African campaign, it set out the principles of close support of land forces by air forces, including pre-arranged and impromptu attacks on the enemy. Indirect air support was defined as attacks on objectives other than the enemy forces in the battle proper.

An Air Support Control headquarters was created for each army corps. These were information exchanges linked by two-way radio to brigades in action. Representing the RAF at brigade was a team called a Forward Air Support Link. The RAF team could assess the action at close quarters and request air support when necessary. On receiving the request, the staff at the Air Support Control team headquarters, with its overview, could work

Above: **Air Chief Marshal Sir Arthur W. Tedder, Deputy Supreme Commander, Allied Forces Western Europe.**

out where best to send its aircraft during a battle for the most effective results.

The principles had already been put into practice on exercises in Northern Ireland as early as September 1940. A developmental Army Co-Operation Command had been set up by the RAF following Dunkirk when the air force received flak for not coming more visibly to the aid of evacuating soldiers.

In Africa, these close-support principles were not only rehearsed but put into action as well, and adopted thereafter to the satisfaction of everyone involved.

THE END OF THE BEGINNING..

'This is not the end. It is not even the beginning of the end. But it is, perhaps, the end of the beginning.'

(Winston Churchill after the Allied victory in North Africa.)

REDS IN THE SKY

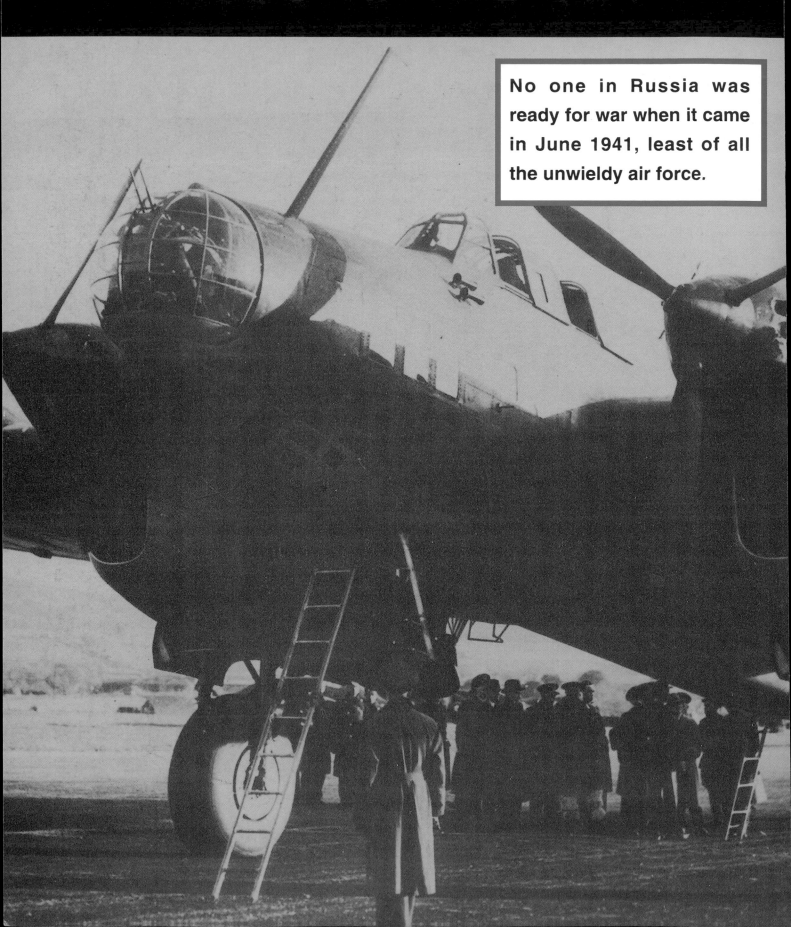

No one in Russia was ready for war when it came in June 1941, least of all the unwieldy air force.

Stalin boasted of a large body of planes. But like the sizeable French air force of 1940, the Red Air Force was ineffectively used and no match for the skill and experience of the Luftwaffe. Its sole four-engined bomber at the outset of the war was the TB-3, slow, underpowered and inadequately armed. It had ten squadrons of MiG, Yak and Lagg fighters. Yet these were far inferior to the Messerschmitts so elegantly handled by German pilots.

In addition, the Russians were partway through a modernisation plan in which their outdated planes would be replaced by more competitive models. The Russian air force, like all branches of the establishment, had suffered its fair share of losses in the purges which Stalin organised to rid himself of potential opponents.

■ AID FROM BRITAIN ■

The pilots of the Red Air Force were trained to support the troops on the ground rather than enter into combat with other aircraft. Many ended up frantically helping to evacuate Russian industry to the east, to save it from falling into German hands – reducing the aircraft available for other duties still further. Indeed, its fighter arm had never been put to the test. The summer and autumn of 1941 brought a succession of disasters for the Red Air Force.

Still being punished by the Germans at home, the RAF nevertheless found the resources to send several squadrons of Hurricanes to the aid of the Russians.

It was Churchill's wish that as much aid should be devoted to the beleaguered and reluctant new ally as possible – despite the fact he was a

Above: Britain provided Hurricanes and know-how to the Russian air force, following the German invasion.

> *The summer and autumn of 1941 brought a succession of disasters for the Red Air Force*

lifelong critic of communism. In a broadcast shortly after Hitler's 'Operation Barbarossa', he explained how the hatred of fascism remained uppermost in his emotions.

Left: Much of Russia's air power was devoted to shipping industry east.
Far left: The TB-7 bomber that brought Russian minister Molotov to Britain.

'The Nazi regime is indistinguishable from the worst features of Communism. It is devoid of all theme and principle except appetite and racial domination. It excels all forms of human wickedness in the efficiency of its cruelty and ferocious aggression. No one has been a more consistent opponent of Communism that I have for the last 25 years. I will unsay no word that I have spoken about it.

■ BRITISH TEACHERS ■

'But all this fades away before the spectacle which is now unfolding. The past, with its crimes, its follies and its tragedies, flashes away. I see the Russian soldiers standing on the threshold of their native land, guarding the fields which their fathers have tilled from time immemorial. I see them guarding their homes where mothers and wives pray . . .

'I see the Russian soldiers standing on the threshold of their native land'

'I see advancing upon all this in hideous onslaught the Nazi war machine with its clanking, heel-clicking, dandified Prussian officers, its crafty expert agents fresh from the cowing and tying down of a dozen countries . . .

'I see the German bombers and fighters in the sky, still smarting from many a British whipping, delighted to find what they believe is an easier and safer prey.

'. . . if Hitler imagines that his attack on Soviet Russia will cause the slightest divergence of aims or slackening of effort in the great democracies who are resolved upon his doom, he is woefully mistaken.'

A British unit was sent with the aircraft to the Soviet Union to teach the Russians how to make and fly Hurricanes and to oass on tactical tips about the escort of bombers and general air operations.

Below: **Royal Air Force Hurricanes pictured in the air over the Russian countryside on their way back to base from escort duty.**

◆ EYE WITNESS ◆

Alexander Pokryshkin, the son of a bricklayer in Novosibirsk in Siberia, emerged as one of Russia's air aces. He flew 550 operational flights, fought 137 aerial battles and had 59 victories to his credit. He became the first member of the Soviet armed forces to be awarded the title 'Hero of the Soviet Union' three times, receiving his third Hero's Gold Star Medal in August 1944.

'I was out with pilot Semyonov as my partner flying on a reconnaissance mission to Jassy where the Germans had an aerodrome. As we approached the town I espied five Messerschmitts flying towards us, three below us and two above. Here, at last, were live Germans. They spotted us. I rocked my wings as a signal to Semyonov that I was going to attack. There were five of them and only two of us.

I was flying a MiG-3. It is a sturdy machine and well armed. It behaves wonderfully at high altitudes when its speed and manoeuvrability increase. I had my plan of action all worked out in an instant. Semyonov was to cover me as we had previously arranged on the ground. I shot up into the clouds and kept on climbing until I ran into one of the two Messerschmitts coming towards me. The German zoomed almost in my face. I did a stall-turn and found myself on the tail of the yellow, blunt-winged craft. I fired at short range. The Messerschmitt burst into flames and plunged downwards. I watched it as it fell and that almost cost me my life. The other German had crept up behind me. White ribbons of his tracers shot by and then my plane shuddered. Its port wing had been torn by bullets.

I dived to zero feet and hedge-hopped all the way home and, feeling that my aircraft was losing stability all the time, with great difficulty got back to the airfield. I made a normal landing, taxied to a stop, shut off the engine and slumped against the armoured back of the seat. I needed a drink. My throat was parched. That was the first German I had bagged.'

Soon, the lessons of the visiting Britons and that of bitter experience began to sink in. Until the Russians became fully conversant with combat know-how and were better equipped, however, a handful of German pilots had a field day.

King of the skies at that time was Erich Hartmann, otherwise known as 'Bubi' Hartmann or the 'Blond Knight'. During World War II he scored a record 352 victories, or kills, all of which were validated, making him an 'ace of aces'. Most were made on the Eastern front.

Hartmann was born in Weissach, near Stuttgart, on 19 April 1922. As a boy, he lived in China where his father was a doctor. When the family returned to Germany Hartmann was encouraged by his mother, herself a pilot, to sample the joys of flight. First qualifying as a glider pilot and instructor, Hartmann then joined the Luftwaffe aged 18.

He revealed the secret of his success: 'My only tactics are to wait until I have the chance to attack the enemy then close in at high speed. I open fire only when the whole

---

During World War II Hartmann scored a record 352 kills, all of which were validated

---

windshield is black with the enemy. Then not a single shot goes wild. I hit the enemy with all my guns and he goes down.'

In his beloved Me-109, he knocked out seven Red Air Force planes above the Battle of Kursk on 7 July 1943. It wasn't unusual for him to return from a sortie with more than one kill to his credit. No Allied pilot even approached such a mighty score.

■ HARTMANN ESCAPES ■

Operating over Russia, his plane was once shot down. Although he was unhurt, he was taken prisoner by Russian soldiers – a fate dreaded by German airmen at the time.

He pretended he was injured and was placed on a stretcher in a truck. En route to find a doctor he sprang up, overpowered his guard and leapt under fire from the lorry into a field of sunflowers. Sleeping by day and walking by night, he finally reached the German lines where he was almost shot by one of the sentries.

His outstanding success and distinctly Aryan features made him a

Above: **Russian pilots are congratulated by their major after completing a mission on the Eastern front.**

Below: **Erich Hartmann was one of the most successful pilots of the war, scoring most of his victories over Russia.**

frequently had cross words with his German superiors. Once he was even drunk enough to begin juggling with the Führer's hat but still remained a 'golden boy'.

■ HARD LABOUR ■

Erich Hartmann scored his last victory on the final day of the war, having flown 1,400 missions. He then came down to earth with a jolt, being captured by Russians. His sentence following the war was 25 years' hard labour – although he was offered freedom if he agreed to settle in East Germany and train their air force. He refused the deal and was finally released in 1956 following negotiations by Chancellor Adenauer of West Germany.

Hartmann resumed his air force career and learned to fly jets under

favourite with Adolf Hitler who awarded him the Knight's Cross and later added the prestigious German military decorations of Oak Leaves, Swords and, finally, Diamonds. Courageous not only in the air, he

ACE PILOTS

In the league table of wartime ace pilots, the first five places are occupied by Germans followed by two Japanese and a Finnish pilot. The first pilot from the West to appear in the league comes in 27th place, South African J. Pattle, who is followed by Richard Bong (below) and Thomas McGuire of the US and J. Johnson of Britain.

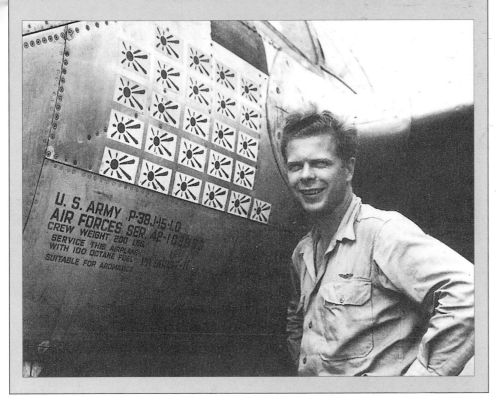

final total of 200,000 men abandoned their air duties to become infantrymen. It left the air crews short of ground staff. They were also to suffer from lack of aircraft and fuel and a diminishing training programme.

Worse was to come for the German air forces remaining on the Eastern front

Russian industry which had moved to the safety of the east was able to produce supplies for the Red Air Force – which was further bolstered by American aircraft through the Lend-Lease Act.

Below: **With much of Russia's powerful industrial muscle in the safety of the east, Stalin was able to provide his air force with vital replacement planes and components when Hitler could not.**

the auspices of the Americans. He was married in 1944 to his wartime sweetheart Ursula Puetsch, and the couple had a daughter. Hartmann died in 1993, aged 71.

As 1941 closed, the prospects improved considerably for the Russians in the air war. The Luftwaffe having deployed the majority of its air power in the opening stages of 'Operation Barbarossa', its strength on the Eastern front soon waned as it became overstretched and struggled to maintain its operations on three fronts.

■ LUFTWAFFE SUFFERS ■

Worse was to come for the German air forces remaining on the Eastern front. Luftwaffe field divisions were created to back up the ground forces as the conflict with Russia dragged on, and a

TIGER, TIGER, TIGER

By 1941, tensions were running high between the Americans and Japan. The United States government looked on uncomfortably as Japan sought to expand its empire by waging a brutal war on China.

Although Japan's leaders pledged neutrality in the European war, alarm bells were sounding across the Western world. Both America and its future allies aided the hard-pressed Chinese.

Seizing a golden opportunity in September 1940, the Japanese pushed the boundaries of their empire back by moving into Indochina at the expense of Vichy France, the colonial rulers of the country. This was a move the European puppet state was powerless to resist. In retaliation the anxious and angry United States and Britain broke off trading relations, which meant a halt to the supply of vital oil to Japan. The exiled Dutch government did likewise. Australia was by now viewing the aspirations of Japan with trepidation.

Without oil, Japan could survive for 18 months at the most despite the huge stockpiles it had imported during the 1930s. At stake was its considerable economic might. The hawks among the Japanese hierarchy quickly argued that time was running out for Japan and that a military strike to consolidate its position was needed sooner rather than later.

■ TRIPARTITE PACT ■

In the same month as the threatening manoeuvres in Indochina, Japan joined with aggressors Germany and Italy in the Tripartite Pact, which set out a code of co-operation between the three. There could be little doubt now that the Land of the Rising Sun was poised on the brink of war. But the question which troubled the Americans was, just how would the inevitable conflict begin?

Japan had sound reasoning behind the desire to enlarge its lands. In 1939, its population reached 99 million and was increasing at the rate of five million a year. Its home islands were becoming overcrowded and overstretched. Britain, France and Holland all enjoyed the benefits of colonies. America, although ideologically opposed to colonialism,

In September 1940 Japan joined with aggressors Germany and Italy in the Tripartite Pact

Left: An aerial view of the US Pacific Fleet's base at Pearl Harbor.
Below: Japan's foreign minister Matsuoka talks with Ribbentrop in early 1941.

had its spheres of influence. Japan felt entitled to the same. It was not unreasonable, the Japanese felt, for their country to hold sway over the Pacific and China.

Japan's transformation from feudal backwater to burgeoning world power had been rapid. It was only in the latter half of the 19th century that Japan had come out of isolation. After that, the Japanese followed the

The Japanese felt cheated, unable to trust the countries they had known as friends

British and American examples and were set on a programme of industrialisation. Yet the new breed of manufacturers struggled to compete on the same terms as the Westerners. Britain had tariffs which discouraged overseas trade while America also followed a policy of protectionism.

Nevertheless, Japan joined the Allies during World War I. After-

Right: **Japanese pilots were hailed as heroes back home after their unannounced attack on the US Pacific Fleet's base at Pearl Harbor.**

wards, the Japanese were anxious to be accepted as part of the New World Order on equal terms with other nations. Bitter disappointment was in store.

At the Paris peace conference the Japanese proposed a clause of racial equality, with the aim of ironing out the discrimination they had previously felt, once and for all. The emissaries from Japan assumed that there would be no controversy over the clause's acceptance.

■ JAPANESE ANGER ■

In the event, it was barred by none other than American president Woodrow Wilson, who went on to place a ban on Japanese people entering the US when immigration by other nationalities was rife. Australia, too, had a 'whites only' immigration policy. The Japanese felt cheated and angry, unable to trust the countries they had hitherto known as friends. Western powers seemed more fraudulent than ever when the Washington Treaty of 1922 was drawn up, limiting Japan to just three capital ships for every five run by both the US and Britain.

The Japanese largely followed Western models of democracy.

Although there was an emperor, he was bound by the decisions of his ministers. Yet the Japanese government differed sharply from others in one vital respect. Its civilian ministers ran civil affairs. But there were ministers from the army and navy entirely responsible for military matters. Without the co-operation of those ministers from the armed services, the government fell. It meant they wielded huge power. To further complicate matters, there was an enormous degree of rivalry between the army and the navy and the two services could rarely agree.

Aside from these wranglings, there was also the sinister threat of assassination. It became a political tool increasingly used among young patriots. Those in power became cautious, corrupt and sly. There came a feeling among the Japanese that politicians

Left: **Admiral Isoroku Yamamoto was the architect of the strike against Pearl Harbor. Yet he feared he had 'awakened a sleeping giant'.**

◆ PEARL HARBOR

On the morning of 7 December 1941, the Japanese attacked on Pearl Harbor. As the US naval base prepared for its day, Japanese carrier aircraft swept in and tore into the US Pacific Fleet at rest. The fleet's carriers were at sea, but the battleships were in. *Arizona*, *West Virginia*, *California* and *Oklahoma* were destroyed; *Pennsylvania*, *Nevada*, *Tennessee* and *Maryland* were damaged. The Japanese lost nine Zeroes, 15 'Vals' and five 'Kates'.

thousands of miles away. The remote islands were economically wealthy, precisely why they were incorporated into empires in the first place. Japan would become stronger than ever before if only it could avail itself of the assets there.

With Japan's vast military might, the islands were easy enough targets. But the Japanese leadership rightly guessed that America was unlikely to sit back and watch as it established a thriving Pacific or Asiatic powerbase. It would, of course, send its big ships to trouble-spots. The answer, it seemed, was to knock out the mighty American navy to obtain the necessary freedom of the seas.

The answer, it seemed, was to knock out the mighty American navy

Conveniently, the pride of the US fleet was based in Hawaii, much closer to Japan than the inaccessible mainland of the United States. And so the infamous attack on Pearl Harbor was conceived.

It was a brilliant short-term strategy drawn up by Admiral Yamamoto. Key to its success was the element of surprise. There was a hard summer of training for the pilots of the fighters, dive-bombers and torpedo-bombers which were to be shipped in for the pre-emptive strike. Most Japanese pilots had seen plenty of action in the war with China.

To ensure the action, code-named 'Operation Z', was effective, powerful six-inch naval shells were adapted for use by the aircraft, sufficient to plough through the armour of US battleships. The Japanese also had a 24-inch torpedo known as the 'Long

could not be trusted. Not only that, there was widespread fear about the encroachment of communism. Together with a growing admiration for the achievements of Nazi Germany, Japan swung towards militarism.

Japan, still cut out from overseas trade by the policies adopted by key trading partners Britain and America, began to feel the pinch during the Great Depression of the 1930s. Japan spent much of the 1930s meddling in internal Chinese affairs. When China became unwilling and belligerent, the two countries finally went to war. In

1937, Japan withdrew from the League of Nations and denounced the Washington Treaty, privately planning to increase its naval strength to compare with that of Britain. And she sought to boost her empire.

■ YAMAMOTO'S PLAN ■

Casting greedy eyes at the colonies in South East Asia and the Pacific owned by Britain, Holland and France, Japanese military leaders realised the outposts were now vulnerable, with the mother countries being embroiled in problems

Right: Japanese aircraft warm up on the deck of the carrier Hiryu before delivering their stunning blow to the US Navy at Pearl Harbor.

Lance', containing 1,000 pounds of explosives; it was among the most powerful weapons in the world.

As early as 26 November 1941 the Japanese navy set off from its base, using an obscure route and maintaining complete radio silence. By 7 December it was in position, 270 miles north of Pearl Harbor in the Kurile Islands.

■ 'TIGER, TIGER, TIGER' ■

The fleet, under Vice-Admiral Chuiki Nagumo, comprised six aircraft carriers, with a capacity of 423 planes. In the attack 360 were used, the force comprising 104 high-level bombers, 135 dive-bombers, 40 torpedo-bombers and 81 fighters. In addition, the escort force consisted of two battleships, three cruisers, submarines and supply ships.

In dock at Pearl Harbor were 96 American ships. Fortunately for the US, the base's two aircraft carriers were at sea. Their destruction may have altered the course of the war.

At Pearl Harbor, a new day was beginning, clouded only by a general fear of war. Still, the beaches were silvery, the sun was warm and the majority of the servicemen based there were looking forward to a day of relaxation. Many were still in bed when the storm broke.

Although America had been forewarned that Japan was planning

The ships in Pearl Harbor were undefended, their ammunition in lockers

a major strike, it didn't know where or when it would take place. Most thought the Philippines the obvious target for Japanese aggression. The ships in Pearl Harbor were undefended, their ammunition safely held in lockers.

The only clue to the carnage to come came in the early hours when a periscope was spotted in the harbour

Left: Pearl Harbor explodes under the onslaught of Japanese bombs. Fortunately, key fuel installations were left intact, so averting utter disaster.

PEARL HARBOR

US Losses

18 ships, including 8 battleships, sunk or badly damaged; 164 aircraft destroyed and 124 aircraft damaged; 2,403 men dead and 1,178 men wounded.

Japanese Losses

29 aircraft downed; 5 midget submarines sunk; 64 men dead or missing; 1 prisoner taken.

Below: US servicemen at Pearl Harbor were staggered at the sight that greeted them. Japanese aggression was dubbed 'treachery' around the Allied world.

mouth. A destroyer duly went out to sink the unidentified submarine.

In fact, few people outside the navy top brass in Tokyo knew what was going on. Unwilling to announce its intentions and give its game away, Japan didn't deliver its declaration of war to America until Pearl Harbor was smoking.

At 6am the first wave of aircraft took off and headed for Hawaii. As they came in sight of Pearl Harbor Captain Mitsuo Fuchida, in command of the first wave, broadcast to his men, screaming 'Tora, Tora, Tora' – 'Tiger, Tiger, Tiger', literally translated. The message

informed them that the Americans were still unaware of what was to come. At 7.56am the first shots rang

> *As they came in sight, Fuchida broadcast to his men, screaming 'Tora, Tora, Tora'*

out. In neat formations, the skilful, well-practised pilots made runs over the lines of vessels anchored along 'Battleship Row', the section of the harbour where the capital ships lay.

Far below them, braving the telltale shallow waters of the harbour, were Japanese midget submarines, each one hoping to bag a battleship.

A stunned commander ordered them to take action, bellowing 'This is no drill!'

Ship after ship was blasted and soon the air was filled with thick, spiralling, oily black plumes of smoke. As the flaming oil from one stricken vessel spilled into the sea, it set light to another. The second wave of Japanese bombers had difficulty locating targets through the fug.

The Arizona was hit and exploded – 1,200 members of her crew died. The battleships West Virginia, Oklahoma, and California were also destroyed, and Nevada, Maryland, Tennessee, and Pennsylvania were damaged. Further casualties included the cruisers Honolulu, Raleigh and St Helena, and the destroyers Shaw, Cassin and Downs. These ships, all symbols of America's greatness, were left tattered wrecks.

In the midst of the chaos a contingent of American aircraft arrived. Their pilots must have gaped in disbelief at the scenes before them. What once was a landing strip had been set ablaze, along with most of the aircraft on it. Then they too were attacked, no match for the nimble Japanese fliers. The same fate was in store for the crews of dive-bombers from the absent carrier Enterprise who returned to base during the attack.

■ 29 PLANES DOWNED ■

At times the Japanese pilots screeched in so low they were clearly visible to the frantic Americans.

The men at Pearl Harbor responded to the onslaught with considerable zest. A stunned commander ordered them to take action, bellowing the words: 'This is no drill!' Despite the shock and disbelief, the Americans soon manned the guns as they had done before in training and claimed 29

Below: 'Battleship Row' at Pearl Harbor provided rich pickings for the carrier-borne aircraft of Yamamoto's strike force.

Above: **Despite the suddenness of the strike, troops rushed to man the guns. A total of 29 Japanese planes – nine Zeroes, 15 'Vals' and five 'Kates' were downed.**

Japanese planes. Others raced to rescue comrades trapped in blazing ships or operated firefighting equipment. Finally, there was calm. The surviving servicemen set about their grim tasks with one ear open for the return of the Japanese.

While the Pacific Fleet's base was extensively damaged, it was not crippled, since the fuelling and repair depots had escaped unscathed. It was to take months, however, and in some cases years, to refloat and repair the shattered bodywork of the damaged ships.

The Japanese did not return to finish off the base, as was widely feared among US servicemen and their families. Well satisfied with the results of the operation, which went better than any of the Japanese commanders dared hope, Vice-Admiral Nagumo decided a quick,

getaway was now in order, particularly as fuel was running dangerously low, and the US carriers Lexington and Enterprise might appear.

In America there was outrage and horror at the loss of life. US secretary of state Cordell Hull was still in conference with Japanese negotiators when news of the attack reached him. They had already presented him with a document purporting to set out the area of debate.

■ A REPEAT OF 1904 ■

Mr Hull furiously declared: 'In all my 50 years of public service I have never seen a document that was more crowded with infamous falsehoods and distortions on a scale so huge that I never imagined until today that any government on this planet was capable of uttering them.'

Although some took the opportunity to condemn President Franklin Roosevelt for his lack of readiness, most American citizens were determined to pull behind him in their fury at the Japanese action.

Ironically, the attack on Pearl Harbor mirrored a military move made by the Japanese against the Russians in 1904. Once again, without an official declaration of war, the Japanese navy carried out a surprise attack on a key Russian base, picking off some prestige targets. Back then, The Times of London hailed it as 'an act of daring' and praised the Japanese for their initiative and vigour.

In Britain, the Daily Mail now voiced the venom of many when it wrote: 'Not even Hitler has yet achieved the infamy of a stab in the back while his envoys were still ostensibly negotiating terms of agreement with his intended victim.

'This is an act which the world will never forget so long as the

> **On 8 December, both America and Britain officially declared war on Japan**

records of history are read. It will stand for all time as an example of the ultimate depths of deceit to which it is possible for any nation to descend.'

On 8 December, both America and Britain officially declared war on Japan. In response to the declaration and the wave of Japanese attacks around the region, the Royal Navy battleship Prince of Wales and battlecruiser Repulse sailed out of Singapore with an escort of four destroyers. Disastrously, 'Force Z', as it was known, ignored the threat of airborne action and left without the protection of an aircraft carrier. Their aim was to prevent the Japanese making landings on British-held territory in South East Asia. But the mission went badly wrong when the

◆ EYE WITNESS ◆

Kazuo Sakamaki was the commander of a midget submarine, one of five which was sent into action at Pearl Harbor.

'Something went wrong. At the moment of release my submarine nearly toppled over into the water. The trim had not worked well. I feared that if we attempted to emerge hastily enemy observers might spot the ship. I remembered that the opening of hostilities was to follow the handing of the notice of war to the US government. If by my own mistake the presence of the Japanese forces should be discovered it would create a grave problem. It would spoil the air attack and every other detail of the carefully worked-out plan. I could not cause such a blunder. No matter how dangerous the condition of my ship I could not let it emerge to the surface.

My aide and I crawled back and forth inside the submarine removing the lead ballast and filling the tanks with water to correct the trim of the craft. It had been our plan that by midnight all five submarines would be inside the harbour and would sink to the bottom and wait for the dawn. But when I looked at the watch it was midnight already. The ship righted itself.

I figured that as long as we entered the harbour during the night no damage would have been done. I drank a bit of wine and ate my lunch.

"Let's do our utmost." My comrade and I held each other's hands and pledged success. I took my position and moved forward with minimum speed.

After ten minutes I lifted the ship slightly to see through the telescope where we were going. To my horror, the ship was moving in the wrong direction.

Moving blindly because my gyrocompass was not working, the ship had gone 90 degrees off her course. If I could manage the ship with the help of the telescope we could get back on our course but this was clearly impossible.

"We must get to the mouth of the harbour" I repeated to myself. My hands were wet with cold sweat. I changed the direction three or four times, hoping against hope that somehow the ship would get going where I wanted to go. The speed was maintained at the minimum as before.

Time ticked away in complete indifference to my predicament. It was almost the moment for attack.

As we came nearer to the enemy ships guarding the entrance I was able to see the white uniforms of the sailors aboard. I concluded they were destroyers.

I pushed the midget submarine toward them, Suddenly I heard an enormous noise and felt the ship shaking. I was hit on the head and lost consciousness. This was my first contact with war.

I came to myself in a short while and saw white smoke in my submarine. I changed the speed to half gear and turned the ship around. I wanted to see if any damage had been done. My comrade was all right. My two torpedoes were all right. I did not want to waste my torpedoes on those destroyers which began again to charge against me. They threw depth charges at us. They fell near us but not as close as the first time.'

two British giants became sitting ducks for the Japanese Naval Air Arm flying out of Indochina.

The Prince of Wales, able to fire 60,000 shells every minute out of its array of 175 anti-aircraft guns, was thought to be impregnable. The cream of Japan's pilots didn't think so.

On 10 December, both ships were sunk off the coast of Malaya within an hour of each other and 800 members of their crews were killed, although 2,000 were saved by the accompanying destroyers. Among the dead was the leader of the ill-fated squadron, Admiral Tom Spencer Vaughan Phillips. There were 34 high-level bombers and 51 torpedo-bombers coming at the ships from all directions. Only three aircraft had to be ditched. The formi-

dable Japanese fliers had struck again. Winston Churchill heard the news by telephone from the Chief of Naval Staff. 'I never received a more direct shock,' he commented.

As militarily admirable as it might have seemed to the Japanese at the time, the long-term consequences of the attack on Pearl Harbor were clearly ill thought-out. Japan had a

Left: **Both Roosevelt and Cordell Hull were disgusted by the Japanese attack.**

magnificent navy, powerful enough to compete with that of America or Britain, with the most modern aircraft carrier fleet in the world. Its army too was large and capable.

■ A GIANT AWAKENED ■

Yet Japan could not have possibly hoped to complete its victory with an occupation of the US. It was a geographical and numerical impossibility. And if the leaders of Japan hoped the action at Pearl Harbor would demoralise the Americans and encourage them to capitulate, they sorely misjudged their foe. The aim seems to have been merely to cause enough damage to keep America at bay while Japan built up its strength in the Pacific.

It is likely they were then hoping for a war of attrition in which America would weary and compromise. Yet architect of the deadly war strike Admiral Yamamoto clearly had

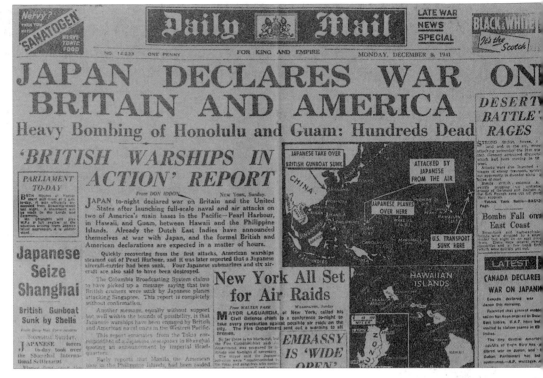

an inclination of what lay ahead when he said: 'I fear we have only awakened a sleeping giant and his reaction will be terrible.'

Above: British newspapers joined the wave of indignation against the war-mongering Japanese after their opening strikes in the Pacific.

◆ EYE WITNESS ◆

A correspondent for the National Broadcasting Corporation gave this account of the bombing of Pearl Harbor.

The most thickly populated air base was attacked by Japanese planes a little after 8 am local time.

After machine-gunning Ford Island the Japanese planes moved to Hickman Field. Observers say that considerable damage was done there but a number of planes were brought down.

Three ships of the United States Pacific Fleet based at Pearl Harbor were attacked and the 29,000-ton battleship *Oklahoma* was set on fire.

All lines of communication appear to be down between the various Army and Navy aerodromes and the Army in the field.

The Army has issued orders for all people to remain off the streets.

The first raiders carried torpedoes and did considerable damage to shipping in Pearl Harbor and off Honolulu. They came in squadron formation over Diamond Head, dropping high explosives and incendiary bombs.

They came over Honolulu itself and were at once met with anti-aircraft from Pearl Harbor, Ford Island, Wheeler Field, Honolulu Municipal Airport, Hickman Field and the new Navy repair base.

A terrific barrage was put up but all the points I mentioned appear to have been attacked.

The chief of fire services has reported that the fires were under control and were not as bad as expected.

FIRES IN THE NIGHT

While German bombers were pounding Britain during 1940 and 1941, the British people huddled night after night in stuffy, cramped shelters and comforted themselves that Royal Air Force bombers were delivering similar punishment to the citizens of the Third Reich.

Sadly, they were mistaken. While British bomber crews were full of sterling young men with an iron resolve, their success rate in the first half of the war was low – and for very sound reasons.

Night bombing was far safer for the aircraft and crew, as the Germans had illustrated in their raids over London. RAF Bomber Command was keen to conserve these valuable assets too and favoured night-time bombing raids instead of exposing its forces to daylight risks.

But the Luftwaffe was operating from occupied airfields a short hop over the English Channel. For the Royal Air Force to strike at the heart of Germany, its pilots and planes had to fly many more miles than their German counterparts, in aircraft that were ill-equipped for long-distance flying or bombing. It took time and investment for new, heavier bombers to be commissioned for the task.

The already limited resources of Bomber Command were also stretched in many different directions. Not only were there the demands of bombing raids over enemy territory but Coastal Command was in constant need of planes to combat the U-boat menace in the Battle of the Atlantic. With Britain under threat of isolation and annihilation if the U-boat peril was not seen to, the need to have planes available for maritime duties was paramount in 1940. In addition, the Middle East and North Africa required a complement of bombers, together with crews and parts – all of which required regular replacements. For a while, night bombing raids over Germany were abandoned altogether so the force could focus on its duties elsewhere.

■ EARLY PROBLEMS ■

Operational shortcomings put the Royal Air Force at a disadvantage, too. For the first sorties were flown, rather informally, on an almost individual level. Following a joint briefing, each aircraft would depart at five-minute intervals following a course chosen by its own navigator to the target. Often, the crews would not catch sight of another plane until after their return. Given that each

> ## For a while night bombing raids over Germany were abandoned altogether

would offload its bombs over a wide area, the effect of single bomb drops on the ground were, of course, much less than an orchestrated raid involving greater numbers.

Added to this, the navigational aids available on planes at the time were wildly inaccurate. Crews conforming to their instructions were sure their bombs were away right on top of the targets. It was not the case. While bomber crews scored hits on clear nights in easily located target areas, bombs dropped on blacked-out Germany or on targets shrouded with industrial haze as often as not fell short. After the war it was discovered that 49 per cent of the ordnance released by the British crews between May 1940 and May 1941 exploded in open countryside.

Navigators used maps, a sextant and a procedure of 'dead-reckoning' to work out their position, all of which could be fouled up by poor weather conditions. It meant that precision bombing by the RAF at night could be successful only on clear, bright, windless nights of which

Left: German planes on a daylight raid of London before night-time tactics were introduced. *Far left:* The Renault works at Billancourt after bombing by the Allies.

Above: A Wellington bomber and its crew pepare for an arduous night's work over Hitler's 'Fortress Europe'.

there were precious few. Once again, it took many months before the difficulties of finding targets under cover of darkness were resolved.

Bomber Command was continuing to sustain losses from the missions over Germany, in exchange for precious few results. It soon became clear a new tactic was in order.

The principles of precision bombing – a technique almost impossible to execute successfully given the constraints of the era – were abandoned for 'area bombing'. For this, not only was the target itself carefully chosen but also its neighbourhood. Thus a large factory producing vital components in the middle of open countryside would be overlooked in favour of a smaller factory among other small factories and industrial workers' housing.

That way enormous damage could be caused for the same amount of effort and risk as was required in precision bombing. It gave a twofold purpose to bombing missions. Not only was there the clear-cut intention of halting Germany's industrial output but, in addition, the chance to demoralise the people by bringing the war to their doorstep, making them homeless or otherwise hampering their daily existence.

The concept was fostered by Air Marshal Sir Richard Peirse, in charge of Bomber Command during 1941. Unfortunately, the failure of his forces to destroy three German warships, Scharnhorst, Gneisenau and the heavy cruiser Prinz Eugen, while they were in dock at Brest, northern France, did little to enhance the ebbing reputation of the force.

■ BREST RAIDS ■

While these three sea monsters roamed, the British suffered terribly. Between them they were responsible for the loss of HMS Glorious, HMS Ardent, HMS Acasta as well as the armed merchant cruiser Rawalpindi and something in the order of 115,600 tons of merchant shipping.

In the spring of 1941, Bomber Command flew 1,161 sorties against the ships, scoring just four direct hits, none of which caused substantial damage. All this for the loss of 43 bombers. Even when the three ships left the dockyard to slip back to

Below: Air Chief Marshal Sir Arthur 'Bomber' Harris, commander of the RAF's Bomber Command.

home ports, the 242 planes sent to destroy them as they sailed failed to dent the pride of the German navy.

It signalled the departure of Peirse and the arrival of Air Chief Marshal Arthur Harris, who adopted the idea of area bombing as his own.

Afterwards, Harris summed up his position. 'I had to prove, and prove quickly, to the satisfaction of those who mattered that the bomber force could do its work if it was large

> # The historic town was engulfed in a firestorm which swallowed up 200 acres

enough and if its efforts were not frittered away on objectives other than German industry as a whole.'

His first priority was to bolster the stocks of planes available to carry out attacks, particularly heavy bombers of which there were fewer than 70 when he arrived.

An opportunity to prove the ability of himself and his men came just a matter of weeks after he was installed at Bomber Command. On 3 March 1942, Harris sent a force of 235 bombers across to Billancourt, France, where a giant Renault factory was turning out tank components for the German war effort.

The planes set off in three waves and now Harris mimicked a successful German tactic. The first wave carried not only bombs but a large number of flares which would light up the target for subsequent attackers. With the River Seine acting as a brilliant marker, 223 of the aircraft found their targets within the space of two hours. This concentrated attack had the desired effect. Enough machinery was put out of action to

SUICIDE BOMBERS

Germany formed its own squadron of suicide bombers known as the Sonderkommando Elbe. They first went into action in April 1945 and engineered mid-air collisions with laden Allied bombers. The 300 volunteers were told they could parachute to safety if possible.

stop the factory working for several months. As a happy spin-off, many completed products were wrecked.

It appeared to Harris that Bomber Command had received the change of fortune it so urgently required. With a new directional aids now in use among navigators, he felt that Germany's industrial heartland of the Ruhr was his for the taking.

Five days after the Renault raid, 211 bombers took off and headed towards the city of Essen. Once again, the technique of using flares and incendiaries was employed. But this time, many had burnt out before the second wave of bombers had got the measure of the area. It finally bore the hallmarks of the haphazard raids which Bomber Command were now known for. Another three attacks made on ensuing nights also failed to produce the spectacular results Harris yearned for although there was widespread damage caused in the city.

Harris had to wait until the end of the month for the next feather in his cap, a raid carried out against Lübeck, a Baltic port comprising many ancient timbered buildings.

When almost 200 aircraft dropped 300 tons of high explosives plus 144 tons of incendiaries on the night of 28/29 March, the historic town was engulfed in a firestorm which swallowed up 200 acres.

■ ROSTOCK RAID ■

At the end of April another Baltic port, Rostock, was given similar treatment. The targets for the bombers were specifically a factory which produced the Heinkel 111 aircraft and in general the town itself. An estimated 70 per cent of the old town was turned to rubble with direct hits being scored against the factory too. Of the 168 bombers that set off for the mission, all but 12 returned safely.

Harris noted with satisfaction that, yard for yard, the destruction wrought in Germany by Bomber Command in those two raids equalled that caused by the Luftwaffe in Britain in 1940 and 1941.

Below: **The Renault works at Billancourt was destroyed after Bomber Command was fired with fresh resolve.**

The Nazi hierarchy was riled by the savage encroachment into the Fatherland. In a fury, Hitler ordered raids against Britain's historic cities to even the score. He picked the targets from a tourists' book of Britain called the Baedeker Guide. Among them were Bath and Exeter.

■ 'MILLENIUM' ■

For one daring raid against a factory producing U-boat parts, Harris was persuaded to return to daylight attack. New Avro Lancaster heavy bombers were brought in for the assault on Augsburg in southern Germany. Together with their fighter escorts they flew in low over enemy territory to avoid radar detection and then began a breathtaking roof-top scrap with Luftwaffe fighters before hitting their target. The cost was high. Seven out of 12 bombers were lost. The crews of the returning battle-scarred aircraft were decorated for their bravery.

It confirmed the general view that daylight raids were unacceptably risky given the aircraft available. In any event, Harris became far too preoccupied with his latest tactical trailblazer to consider further daylight sorties. The continued all-out efforts to obliterate the Ruhr were proving frustrating. With the lack of truly efficient navigation and the industrial smog it was impossible to co-ordinate a successful mission. He had pondered long and hard about pulling off a single operation which would earn the admiration of those doubters at home and the trepidation of the Germans.

The answer, he decided, was a thousand-bomber raid against a prime target in Germany. But, given that the most he had been able to rally for an attack to date was 235 bombers, it seemed this was nothing more than a flight of fancy. That was until Harris's deputy Air Vice Marshal Saundby got to work.

With the use of borrowed aircraft from Coastal Command and the entire stock of his reserves flown by trainee pilots and instructors alongside existing crews, it was conceivable that 1,000 bombers could be summoned for an epic raid.

Code-named 'Operation Millenium', the first thousand-bomber raid took place against Cologne on 30 May 1942. All the planes were to strike within an hour and a half.

The raid represented a new departure in aerial warfare. The largest force of aircraft dispatched to Britain at any one time had numbered 487 while the British had never been able to gather together more than 235 bombers at any one time.

Churchill himself was captivated by the idea of such a mighty strike. He

Below: An RAF Wellington bomber is loaded with bombs before setting off on another mission.

was under pressure from fellow politicians who saw the largely inconclusive night raids against Germany as a waste of time and effort. Stalin was also waiting in the wings, always demanding a decisive attack by the British

> *Ground crews worked flat out on damaged aircraft to furnish Harris with the required number*

against Germany. It was realised that there would be too few German fighters in the air to halt the impact of the raid. The possiblity of collision was to be diminished by dividing the planes into three groups operating in parallel lines against different targets. Despite the immense commitment, it seemed the risks were calculated. The raid could not end up as the swansong of Bomber Command.

■ 1,046 BOMBERS ■

For a while, 'Operation Millenium' appeared under threat when Coastal Command refused to release the 250 planes it had promised. Its chiefs had got cold feet. They decided the risk of releasing their aircraft was too great. Saundby was left scraping the barrel

to fill the ranks for the raid. A spell of poor weather which caused the operation to be postponed proved a saving grace. Ground crews worked flat out on damaged aircraft to furnish Harris with the required number. On the morning of 30 May the magic 1,000 was surpassed.

The 1,046 bombers departed from 53 airfields across Britain and assembled in a 70-mile convoy across the North Sea. Before them went 50 fighter planes ready to duel with the defending Luftwaffe.

Mechanical difficulties accounted for 100 planes in the force even before it had reached the target and they turned back to base.

Still, the first bombs and incendiaries were dropped at 12.47am on 31 May. The rest of the operation went according to plan. Land-based defences and intercepting Luftwaffe fighters were overwhelmed and the last bomber dropped its load over Cologne at 2.25am.

As they flew homewards, rear gunners could see the city burning from 150 miles away. The night's work destroyed 18,432 buildings, killed nearly 500 people, injured 5,000 more and rendered almost 60,000 homeless. Forty bombers did not return, which meant the loss of 40 instructors and 49 pupils.

Above: Sir Barnes Wallis, inventor of the bouncing bomb, which proved a huge morale-booster in Britain.

At home it was hailed as a triumph. Yet the success in itself put pressure on Harris to produce more of the same. Now the British public expected many more raids of similar dimensions to lambast the enemy.

An attack against Essen on 1 June involving 956 bombers failed to achieve the same degree of destruction. Key industrial centres escaped from the raid unscathed.

It wasn't until 25 June that another large-scale attack was attempted, this time against Bremen. Poor weather once again hindered the 1,006 bombers as they sought their targets. It was a resounding success except for the higher number of casualties claimed by Germany. This time 49 aircraft didn't come home.

The Luftwaffe, in charge of ground defences as well as airborne, quickly realised the intention of Bomber Command. Now it set about denying the British an opportunity to hammer German industry.

To combat the upsurge in Luftwaffe fighters and improve the success of the night bombing raids, a

---

◆ EYE WITNESS ◆

Dennis Golding, of Gosport, near Portsmouth, England, was a British rifleman with the King's Royal Rifle Corps. As a light infantryman he was engaged in hand-to-hand combat with German troops throughout the 1944 advance across Western Europe.

❝ On VE day we marched into Hamburg to find everything devastated except the roads. The Germans had cleared them and stacked up all the re-usable bricks they could salvage. It was typical German efficiency and I suppose it also helped improve their morale.

The civilians were more or less glad to see us. There was certainly no hostility and, like our own people, they were just glad it was all over. We weren't allowed to fraternise with them at first. If you were caught you were put on a charge. That rule soon broke down. When they spoke to you you felt you had to talk back. ❞

Pathfinder force was created. In charge was Australian Group Captain D.C.T. Bennett, a first-class pilot and skilled navigator.

Their aim was to fly 'finder' aircraft over the target on parallel tracks two miles apart dropping flares, creating a 'runway'. Behind them came 'illuminator' aircraft, dropping further flares picking out the target area precisely. Then came the 'marker' group which started fires with incendiaries to pinpoint the targets for following bombers. When it was cloudy the Pathfinders dropped 'sky-markers', parachute flares which lit up the target beneath the cloud cover. In response the Germans used fires on the ground as decoys in much the same way as the

The Air Ministry favoured a plan to knock out three giant dams

British did during the Battle of Britain. The Pathfinders proved a massive boon to the night bombing raids, with the additional attraction that their loss rate was a smaller-than-average three per cent.

At the end of 1942 Bomber Command diverted resources to the 'Torch' landings in North Africa and provided valuable support. At the same time it carried out some successful raids over Italy, finding the air defences there far lighter than those in Germany.

Still, Harris was determined to kill off German industry in the Ruhr. By March 1943 he was set upon a concerted attack on the region. The Battle of the Ruhr got underway on the night of 5 March with a 442 aircraft raid and continued for six

weeks more or less relentlessly. During the battle the famous Dambusters raid was carried out. Although Harris himself was opposed to it, the Air Ministry favoured a plan to knock out three giant dams which would deprive the region of vital hydroelectric power. To do it, Wing Commander Guy Gibson and his squadron had to drop new 'bouncing bombs', designed by engineer Barnes Wallis.

■ DAMBUSTERS ■

Each bomb weighed five tons, measured five feet in length and four feet across. Carried in a special cradle beneath a Lancaster bomber, it went into action with backspin imparted, which would cause it to skip along the surface of the water until it met the dam wall.

The targeted dams – the Möhne, the Eder and the Sorpe – were 150 feet high and their concrete walls were almost the same again in thickness. The skill required by Gibson and his crews was enormous. They had to fly in at low altitude to evade German radar and drop their bombs at

Above: A Lancaster of 617 Squadron, loaded with its 'bouncing bomb' before heading for the German dams.

precisely 60 feet above the water and exactly 425 yards from the perimeter of the dam.

On the night of 16 May 1943 the 19 Lancasters took off in three waves. In the first wave of nine planes, headed by Gibson, one plane was lost to flak and several bombs went astray before three explosions ripped through the Möhne Dam and a flood poured down the valley.

In the second wave just one of the five Lancasters reached the Sorpe Dam, under the guidance of Flight Lieutenant McCarthy, an American serving with the RAF. His bomb load damaged the dam but failed to breach it. Meanwhile, the third wave scythed a gap in the Eder Dam.

Eight of the Lancasters together with their 56 crew members failed to return. And, although it was a feat of undoubted heroism, the damage took the Germans just three months to repair. Perhaps it was most successful in capturing the public's imagination

◆ EYE WITNESS ◆

George Funnell joined the 55th Kent Regiment in 1939 aged 17, after lying about his age. He witnessed the Blitz in London when he was stationed at an anti-aircraft battery – and later saw the destruction caused by air raids in Germany after fighting his way through Normandy, Belgium and Holland to Hamburg in 1944.

‘In Hamburg there was mile after mile of devastation. I lived through the London bombing but it was nothing like as bad as that over Germany.

Even when we got to Hamburg, long after the air raids had taken place, there was still the stench of death coming from crumbled buildings. It took ages to find some of the buried remains.

On the streets we only found a few old men and young boys. The rest of the male population had been called up into the army. The vast majority of the people we met were women struggling to survive as best they could.’

in terms of a morale-boosting coup and depriving the Atlantic Wall in northern France of some labour. This was redirected instead to the Ruhr to repair the damage there.

Harris returned to his bombing campaign, this time picking Hamburg as the target for prolonged attack . 'Operation Gomorrah' began on 24 July with the first use of aluminium foil. It had been known for years that a simple device like this would fog the German radar screens. But the Air Ministry held back from using it in case that same device was used in retaliation. In fact, Germany was well-acquainted with the technique and also refrained from using it, for the same reason. Called 'Window', it was brought in to play on the orders of Churchill in a bid to counter the Luftwaffe defences.

■ HAMBURG HORROR ■

At midnight 740 bombers dropped 92 million strips of tin foil, creating the desired effect. The planes went on to deliver almost 3,000 tons of bombs. Subsequent attacks made by night and day virtually unremittingly devastated the city's defences. Fine weather had left the city dry as paper. As new fires were sparked by existing blazes, the perpetual heating of the

air which funnelled into the sky caused a firestorm, akin to a tornado with wind speeds of 150 miles per hour. Delayed detonators on some of the bombs wrought havoc among the rescue workers as they attempted to deal with the blazes.

The melting temperatures achieved in the raid scorched buildings and bomb shelters, water mains and electric cables. Hamburg endured the horror for nine days by which time ten square miles of the city was laid waste. In total 2,630 bombers unleashed more than 4,300 tons of incendiaries and a similar amount of high explosives, creating in total three firestorms. The death toll was an estimated 42,000.

Harris continued to work through the list of German cities he hoped to destroy. His armoury now included a 12,000lb bomb and some excellent new nagivational aids and target-finders. Now his sights turned towards Berlin. The German capital was a far-distant target from British airfields across hostile territory. The Battle of Berlin opened in November 1943 and a further 15 attacks were launched against it. Although the demands on the participating crews of Bomber Command were eased when airfields were opened in Europe

following D-Day, those raids cost no less than 587 aircraft together with 3,640 men killed or missing. When reconnaissance photographs proved little was being gained from the attacks, they were suspended.

If Harris hoped to end the war with his tactics bathed in a blaze of glory, he was disappointed. At last, public opinion both in Britain and overseas began to question the wisdom of saturation bombing. (The phrase 'terror bombing' was constantly rebuffed by air chiefs.)

On 30 March 1944 a night raid by Halifaxes and Lancasters was sent awry by a strong wind which sent them into the arms of defending Luftwaffe fighters. Out of the 795 aircraft that set off, 95 failed to return and another dozen crashed in England. Night bombing raids afterwards came to an end.

Below: **A reconnaissance photograph reveals the damage done to the Möhne Dam by Wing Commander Guy Gibson and his Dambusters.**

DAYLIGHT RAIDING

By the time America entered the war, the British had some fixed ideas about aerial combat.

The Royal Air Force had learned the hard way that aircraft employed on daylight raids were more vulnerable to the enemy, that bombers had a better survival rate when they were accompanied by fighters. Harris and the other British air supremos thought it best that the US fliers reinforced the existing night bombing expeditions being carried out by the RAF.

Novices at warfare in the air they may have been, but the Americans had thoughts of their own on the issue. US pilots were untrained for night missions. Not only that, they had a different bombing philosophy from that of their British counterparts, that of precision bombing.

▪ FIRST ACTION ▪

Given that their Flying Fortresses were, in their opinion, well defended and that the aircraft were equipped with a revolutionary new bombsight called the Norden which 'could drop a bomb into a pickle barrel from 20,000ft', it was their preferred plan to fly during the day. No amount of friendly persuasion from the British could dissuade the US air chiefs from their stated aims.

The Royal Air Force held Flying Fortresses in low regard. During experiments with the new aircraft in 1941, pilots felt they became large targets for German defences. For their part, the US air chiefs believed the RAF had used the Fortresses wrongly, sending them out in twos and threes instead of in a large formation when they performed best.

First taste of action for the US pilots came on 17 August 1942 when a dozen Flying Fortresses flew out of Grafton Underwood aerodrome, heading for Rouen, northern France.

With protection from four squadrons of RAF Spitfires, they made the flight, dropped the 18.5 tons of bombs on railway targets and returned home intact but for slight damage on two Fortresses caused by flak.

On the mission was Ira C. Eaker, a brigadier-general, and superb pilot, who set up the headquarters for the US 8th Air Force in Britain and was soon given command of its European flight operations.

There followed a succession of small-scale bombing raids. The success of precision bombing was trumpeted by Eaker although, like the number of victories claimed against the Luftwaffe on such outings, the statistics had to be

The Norden bombsight 'could drop a bomb into a pickle barrel from 20,000 ft'

treated with caution. Nevertheless, in 13 missions, just two planes were lost – an enviable record.

Still, their operations had been strictly 'local' on missions regarded as workaday 'milk runs' by the British pilots.

Left: A US Flying Fortress carries out a daylight bombing raid over Germany.
Below: By the middle of 1942, US aircraft were a familiar sight in Britain.

Above: US B-17s plough on towards their targets while fighter escorts fend off marauding enemy interceptors. The range of escorts increased during the war.

Then poor weather began to not only hamper the efficiency of the Norden bombsight – which had earned its colours in the cloudless skies above New Mexico and frankly struggled in the cloud- and smog-filled heavens above Germany – but brought about the wholesale cancellation of planned raids.

Like the RAF, the USAAF had to do its bit for the 'Torch' landings in North Africa in late 1942, which cut aircraft and crew stocks by a third.

Then the Luftwaffe hit on a new tactic which took its toll among the American fighters. Canny German pilots spotted the Achilles heel of the Flying Fortresses, which was head-on attack. There were no defences on the nose of the plane and the Germans had enough guts to mount daring frontal assaults despite the obvious risk of collision. It appeared that the 8th Air Force, clinging to its belief in daylight raids, was on a hiding to nothing.

Churchill was among those who strongly objected to the Americans going their own way. He believed that precision bombing being executed by the Americans, which needed daylight to succeed, was the height of folly. Area bombing under the cover of darkness appeared a far better bet and might encourage the Americans to venture for the first time over German territory.

At the Casablanca Conference of January 1943, the British leader was hoping to persuade Roosevelt that daylight bombing raids should be dropped in favour of night bombing operations by both air forces.

Eaker had one chance beforehand to convince Churchill otherwise. Finally, it only took one sentence. His proposal in favour of the continua-tion of daylight raids contained the words: 'By bombing the devils around the clock we can prevent the German defenses from getting any rest.' The idea instantly caught Churchill's imagination. He vowed to give Eaker the opportunity to prove his point.

■ THE B-24 ARRIVES ■

Afterwards there came the Casablanca Directive, backing orchestrated day- and night-time bombing raids and listing top targets, namely centres of German industry.

On 27 January that year the US airmen were at last sent to Germany to produce the goods. Their target was Wilhelmshaven on the North Sea, where U-boats were made. By now B-24 Liberators had joined the Flying Fortresses in the ranks. Of the 53 which left for Wilhelmshaven, three were lost and the remainder had to battle at close quarters with Luftwaffe fighters while achieving only moderate success in their mission. The difficulties of daylight raids over hostile territory were crystallised for the Americans.

Danger from flak and enemy fighters was not the only problem faced by the Americans on their daylight raids. To stay out of reach of the enemy, they flew at high altitudes, usually above 20,000 feet. The chill of the air

Area bombing under cover of darkness appeared a far better bet

numbed their faces, crammed as they were in small cockpits. Tension mixed with boredom as another lengthy mission got underway. For a while each member of the crew remained vigilant for the enemy, but there were long hours when the Luftwaffe didn't

EYE WITNESS

Burdsall D. Miller, from Sacramento, California, joined the US Army Air Force, aged 24, following the Japanese raid on Pearl Harbor. Based in Sudbury, England, he became a colonel and flew 32 missions.

'I flew ten missions in a B-24 Liberator and then switched to B-17s for a further 22 raids. Most of them were daylight raids over Germany although we also hit Italy and Norway. I got shot up but never enough to bale out or crash land.

As command pilot, I sat in the co-pilot's seat and made all the decisions as far as the group or squadron were concerned that day. I was scared but I was trained to do a job. The thing that made the biggest impression on me was flying in formation and seeing a wing man shot down in flames. It was very upsetting.

But we all got fatalistic and figured when our time came we were going to get it. Perhaps that made us seem like we had nerves of steel. Otherwise we would not have lasted. We had some men who didn't last. They refused to fly, but it was very few out of a considerable number of men.

As soon as we dropped our bombs we got out of the target area as most were heavily defended. As we turned we could see bombs hitting and we could usually tell if we had hit the target.

I have a big picture at home. It was taken on a raid over Germany on one of the most heavily defended targets. We had turned to start our bombing run. We just opened our bomb bay doors. To the left of us, another plane was doing the same when some flak went right into the bomb bay. The plane just exploded. Nobody got out alive. At the moment the plane blew up, my waist gunner took the picture.'

appear in which there was little to do but study the clouds.

Every US airman wore a steel chain vest to protect himself from flak. His flight suit was thick to protect him from the cold. Each wore a parachute and an oxygen mask, itself deeply uncomfortable. Despite the elaborate precautions, there was at least a one in ten chance of dying.

Americans adopted different flying patterns to suit the daylight nature of the raid. Up to 21 planes would form a box which was staggered both vertically and horizontally for protection. Three boxes lined up in the air to form a combat wing.

To improve the accuracy of bombing, the most skilful men were placed in the lead planes and gave the signal for the rest of the aircraft in the box to drop their bombs.

> **Historically the US Army Air Corps was treated as the poor relation by the White House**

On the ground, Eaker had his own problems. Historically, the US Army Air Corps, as it was first known, was treated as the poor relation by the White House. Priorities changed only slowly during the war and Eaker spent many fruitless hours harrying his bosses in America for extra planes and crews. It wasn't until mid-1943 that his efforts paid off. The US 8th Air Force could at last increase the size and effectiveness of its attacks.

■ DANGEROUS GAME ■

Perhaps the biggest bonus of all to the US airmen was when fighter aircraft increased their range, although it was late in the conflict when a combat aircraft which could escort bombers into the heart of Germany and back came into use.

Daylight missions were stepped up in 1943 and the heavy bombers recorded some admirable successes. Assisting their cause was the decision to scale down Luftwaffe defences in France by withdrawing two groups back to the Reich to improve air security there. The Allies were now

Left: Despite damage from a German rocket in the Battle of Berlin, this US B-17 still managed to land safely.

making a concerted effort to draw the Luftwaffe aircraft into the sky at every available opportunity, trying to shoot down as many as possible. Of course, a considerable number of Allied planes fell victim while playing this dangerous game.

■ PLOESTI RAID ■

The US medium bombers fared less fortunately. A flight of B-26C Marauders which set off from Great Saling on 17 May was virtually wiped out during a raid on Haarlem.

And raids later in the year proved yet again the perils of daylight raiding. On 1 August 1943 the target was Ploesti, the oilfields in Romania which fed Germany's war machine. The Americans had planned a surprise attack, keeping radio silence and flying at low altitudes to avoid radar detection. Their approach was to be over a lightly defended sector and their escape route was to North Africa. Alas, the planes were picked up in Germany as soon as they left the runway. Navigational errors brought them in over the thickest of the anti-aircraft gunfire. Fifty three of the Liberators on the raid were shot

down in enemy territory. A further 55 reached Libya in such appalling condition that they were fit only for scrap. The results were disappointing, too, with only a small dent being made in the oil production levels.

In the same month, the Americans tackled Regensburg and Schweinfurt, key centres for aircraft manufacture and the production of that tiny but indispensible engineering component, the ball bearing. The raids would be without fighter escorts. So deep were the targets inside Reich territory the

> ## The German pilots were under no illusions. They were no longer the favoured elite

existing fighters did not have the capacity to fly there and back.

When the 146 Flying Fortresses dispatched for Regensburg crossed the German border they met a hail of fire from a host of defending Luftwaffe planes. The German pilots were under no illusions. They were

Above: **A German tank factory is ruined and its new stock in tatters following a daylight raid by the United States Army Air Forces. The Americans specialised in precision bombing by day.**

no longer the favoured elite. Hitler was once again frustrated at the lack of success brought home by the Luftwaffe which once had seemed invincible. Now fewer resources than ever were being ploughed into aircraft manufacture and the training of crews. Without this investment, the entire force would surely be strangled. Luftwaffe production chief Ernst Udet had already committed suicide in despair at the plight of the force. The pressure was on to prove the worth of the air force before the unpredictable Führer sought his own revenge against it.

Those Flying Fortresses that survived the arduous 90 minutes to Regensburg dropped their bomb loads and made off in haste towards Algiers, saving themselves a possibly fatal return journey.

Now it was the turn of 230 Flying Fortresses to run the gauntlet across Germany en route to Schweinfurt.

The fierce firepower of 300 Luftwaffe fighters battered and buffeted the American planes. While the Germans lost 25 fighters that day, the US bombers were down by 60 and another 47 were so badly damaged they could not be salvaged.

The figures were bleak for the USAAF. In October 1943, 153 aircraft were lost in a single week. It led to the halt of bombing raids without fighter escort.

■ DROP TANKS ■

Fortunately the drop tank appeared, a suspended fuel tank which could be jettisoned when empty. This was attached beneath the wing to vastly increase the range of fighters. Hot on

its heels came the P-51 Mustang, a fighter with an 850-mile range. It helped tip the balance of the air war over Europe in favour of the Allies.

By 1944 the Allies were producing twice the number of aircraft as the Reich was. The Luftwaffe's difficulties were compounded by the damage each fighter was sustaining which wasn't being repaired. Hitler was punishing the disappointing Luftwaffe by depriving it of essential materials to stay alive.

Yet the theories adopted by 'Bomber' Harris for the RAF and Eaker for the USAAF cannot be said to have been an outright success. Harris hoped to defeat the Third Reich by saturation bombing, destroying the will

of the German people. The question of the morality of carpet-bombing civilian centres, including the ancient city of Dresden late in the war, raged long after the conflict had ended.

Eaker targeted industrial centres, certain that concerted bombing raids would cause Hitler's regime to topple. Despite the bravery and commitment of the pilots, the principles were flawed. In fact, Hitler illustrated only too well over Britain in 1940 that air power by itself was not sufficient to win a war. Bombs from above failed to break the will of the Germans in just the same way as they had failed to crack the British. And damage sustained by industry could inevitably be repaired – particularly in Germany with the use of forced labour.

The liberation of Europe came with the arrival of the ground troops, albeit with priceless assistance from their colleagues in the air forces.

Hitler was punishing the disappointing Luftwaffe by depriving it of essential materials

◆ EYE WITNESS ◆

Lieutenant Harmon Cropsey, a former state senator from Decatur, Michigan, served with VB110, a US Navy squadron, navigating Liberators on 12-hour anti-submarine patrols into the North Atlantic. He was based at Dunkeswell in Devon under RAF Coastal Command.

'One of my fellow officers was Joe Kennedy, John's elder brother. We used to meet quite regularly in the mess and swap notes. He was flying the same aircraft as me.

It was Joe who volunteered for one of the most dangerous missions of the war. The idea was to strip everything out of one of the Liberators and pack it full of TNT. He was to fly this out over the North Sea to a prearranged navigational point and bale out. The plane would then be radio controlled to crash-land on its target – a 40-foot layer of reinforced concrete around some U-boat pens in Holland.

But something went wrong and the plane exploded in mid-air over England. We never found out what the problem was, and obviously there was nothing left of his body. He was a very brave man.

Our base lost an awful lot of airmen. The other two squadrons, 103 and 105, had around two-thirds of their crews killed in the first few months of our arrival in 1943. There was a German advanced training base at Brest and they were sending up the twin-engined Junkers 88 which had a 50-knot advantage on our planes. If you got caught out over the sea on a clear day you were a dead duck. Your only hope was to find cloud cover.

I know of only one plane, flown by a Free Czech crew, which made it home after being attacked. We were just fatalistic about it.

Every mission you were handed a top secret chart showing where all the Allied subs and ships were supposed to be. It was absolutely vital. One day I'd got this thing spread out inside the plane with the door still open. Suddenly the engines start and the whole thing blows right out into a field. I go haring after it and my flight suit gets caught on some barbed wire. As a result, I fall and dislocate my shoulder.

That really extended my war. You were allowed to go home after 25 missions but because of my injury I stayed behind when all my chums left. Then they decided they needed an experienced navigator to show the new crews what to do. I ended up flying 42 missions.'

THE ULTIMATE WEAPON

In Japan, the people were preparing for all-out war against invading Americans.

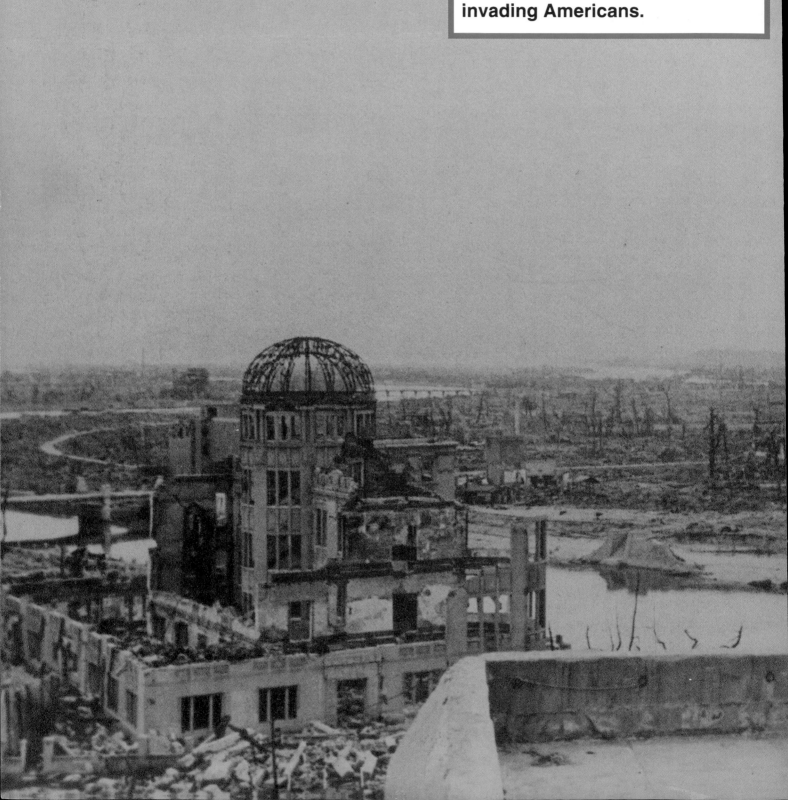

As early as November 1944 all Japanese men aged between 14 and 61 were conscripted. Women between the ages of 17 and 41 were on standby for military service, too. This new militia was being schooled in beach defences and guerrilla warfare. Those that were left unarmed – the vast majority – were told to practise martial arts skills as a form of defence. The message from the rulers of Japan was to be seen on giant posters hung around towns and villages. 'One hundred million will die for Emperor and nation!'

Key installations in Japan had been destroyed by the American bombing campaign. Much of the Japanese shipping had been sunk already by US ships, aircraft and submarines, which were now operating a tight blockade of the island coastlines. Japan was being starved of everything she needed to survive – yet still there was no sign of surrender.

In fact, various feelers had been extended by the Japanese through Swedish and other neutral sources for a negotiated peace, all cloaked in secrecy. Finally, the Japanese foreign ministry approached Russia to act as an intermediary, partly in a bid to divert Stalin from opening another battlefront with the war-weary country. But Japanese demands were unacceptable to the Allies who would agree to nothing less than an unconditional surrender.

Not for the first time, the lack of a cohesive war leader in Japan was keenly felt. Emperor Hirohito was a figurehead who could apparently do little without the say-so of his government. Prime minister Admiral Suzuki was eager to sue for peace but there still remained in opposition hardliners who were willing to fight to the death. No one, it seemed, was in outright control and nobody dared utter the word 'surrender' without the prospect of assassination, political retribution or military uprising looming large. So Japan struggled on as best it could in a vacuum of indecision.

The losses among the American troops in the landings around the Pacific islands had horrified and shocked the commanders. By now painfully aware of the Japanese resilience to attack and reluctance to surrender, they viewed invasion of the home islands as a tall order. The estimates for the number of US casualties appeared virtually open ended.

Later Truman confided that America had developed a new bomb which could end the war

When Truman met with Churchill and Stalin in Potsdam in July 1945, they discussed the inadequate peace overtures from the Land of the Rising Sun. Later Truman confided that America had developed a new bomb which could finally end the war.

■ ATOMIC POWER ■

He was referring to the end result of the Manhattan Project, begun back in 1942, in which a band of elite scientists, the most admired brains of the free world, had got together to probe the possibilities of atomic power.

By December of that year, the scientists under the leadership of Professor Enrico Fermi made a significant breakthrough in understanding how to spark a man-made chain reaction.

At two big plants – Oak Ridge, Tennessee, and Hanford, Washington – work continued in the bid to extract the essential substance known as U-235 from uranium for the manufacture of plutonium.

It wasn't until 5.50am on 16 July 1945 that the theory was finally put into full-scale practice. In the scorched sands of the New Mexican

Far left: Scientists knew they had created the ultimate weapon when it was tested.
Left: Truman confided in Churchill about the bomb at Potsdam.

Above: A weapon similar to that detonated at Nagasaki. Its weight was 10,000 pounds and it was equivalent in power to 20,000 tons of TNT.

Below: Dr Albert Einstein (left) was the initial innovator. Dr Robert Oppenheimer (right) took up his theories and made them reality.

desert the plutonium bomb called 'Fat Man' was detonated. (It won the name by having a passing resemblance in profile to Churchill.) Observing scientists could barely hide their awe at the intense power man had created.

Dr Robert J. Oppenheimer, the physicist directing the project, instantly realised the shattering effect it would have on the world.

■ TRUMAN INFORMED ■

A telegram detailing the precise results of the 'Fat Man' experiment was sent to the Potsdam Conference for the consumption of President Truman – who himself had only found out in April the full scope of the Manhattan Project.

Two further atomic bombs were made and dispatched to the Pacific while the politicians pondered. Was the world ready for the atomic age? Once unleashed, would this mighty new force return to act as a Sword of

> *Observing scientists could barely hide their awe at the intense power man had created*

Damocles poised over the heads of free and fair countries?

Churchill for one was in no doubt that it should be used. Afterwards, he wrote: 'To avert a vast, indefinite butchery, to bring the war to an end, to give peace to the world, to lay healing hands upon its tortured peoples by a manifestation of overwhelming power at the cost of a few explosions seemed, after all our toils and perils, a miracle of development.

'British consent in principle to the use of the weapon had been given on 4 July, before the test had taken place. The final decision now lay in the main with President Truman, who had the weapon. But I never doubted what it would be nor have I ever doubted since that he was right.'

In his memoirs, Truman wrote: 'Let there be no mistake about it. I regarded the bomb as a military weapon and never had any doubt that it should be used.'

Still, there was debate about whether Japan should be warned about its terrible fate. A chain of events finally overtook these talks.

The Potsdam Conference finally closed on 26 July with an ultimatum for Japan. It called for unconditional surrender. In the absence of such a surrender, Japan would face complete destruction. Just two days later Premier Suzuki announced his country would be ignoring the Allied threat.

Such belligerence was enough to confirm an order sent to Lieutenant-General Spaatz, commanding general of the US Army Strategic Air Forces to prepare a B-29 to carry the newly fabricated atomic bomb.

Below: **Smoke rises more than 60,000 feet into the air following the explosion of the atomic bomb at Nagasaki.**

The hour was early, the morning still warm and beautiful. Shimmering leaves reflecting sunlight from a cloudless sky made a pleasant contrast with shadows in my garden as I gazed absently through wide-flung doors opening to the south.

Clad in vest and pants, I was sprawled on the living room floor exhausted because I had just spent a sleepless night on duty as an air raid warden in my hospital.

Suddenly a strong flash of light startled me – and then another. So well does one recall little things that I remember vividly how a stone lantern in the garden became brilliantly lit and I debated whether this light was caused by a magnesium flare or sparks from a passing tram.

Garden shadows disappeared. The view where a moment before all had been so bright and sunny was now dark and hazy. Through swirling dust I could barely discern a wooden column that had supported one corner of my house. It was leaning crazily and the roof sagged dangerously.

Moving instinctively, I tried to escape but rubble and fallen timbers barred the way. By picking my way cautiously I managed to reach the roka and stepped down into my garden. A profound weakness overcame me so I stopped to regain my strength. To my surprise, I discovered that I was completely naked. How odd. Where were my vest and pants. What had happened?

All over the right side of my body I was cut and bleeding. A large splinter was protruding from a mangled wound in my thigh and something warm trickled into my mouth. My cheek was torn, I discovered, as I felt it gingerly with the lower lip laid wide open. Embedded in my neck was a sizeable fragment of glass which I matter-of-factly dislodged and with the detachment of one stunned and shocked I studied it and my blood-stained hand.

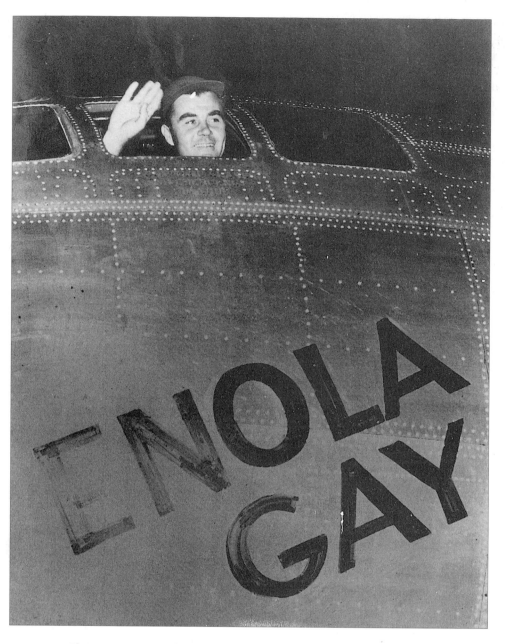

growing up and we watched it blossom. And down below it the thing reminded me more of a boiling pot of tar than any other description I can give it. It was black and boiling underneath with a steam haze on the top of it. And, of course, we had seen the city when we went in and there was nothing to see when we came back.'

On 8 August further pressure was exerted on Japan when the Soviet Union declared war and launched an invasion of Manchuria.

'We had seen the city when we went in and there was nothing to see when we came back'

A day later a further atomic bomb dropped, this time on Nagasaki. It came from the bowels of another B-29, this one christened 'Great Artist', under the command of Major Charles Sweeney. About 40,000 people died this time with a further 60,000 injured.

It is doubtful whether the introduction of atomic weapons had a huge effect on the people of Japan. The scale and horror of the previous bombing campaigns had claimed victims by the thousand and caused acres of destruction. Wholesale killing, burns and homelessness was nothing new for them. The only fresh aspect was the radiation sickness spread among the survivors, the wide-ranging effects of which were not immediately apparent.

For the rest of the world, the double bombing was like a macabre sideshow

On 6 August 1945 the first atomic bomb, called 'Little Boy', was released over Hiroshima. A mammoth 120 inches long and weighing 9,000 pounds, beneath its shell it contained the power equivalent to 20,000 tons of TNT. It was carried to its target in a B-29 called 'Enola Gay' which took off from the Marianas. In command was Colonel Paul Tibbets.

The uranium bomb exploded 2,000 feet above the centre of Hiroshima. Four square miles of the city was instantly wiped out. Those at the epicentre of the bomb were reduced to ashes along with buildings and cars. Beyond that immediate area, many more died and tens of thousands were horribly burned.

■ SHOCK WAVES ■

The authorities could only estimate the numbers of people who had perished in the ferocious cauldron. The final figure was put between 70,000 and 80,000 persons.

Colonel Tibbets later described how his plane was shaken by the shock waves as it sped away and told of the scene of devastation he left behind: 'There was the mushroom cloud

◆ EYE WITNESS ◆

Tsutomu Yamaguchi worked in the Hiroshima yard of the Mitsubishi shipbuilding company and was on his way to work when the bomb dropped more than a mile away.

❝ Suddenly there was a flash like the lighting of a huge magnesium flare. As I prostrated myself there came a terrific explosion. I was lifted two feet from the ground and I felt a strong wind pass my body.

How long I lay in the road dazed, I don't know, but when I opened my eyes it was so dark all around me that I couldn't see a thing. It was as if it had suddenly become midnight in the heat of the day. When my eyes adjusted to the darkness I perceived that I was enveloped in an endless cloud of dust so thick it was black.

As the dust blew away and my surroundings became visible I saw what seemed to be thousands of tiny, flickering lamps all over the street and in the fields. They were little circles of flame, each about the size of a doughnut. Myriads of them were hanging on the leaves of the potato plants.

I looked toward the city and saw a huge, mushroom-shaped cloud rising high into the sky. It was an immense evil-looking pillar. It seemed to be reflecting every shade in the spectrum turning first one colour then another.

Feeling terribly weak and suffering intense pain from the deep burns on my face and arm, I stumbled into the potato field. There was a big tree out in the field and I headed for that. Sometimes I could only crawl, creeping from bush to bush. When I finally reached the tree I had no more strength to go on. And I had acquired a terrible thirst.

I saw a group of teenage boys unclothed except for torn underpants. As the boys came near I saw that they were pale and shaking severely. I had never seen such a horrifying sights as those five shivering boys. Blood was pouring in streams from deep cuts all over their bodies mingling with their perspiration and their skin was burned deep red like the colour of cooked lobsters.

At first it seemed strangely that their burned and lacerated backs and chests were growing green grass. The I saw that hundreds of blades of sharp grass had been driven deep into their flesh, evidently by the force of the blast. ❞

with people riveted by the footage and photos of the vast mushrooming cloud that rose up some 20,000 feet as the bomb was detonated.

■ JAPAN SURRENDERS ■

In any event, it was clear that Truman's pledge to 'obliterate' Japan was no empty threat. Hirohito himself was sickened at the sight of the suffering among his people. Finally, he found the leverage inside his government to bring the conflict to an end.

The day after Nagasaki was bombed, Japan broadcast a willingness to surrender 'on the understanding that it does not comprise any demand which prejudices the prerogatives of the Emperor as Sovereign ruler.'

Yet still the hawks in the regime dragged their feet. A flight of US Navy carrier-borne planes flew over Japan on 13 August dropping leaflets spelling out the surrender so the people would understand that it was all over.

The following day at 11pm the Emperor himself told his people the war was over

The following day at 11pm the Emperor himself told his people the war was over. Even at this late stage, 1,000 militant soldiers stormed the Imperial Palace in a bid to prevent the surrender. They were beaten off by the Emperor's own guard.

VJ day was then declared on 15 August. The pockets of Japanese resistance around the Pacific and

Left: **The atomic bomb scarred the landscape of Nagasaki so deeply it was beyond recognition.**

Left: The luckier victims of the atomic bomb blasts suffered burns to their bodies. The remains of many of the victims were never found.

South East Asia surrendered through the following month, ending with Hong Kong on 16 September.

In the meantime the official ceremony marking the outbreak of peace came on 2 September aboard the USS Missouri in Tokyo Bay. The Japanese delegation was led by the

Sailors squeezed into every available inch of the deck to witness the historic moment.

After the signing was over, General MacArthur gave a stirring speech opening the door to a new order.

'We are gathered here, representatives of the major warring powers, to conclude a solemn agreement whereby peace may be restored. The issues involving divergent ideals and ideologies have been determined on the battlefields of the world and hence are not for our discussion or debate.

■ PRAYER FOR PEACE ■

'Nor is it for us here to meet representing as we do a majority of the people of the earth in a spirit of distrust, malice or hatred. But rather it is for us both victors and vanquished to serve, committing all our peoples unreservedly to faithful compliance with the understandings they are here formally to assume. It is my earnest hope... that from this solemn occasion a better world shall emerge... a world dedicated to the dignity of man... Let us pray that peace be now restored to the world and that God will preserve it always.'

'Let us pray that peace be now restored to the world'

one-legged foreign minister Mamoru Shigemitsu, who wore a top hat for the occasion. The military wing of the country was represented by General Yoshijiro Umezu. There to receive them were dignitaries from all the countries that had taken part in the war against Japan – America, Britain, Australia, New Zealand, Canada, China, France and Holland.

Right: Servicemen greeted news of the atomic explosions with relief. The blasts probably saved thousands of US troops.

Horrors of War

THE CAMPS

Internment has long been used to curtail the activities of so-called 'undesirables' by countries across the globe.

In this respect, concentration camps – although the very name now chills the heart – were nothing new in the Thirties. Unsavoury though the idea appears, they were to pen people without trial on account of their race or beliefs.

Indeed, during World War II both Britain and the US used similar devices to curb the movements of potential enemies on the home front. In Britain those with German ancestry or Fascist sympathy were targeted while in America the residents of Japanese descent were rounded up. In Russia, dissidents were put in Gulags.

The argument for such action in times of war is that of national security and it is a valid one. Concentration camps in Germany were different entirely because of the barbarity that became inextricably associated with them.

Concentration camps became a covert fact of life in Germany soon after Hitler came to power. The first was Dachau which opened on 22 March 1933 just 12 miles outside the centre of Munich.

■ ANTI-SEMITISM ■

Their main purpose was to cage 'enemies of the state'. Into this category fell Communists, Socialists, homosexuals, gypsies, pacifists, opposing politicians and intellectuals – and just about anyone else conceivably opposed to the Nazi regime. They were to become most notorious for housing Jews.

Anti-semitism was not invented by Hitler. He merely made a stake in a middle Europe movement which flourished among the ignorant and was expounded in pamphlets.

Some have suggested that Hitler's own vociferous brand of Jew-hating

was inspired by him having caught venereal disease from some dubious sexual relations with a Jewess.

The theory has never been proven. But certainly there is not a single fact contained in 'Mein Kampf' and his anti-semitic rantings which give the remotest credibility to his arguments. His depictions of Jewish people were so far-fetched as to be laughable. Perhaps it was this very extremism that captured the imagination of his supporters, who were tunnel-visioned people looking for a scapegoat in society on which to vent their otherwise aimless fury.

In 'Mein Kampf' Hitler wrote of his hatred of Jews: 'Thus I finally discovered who were the evil spirits leading our people astray... My love for my own people increased correspondingly. Considering the satanic skill which these evil counsellors

Hitler claimed that the German people had been tricked by the Jews in World War I

displayed, how could their unfortunate victims be blamed?'

So Hitler sought to excuse the weaknesses as he saw them of the Social Democrats and trade unionists, whom he had previously despised, at the expense of the longtime scapegoats, the Jews.

The steps taken against Jews increased gradually from 1933 and did so with the full force of law. By the time the 1935 Nuremberg Laws were passed, German Jews were

Left: Russian children, parted from their parents, were among those caged by the Nazis. Right: A prisoner at Buchenwald after liberation by the Americans.

stripped of their citizenship and the many still remaining at liberty endured a precarious existence.

■ NAZI SADISM ■

Following 1933, violence against minorities and dissidents became an accepted part of German society. The government itself was not beyond imposing law by terror and intimidation. There was a wide range of potential targets and many of the acts of thuggery carried out by Nazi bully-boys were pure acts of revenge or sadism. Too many people in the battered and buffeted state of Germany construed this to be a hallmark of strong government and favoured it.

Above: Britain also had its concentration camps, like this one at Ramsey on the Isle of Man.

Below: Himmler (*second right*) visits Dachau. He personally engineered much of the suffering.

When they could, German Jews fled. In the Thirties some 250,000 Jews left Germany, abandoning all hope of a peaceable existence when daily they read slogans and posters bearing the messages 'Let Judah perish' and 'Jews not wanted here'.

Inmates worked from morning till night, usually on futile tasks, always at jogging pace

Sooner or later, those who remained were destined to be sent to a concentration camp. Joining them were the much-despised Slavs, particularly the intelligentsia.

The first inspector of concentration camps was SS recruit Theodor Eicke who made it his business to breed out any signs of compassion in his men

Top right: Hitler's 'Mein Kampf', heralded around Germany, was full of anti-semitic rantings without a shred of fact.

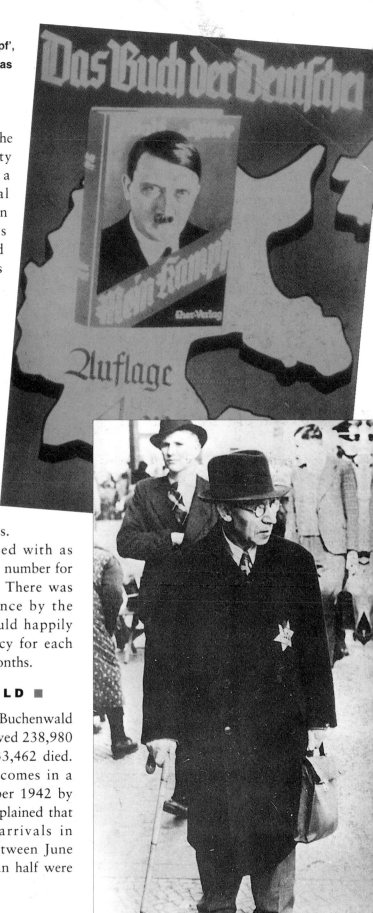

who would be guarding the camp prisoners. Cruelty and sadism became a matter of professional pride. SS men involved in the running of camps boasted of their work and named themselves Death's Head units.

Helping the SS to run the camps were German criminal prisoners dressed in blue and white striped uniforms and just as willing to mete out beatings as their legal overlords. In fact, they were frequently more vindictive to impress their SS masters and avoid a beating themselves.

Names were dispensed with as each detainee was given a number for identification purposes. There was little attempt at pretence by the prison guards who would happily reveal the life expectancy for each prisoner was but three months.

■ BUCHENWALD ■

Between 1937 and 1945 Buchenwald concentration camp received 238,980 prisoners out of which 33,462 died. A grim note of reality comes in a letter written in December 1942 by an SS official which complained that out of 136,870 new arrivals in concentration camps between June and November, more than half were already dead.

Bottom right: Jews were marked out by a yellow star in Germany, one of the milder measures taken against them.

Above: Concentration camp survivor Maurice Goldstein reveals the number he was identified by as an inmate.

Discipline was harsh and the beatings regular, particularly for the old or infirm. Frequently the sadistic lashings carried out by the guards were enough to kill. Medical treatment for those who survived was a case of make-do-and-mend by fellow prisoners with a modicum of training.

Inside the wooden huts that housed the prisoners, beds were made of straw and their occupants were crammed together, forbidden to speak. In the summer the huts were acrid and airless, in the winter, damp and cold.

For inmates, the days were filled, morning until night, with unrelenting work. The tasks chosen by their captors were frequently pointless or futile. Nevertheless, all the jobs had to be done at a jogging pace.

In addition to all this, there were regular singing lessons in German complete with beatings for those who were judged to have performed poorly because they were too tired, too scared or because they couldn't speak sufficiently good German.

Inmates were colour-coded to denote the reason for their incarceration. Jews wore yellow stars. The others wore tags which were coloured pink for homosexuals, orange for political prisoners, purple for pacifists, green for criminals and black for those found guilty of anti-social behaviour.

Escape was rare – which was fortunate for the prisoners, because the retribution dished out to those left behind was terrible and merciless. For a single escape, hundreds of prisoners might be made to stand in the compound naked and still for an entire night, summer or winter. It was enough to claim the lives of those growing increasingly frail with the everyday rigours of camp life.

■ HEINRICH HIMMLER ■

The atmosphere bred tension, fear and despair. The terrorised inhabitants forced to witness the punishment of others and suffer the endless, undeserved beatings themselves felt their spirits crumble. Many had never seen a dead body before going into a concentration camp. Now they were seeing many each day who gave up the fight for survival.

There were those who collaborated with the Germans in a bid to save their own skins. At first they were despised and killed by the guards or exposed and slaughtered by fellow prisoners. Finally, the guards relied on such assistance and the inmates had no energy to strike back at the traitors.

Now inmates dreamed of dying a peaceful death in a comfortable hospital bed rather than be killed in such sordid surroundings. There seemed little hope of this small dream coming true.

Amid the despondency were a few glimmers of hope. Working parties sent outside the boundaries of the camp sometimes found local people bearing food and drink for them. When the residents of local towns were in evidence, the harsh treatment from the guards usually diminished for a while.

In 1942 Himmler drew labour from the camps to prop up German

> ## 'We Germans are the only people in the world who have a decent attitude towards animals'

industry. Some prisoners, he maintained, could be worked to death.

'Whether 10,000 Russian females fall down from exhaustion while digging an anti-tank ditch interests me only in so far as the anti-tank ditch for Germany is finished. We shall never be rough and heartless when it is not necessary, that is clear.

'We Germans, who are the only people in the world who have a decent attitude towards animals, will also assume a decent attitude towards these human animals. But it is a crime against our own blood to worry about them and give them ideals thus causing our sons and grandsons to have a more difficult time with them.

'When someone comes to me and says: "I cannot dig the anti-tank ditch with women and children, it is inhuman, for it would kill them",

'If the anti-tank ditch is not dug German soldiers will die and they are the sons of German mothers'

then I have to say "you are the murderer of your own blood because if the anti-tank ditch is not dug German soldiers will die and they are the sons of German mothers. They are our own blood." We can be indifferent to everything else.'

■ FINAL SOLUTION ■

By the end of September 1944 there were a staggering 7,500,000 civilian foreigners in harness for the Reich alongside two million prisoners of war. Often, the civilians who had been rounded up, herded on to insanitary railway trucks and shipped miles from their homes and families, were housed in concentration camps.

As the numbers deemed suitable fodder for concentration camps grew, so did the number of camps across Germany, Austria and, later, occupied Poland. The tentacles of the Reich spread still further, across the Low Countries, France and Norway, bringing in ever larger crowds of prisoners. When the camps could hardly cope with the daily influx, there seemed little option for the authorities. Tough measures were needed to deal with a tough situation. A systematical extermination would be necessary.

◆ EYE WITNESS ◆

Ron Tansley, a pacifist volunteer doing humanitarian work with the Friends Ambulance Unit, helped to clear Belsen and Neuengamme concentration camps.

'We took the victims from there to various hospitals. It really was shocking. The atmosphere, the stench of death, the dead bodies, the poor victims on their last legs. The barbarity of it all was in each person who existed there. When we had cleared Belsen we were sent to Hamburg.

The worst people I met the entire time I was in Germany were in the Gestapo. They were not all Germans, there were Rumanians, Latvians, Hungarians and all nationalities. They couldn't care less about what had happened in the concentration camps.

From Hamburg we went past Lubeck to Neuengamme concentration camp. All the victims had gone but there were still piles of bones 10ft high and bones left partly in the furnace.

We had to get the camp ready for 5,000 Russian labourers on their way back to their homeland. I went down to the nearest town and asked for the mayor. He had run off so I spoke to the priest instead. I wanted 100 local people to help clear out this camp.

I told him: 'I'm surprised that you, a man of God, could allow that (the events at the camp) to happen'.

He turned up his sleeve and there was a concentration camp number tattooed on his arm. He had spoken out against it and a few days later he was inside the gates himself.

Then he turned to me and asked: 'What would you have done?' I have often thought about that since.

The Russians duly arrived. We fed them as best we could on cabbage and potatoes. On the day we had order papers saying the Russians were to go back, we posted notices and prepared them. The next day half of them had disappeared. They knew they would be killed in Stalin's Russia. All the Allied leaders knew it too.'

NAZI MURDER SQUADS

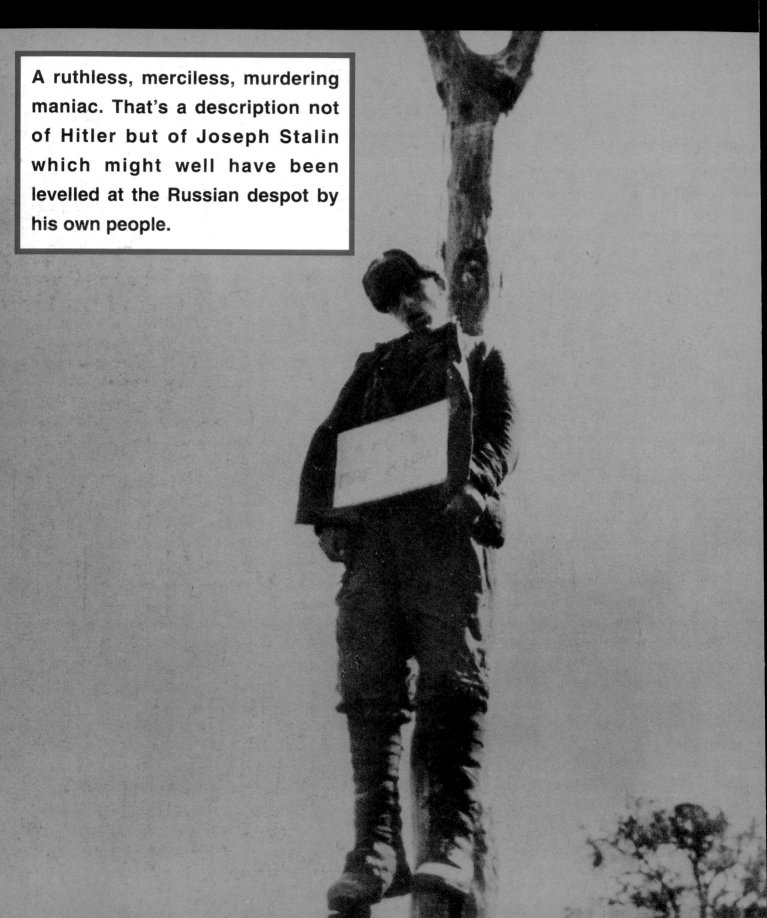

A ruthless, merciless, murdering maniac. That's a description not of Hitler but of Joseph Stalin which might well have been levelled at the Russian despot by his own people.

For years they had suffered under his harsh and barbaric rule. Thousands had died as the 'man of steel' had sought both forcibly to improve Russian industry and eliminate possible opposition. Crude Gulags, state-run labour camps which were the forerunners of Germany's own concentration camps, housed thousands of dissidents.

All the passion so evident in the Russian Revolution of 1917 had evaporated. Society had been dulled by fear and repression together with a sense of helplessness.

A clever man determined to invade Russia might have made capital out of this, portraying himself as a liberator and winning the support of the downtrodden masses. Given the vast area to conquer, widespread support of the people would have made the task considerably easier.

■ NAPOLEONIC PLAN ■

Hitler wasn't smart enough to see the golden opportunities he was passing up. Blinded by his rabid racism which extended to Slavs, he ignored the easy path in favour of the outright hostility necessary for an ideological war of destruction.

The Führer considered Russia a stronghold of Jewry and Bolshevism, his twin loathings

His plan was to incorporate the Crimea into the Reich along with the Baltic states. Further mineral-rich areas were ear-marked for the Fatherland. Germany would dominate Russia as far as the Urals and would

tolerate no armed resistance in the entire area. It was an ambitious plan, one which the Emperor Napoleon had found impossible to achieve. Much taken with the pint-sized despot of the previous century, Hitler was determined to retrace his steps but emerge as victor.

Left: Partisans were usually hanged as an example. Above: These starving Russian soldiers were later executed.

The Führer considered Russia a stronghold of Jewry and Bolshevism, his twin loathings. There is even a school of thought which says he

◆ EYE WITNESS ◆

Vera Inber, trapped inside Leningrad when it was under siege by the German army, kept a diary of the city's sufferings.

25 Jan 1942
❝ Our position is catastrophic. Just now a crowd destroyed the wooden fence of the hospital grounds and carried it away for firewood. There is no water and if the bakery stops even for a single day, what happens? We have no soup, only porridge. In the morning there was coffee but there won't be any more to drink.

26 Jan 1942
For the first time I cried from grief and fury. Inadvertently I overturned the saucepan of porridge on the stove. We nevertheless swallowed a few spoonfuls mixed with the ashes. There is still no bread.

27 Jan 1942
The bakery did not stop work after all as we were afraid it would. When the water mains packed up, eight thousand Young Communist League members – weakened like everyone else from starvation and chilled to the bone – formed a chain from the Neva to the bakery tables and passed to them the water from hand to hand.

Yesterday there were enormous queues at the baker's shops. Bread wasn't delivered till the evening but still it was there. ❞

Above: **Russian citizens were murdered in cold blood by rabid Nazis as they forged through following Barbarossa.**

Russian schoolmistress Genia Demmianova tried to negotiate with invading Germans who were in search of food when they occupied her home village of Povsk in August 1941. Her attempts to speak for an old man found herding his calf on the outskirts of the village were frustrated.

' I was seized by two soldiers. I fought to get free but I could not even move. I was screaming all the time but suddenly I stopped. It flashed into my mind that this was just a nightmare and that I should wake up in a minute. My eyes fixed on old Serge. He looked horrible. One of his eyes looked terribly big and staring and he was whimpering just like a young puppy dog. His face was one mass of blood and there was blood dripping from the gnarled hands he was holding up in front of it.

Two Germans tore the shirt off Serge's back, pulled down his trousers and topboots and left him standing half naked with is bloody hand covering the staring eye. The sergeant picked up a short whip from the table and stepping up to the old man he bawled: 'For the last time, where is the food depot?'

The interpreter quickly translated this. The old man tried to speak but only brought out a hoarse grunt.

All the Germans stepped aside. They knew what was coming. The sergeant raised the whip and brough it down on the old man's back with terrible force. It made Serge's dirty shirt split. The next blow and the next cut it to ribbons which were dyed crimson at the same time. The old man fell to one knee, with on bare bloody arm held in front of his face then he just collapsed on the floor.

The sergeant kept repeating with horrible gentleness: 'Where is the food?'

Two soldiers entered with a tub of water. They flung the water over old Serge. He made a faint movement and moaned once or twice but that was all.

'Take him out,' ordered the sergeant, 'and hang him on that tree.' He spoke casually without the slightest expression in his voice and asked the interpreter to explain why.

The sergeant forced me to look out of the window. The interpreter said old Serge was charged with food smuggling and would be hanged unless the people revealed where the food was hidden. I saw people being driven along to the school by soldiers from all directions. The interpreter kept talking on and on but I knew that the people did not quite understand him not only because his Russian was bad but also because they were dazed. They only began to understand when a German soldier came out with a long rope and tied it on a branch of the chestnut tree.

Immediately poor Serge was brought out. I do not think he was conscious. When people saw his battered bloody old body there was a murmur, then an old woman gave a scream, an old man shook his fist at the Germans and someone threw a stone. The old man was at least ninety.

The stone thrower could only have been a boy. But the Germans responded like beasts. They used their rifles blindly hitting out right and left like mad dogs. It all happened in a few seconds. The air was full of screams, groans, brutal curses. The people ran in all directions. '

carried out 'Barbarossa' not to provide 'Lebensraum' or 'living space' for his people as he professed but merely as a major thrust in his policy to rid Europe of Judaism. The diabolical excesses of Hitler and his forces surely saved Stalin's bacon.

Russia's vast Jewish population which in its history had already known so much about bully boy authorities was to be subjugated again. Although the task was immense, it became a military consideration for Hitler. The Slav people were equally unworthy and were to be extinguished as necessary.

■ KILLING SQUADS ■

Hitler gave his troops an amnesty for atrocities committed on the Eastern front before they even left German soil. Soldiers – and not just SS troops – were encouraged to treat Russian people, prisoners and Jews as nothing better than vermin. However, there was a special role for the SS.

Almost immediately after invasion, more Einsatzgruppen were formed, special killing squads which had cut their teeth in occupied Poland. They moved eastwards in the wake of the front line rounding up Jews and Bolseheviks and shooting them. Those Jews involved in the state or party machine were most at risk.

One Einsatzgruppe leader Otto Ohlendorff estimated that his unit alone killed 90,000 men, women and children in southern Russia in a year. Later, at the War Crimes Trials at Nuremberg, he explained his orders:

'The instructions were that Jews and Soviet political commissars were to be liquidated; the Jewish population should be totally exterminated.'

In the north, another Einsatzgruppe boasted of killing 135,000 victims in just four months. Adolf Eichmann once said that over the course of the war these killing squads claimed two million lives, probably a slightly exaggerated estimate but nevertheless a shocking one.

Above: SS men didn't hesitate to mete out summary justice to those suspected of anti-German activities.

As the idea of efficient extermination in order to achieve the Final Solution gripped the Nazis, mobile gas vans were eventually supplied for use around Russia.

■ THE WINTER WAR ■

For the first time, German soldiers became involved in atrocities which in the west had been the preserve of the Gestapo and the SS. At first, the army were simply encouraged to

> In White Russia, the German 707th Infantry Division shot 10,431 prisoners out of 10,940

trigger action by the local communities against their leaders. This was soon set aside. Although commanders feared individual action by

soldiers against the Russians would result in a catastrophic break-down in discipline, they did little to curtail the killings.

The invading German soldiers themselves were experiencing trying conditions, which were to become more acute in the winter months.

They found Russia to be a primitive country compared to their own. And they found actions by the rapidly expanding partisan movement which claimed many German lives almost intolerable. Before long, German soldiers were no longer able to tell the difference between partisans, Jews and communists.

In White Russia the 707th Infantry Division shot 10,431 people in one month, out of a total of 10,940 taken prisoner. Partisan action had inflicted just two dead on the division and five more men were wounded.

Below: Russian citizens standing before a deep pit are gunned down by a German army firing squad.

◆ EYE WITNESS ◆

Herman Graebe, a German civilian engineer building roads in the Ukraine, witnessed the modus operandi of an Einsatzgruppe. His account to a rapt courtroom at Nuremberg portrays the misery brought about at the whim of the 'master race'.

'Armed Ukrainian militia were making people get out, under the surveillance of SS soldiers… The people in the trucks wore the regulation yellow pieces of cloth that identified them as Jews. I went straight toward the ditches without being stopped.

When we neared the mound I heard a series of rifle shots close by. The people from the trucks – men, women and children – were forced to undress under the supervision of an SS soldier with a whip in his hand. They were obliged to put their effects in certain spots, shoes, clothing and underwear separately.

I saw a pile of shoes, about 800 to 1,000 pairs, great heaps of underwear and clothing.

Without screaming or weeping, these people undressed, stood around in family groups, kissed each other, said farewells and waited for the sign from the SS man who stood beside the pit with a whip in his hand.

During the 14 minutes I stood near I heard no complaint or plea for mercy. I watched a family . . . . an old woman with snow-white hair was holding a child of about one in her arms, singing to it and tickling it. The child was cooing with delight.

The parents were looking on with tears in their eyes. The father was holding the hand of a boy about ten years old and speaking to him softly: the boy was fighting back tears. The father pointed to the sky, stroked his head and seemed to explain something to him.

At that moment the SS man at the pit started shouting something to his comrade. The comrade counted off about 20 people and instructed them to go behind the earth mound. Among them was the family I have just mentioned.

I well remember a slim girl with black hair who, as she passed me, pointed to herself and said : 'Twenty-three'.

I walked around the mound and stood in front of a tremendous grave. People were closely wedged together and lying on top of each other so that only their heads were visible. Nearly all had blood running over their shoulders from their heads.

Some were lifting their heads and moving their arms to show that they were still alive. The pit was nearly two thirds full and I estimated that it contained about 1,000 people.

I looked at the man who did the shooting. He was an SS man who sat at the edge of the narrow end of the pit, his feet dangling into it. He had a tommy-gun on his knees and was smoking a cigarette.

The people, completely naked, went down some steps which were cut in the clay wall of the pit and clambered over the heads of the people lying there to the place to which the SS man directed them. Some caressed those who were still alive and spoke to them in low voices.'

The SS Cavalry Brigade clearing the Prypiat Marshes in August 1941 shot 699 Russian soldiers, 1,001 partisans and 14,178 Jews. All this killing was in retaliation for 17 dead and 36 wounded Germans. A report from the Second Army revealed it shot 1,179 people out of the 1,836 arrested between August and October 1941.

German soldiers readily believed tales of Jewish and Bolshevik barbarity. One story circulated about innocent Lithuanians having their homes burned, their hands and feet chopped off, their tongues torn out and their children nailed to the walls.

■ RACIST SENTIMENT ■

In letters home, the German soldiers who were anyway programmed by years of Nazi propaganda revealed their racist sentiments.

German Captain Hans Kondruss wrote: 'Here clearly a whole people has systematically been reared into subhumanity. This is clearly the most Satanic educational plan of all times which only Jewish sadism could have constructed and carried through.'

Lance-Corporal Hans Fleischauer wrote: 'The Jew is a real master in murdering, burning and massacring…

Left: On Wulecka Hill in Lvov, eminent scientists were shot by the Nazis.

These bandits deserve the worst and toughest punishment conceivable. We all cannot be thankful enough to our Führer who had protected us from such brutalities and only for that we must follow him through thick and thin, wherever that might be.'

Another soldier described Russian prisoners of war. 'Hardly ever do you see the face of a person who seems rational and intelligent. They all look emaciated and the wild, half-crazy look in their eyes makes them look like imbeciles.'

He went on: '[It is] almost insulting when you consider that drunken Russian criminals have been set loose against us. They are scoundrels, the scum of the earth!'

It wasn't until after the war that many soldiers questioned the brutality which occurred on the Eastern front.

'The Russian fights today... for nothing more or less than... his human dignity'

One junior officer who had served in Poland and Russia explained: 'Well, of course, what they [the Nazis] did to the Jews was revolting. But we were told over and over again that it was a necessary evil. No, I must admit, at the time I had no idea we had fallen into the hands of criminals. I didn't realise that until much later, after it was all over.'

One man in Germany spoke out about the folly of the campaign. Dr Otto Brautigam, a diplomat who became deputy leader of the Political Department of the Ministry for the Occupied Eastern Territories, pinpointed the mistakes being made in a 13-page memo written in October 1942. 'In the Soviet Union

we found on our arrival a population weary of Bolshevism which waited longingly for new slogans holding out the prospect of a better future for them. It was Germany's duty to find such slogans but they remained unuttered. The population greeted us with joy as liberators and placed themselves at our disposal.

'...The worker and peasant soon perceived that Germany did not regard them as partners of equal rights but considered them only as the instrument of her political and economic aims...

'...Our policy has forced both Bolshevists and Russian nationalists into a common front against us. The Russian fights today with exceptional bravery and self-sacrifice for nothing more or less than recognition of his human dignity.'

■ NAZI INVASION ■

The invasion of the Nazis wasn't entirely unwelcome. Ethnic Ukrainians, Lithuanians, Latvians and Estonians were thrilled to be free of Stalin's choking communist yoke. They even held parades and sported the Swastika. At least for them the German slogan of 'Liberation from Bolshevism' had some credibility.

Above: After liberation, women work to identify bodies.

Their young men rushed to volunteer for the SS and became in many cases some of its most ardent and hardline members.

Predictions that the Red Army would be beaten in ten weeks turned out to be wildly optimistic. Although it took two years, Stalin's men got the upper hand against the invaders and began pushing them back into their own territory and beyond. Here was their opportunity to pay back in kind the treatment their own people had endured.

German troops were now faced with the appalling prospect of giving themselves up to the Red Army and went to elaborate lengths to surrender to American and British forces instead.

British soldiers released from prison camps by the Russians were appalled at the behaviour the liberators displayed towards German civilians, little realising the horrors that had gone before on the Eastern front.

The horror inspired by senseless Nazi doctrine that had taken place in Russia makes up yet another shameful chapter in history from which neither side could easily recover.

FINAL SOLUTION

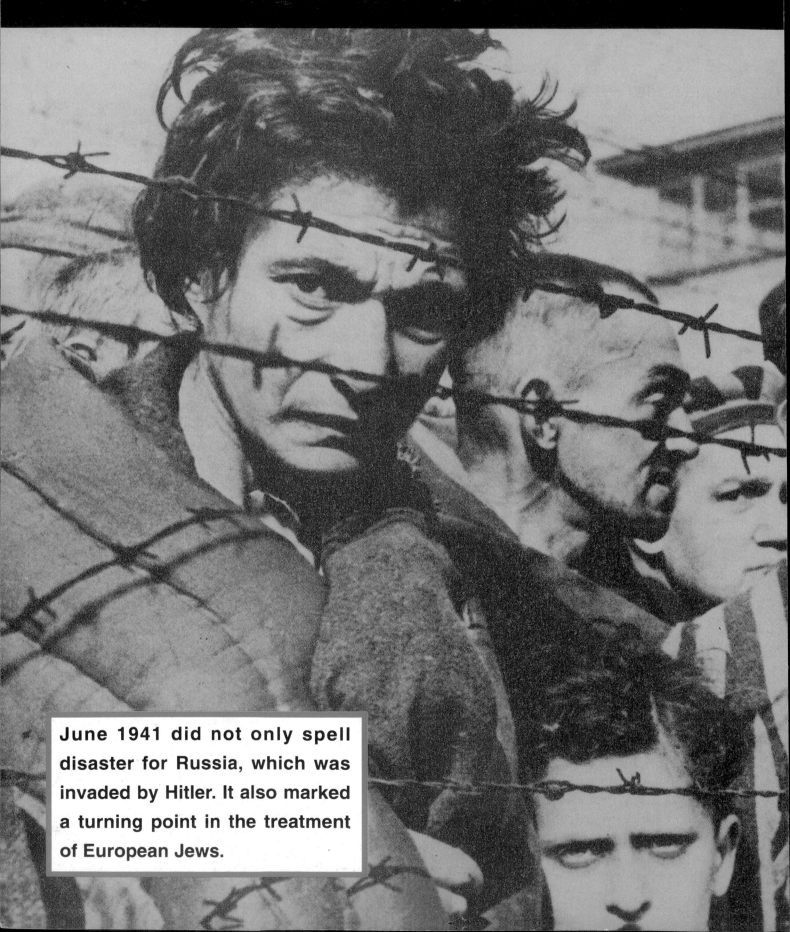

June 1941 did not only spell disaster for Russia, which was invaded by Hitler. It also marked a turning point in the treatment of European Jews.

The drive against Jews had escalated with dynamism. As each new European territory was incorporated into the Reich, there were thousands more shipped in cattle trucks to the concentration camps of Germany, Austria and Poland.

As they saw the countryside race by through the slits and cracks in the uncomfortable carriages, they knew they were facing their doom. The existence of concentration camps where only the supremely fit could survive was now no secret. Yet few could have been prepared for the state-sponsored horror which awaited them.

The death squads in Russia went about their task with the fervour of the zealot

Concentration camps and ghettos which by now had become the chosen route to 'free' Europe of Jews were both haphazard methods which took time to win results. The emigration of Jews to freedom, both voluntary and forced, had been curtailed in Palestine and was occurring at little more than a dribble. (It was finally brought to an end by the Germans themselves.)

Now the sheer volume of 'Untermenschen' or 'sub-humans' being deported into the Reich was multiplied many fold. The satellite death squads which went into Russia went about their task with the fervour of the zealot. Although as many as half a million died in total, it wasn't sufficient for the barbaric regime. Ideas of the 'Final Solution' were formulating

in the heads of the most ardent Nazis; that is, the wholesale extermination of the Jewish people in Europe.

There is no exact date for the start of the Final Solution, though operations against the Jews were stepped up after the end of July 1941.

To that end, a range of experiments were tried. The first guinea pigs at Auschwitz were the much-despised Russian prisoners of war, who, alongside 300 Poles, were herded into a sealed cellar one night in September 1941. Through a grating, the callous guards pumped poison gas, oblivious to the screams of the men inside. It took hours for the cries and groans to stop. At dawn, other camp inmates were ordered to carry the bodies from the chamber to the crematorium.

In November 1941 another experiment in mass killing took place, this time in Berlin. The victims were Jewish slave labourers taken from Buchenwald concentration camp whose destination was the infamous Euthanasia Institute where they were gassed to death. The experiment was once again deemed a success. The answer to the Nazi problem was by now apparent.

On 8 December 1941 several hundred Jews were taken from three Polish towns to a wood outside the village of Chelmno and gassed in a specially constructed building.

The Wannsee Conference scheduled for 9 December 1941 was a top level debate on what to do with Jews in the Third Reich. It was sponsored by SS-Obergruppenführer Reinhard Heydrich, one of the authors of Nazi policy against the Jews.

■ WANNSEE ■

In fact, the conference was postponed after Japan's attack on Pearl Harbor. It didn't take place until 20 January 1942 when the representatives of seven high offices – including the Ministry of the Occupied Eastern Territories, the Interior Ministry, the Ministry of Justice, the Foreign Ministry and SS departments – gathered to hear about the Final Solution.

Heydrich made no secret of his desire to deport the entire Jewish

Left: Hopeless and helpless, inmates at Auschwitz concentration camp wait for the end. *Below:* Windowless huts in the Auschwitz camp housed thousands.

Historians have since debated long and hard the significance of the Wannsee Conference. Today it is regarded as little more than a platform sought by Heydrich to broadcast his radical views. It was, nevertheless, the precursor to genocide and the holocaust for which

Mass murder was now sanctioned as an official Third Reich policy

population into the east where they would be quite literally worked to death. Those who remained would be 'dealt with'. Here, the policy on procreation was acidly clear. It was the germ that led to the sterilisation programme later brought in by the Nazis to stop the spread of the Jewish population. Among those present at the Wannsee Conference were Himmler, Adolf Eichmann and Ernst Kaltenbrunner.

the Nazis are best remembered today. The mainly localised examples of mass murder carried out on the initiative of individuals was now sanctioned as a Reich policy.

In a speech given by Hitler at the end of January 1942, he told the German people the war could only end when the Jews had been 'uprooted' from Europe.

Hitler said: '…The war will not end as the Jew imagines it will, with the uprooting of the Aryans, but the result of this war will be the complete annihilation of the Jews. 'Now for the first time they will not bleed other people to death but for the first time the old Jewish law of "an eye for an eye, a tooth for a tooth" will be applied.'

Left: In Auschwitz camp the inscription on the main gate read 'Work brings freedom'.

It seems clear, therefore, that not only the Nazi officials but also the general public knew of Hitler's desire to kill off Jewry in Europe.

There has been much debate since about the passive acceptance of the German people to this sickening policy. Yet it is clear that the Germans had suffered a degree of brainwashing by Hitler. Thrilled at the emergence of a strong state in which their personal fortunes had improved tremendously, most

Above: Zyklon-B was the gas used to kill thousands in Auschwitz after they were herded into fake shower rooms.

Germans accepted the arrival of concentration camps as necessary to suppress revolutionaries and to house the mentally deranged. There was confusion in the minds of many people who felt being anti-Hitler was tantamount to being anti-German.

As the activities against those targeted minorities like Jews, gypsies, the mentally or physically handicapped and homosexuals increased, the brutalised Germans were already well-practised in turning a blind eye. The punishment for showing any kindness to Jews was severe. Victims of an expert Nazi propaganda machine, native Germans believed they themselves were at risk from a resurgent Jewish force.

■ NO FREE SPEECH ■

If lively discussion of the Jewish question and the extreme measures taken by the regime had been permitted, perhaps a group of people

opposed to exterminations would have found expression. But free speech was impossible. A Berlin butcher who whispered to a customer that Hitler had started the war was sentenced to death and dispatched to a concentration camp. Germany was, after all, a militarised state which would brook no opposition.

People were subject to the same tools of terror as the so-called 'enemies' of the people. The German underground could operate with only the same degree of effectiveness and in much the same sphere as those resistance movements set up in occupied countries. Veterans of the

Eastern front were no longer shocked by extermination and were even convinced of its necessity.

After the war, American interrogators discovered a broad sense of guilt about the fate of the Jews among everyday Germans. But generally people feared revenge, blocked out

203

KRISTALLNACHT

German citizens chuckled and cheered when Jewish businesses were smashed and businessmen were beaten during a night of horror in November 1938.

Organised by propaganda chief Goebbels, a wave of anti-Semitic attacks took place across Germany apparently in reprisal for the killing of a German diplomat in Paris by a young Jew. On account of the amount of plate glass shattered it was dubbed the Kristall-nacht, or Crystal Night.

More than 7,000 Jewish shops were looted and scores of synagogues were set ablaze. An unknown number of Jews died with many more suffering appalling injuries at the hands of thugs employed by the Nazis. Yet as the terror unfolded, middle-class passers-by stopped to applaud the actions of the bully boys and even held up their babies to see the violence administered to Jews.

In order to prevent a recovery by the Jewish faction, the government plotted to confis-cate insurance cash paid out following the Kristallnacht and return it.

unsavoury information and put the blame squarely on the shoulders of the Führer.

Abroad, governments had long known about the threat to the Jewish population. There was, however, an unwillingness to believe that system-atic murder of a race was taking place. Allied leaders were unwilling to use the facts as they knew them in

Below: **One of the devices which was used to boil human remains down to soap by the Nazis.**

the propaganda war against the Axis powers. The stories of extermination seemed too terrible to be true. Surely no modern nation could be that vile and cruel? Horror stories about Germans had been circulated during World War I which had later been shown to be false.

Torn by political considerations, the British government even went as far as restricting Jewish immigration into Palestine, a vital escape route, to pacify the Arab populations of the Middle East. By 1942 the Swiss

authorities also closed their borders, barring the way to freedom for scores of Jews in Vichy France. Despite its reported independence from Germany, the anti-semitic measures common to the rest of the Reich were also instituted there.

There was enormous sympathy for the plight of the Jews in Britain, reflected in pontifications by the politicians who urged that Britain house more than seven million dispossessed Jews at the end of the conflict. The fact that, given the savage Nazi actions against them, far

> **By August 1942 news of the mass killings in the Reich reached the free world on a daily basis**

fewer Jews than that would remain alive at the end of the war appeared to have escaped them.

Britain's Foreign Office first began hearing about the use of gas chambers in February 1942. A Swedish doctor returned from a visit to the Third Reich confirming that asylums were being cleared by the use of poison. Further reports leaked out of Germany to the same effect. By August 1942 news of the mass killings reached the free world on a daily basis.

■ RIGA MASSACRE ■

On 19 August the Foreign Office in London received via the Belgian Embassy an eyewitness account of a massacre that had taken place outside Riga in Latvia.

'The order was given for the Jews to undress completely. There foll-owed a scene impossible to describe; men and women weeping, falling on their knees, beseeching the German executioners to desist. But all in vain.

'These unfortunate people, among them young children, were lined up at the edge of the trench and machine-gunned. The execution over, the trench was searched to ensure that there was no one alive among the victims. One of the Latvian officers present was unable to stand it and went suddenly mad.'

■ AUSCHWITZ ■

Now some concentration camps had turned into extermination camps, the largest of which was Auschwitz, with its annexe camp of Birkenau. The rate of killings here far exceeded that in other camps of Treblinka, Sobibor, Lvov, Kaunas, Minsk, Vilnius, Riga and Belzec. It was into here that vast numbers of people snatched from their homes in occupied territories disappeared, never to be seen again.

Train loads of deportees arrived to be gassed immediately. On 2 Septem-

---

Everything of value was stripped from them, including gold fillings from the teeth

---

ber 1942, 957 Jewish men, women and children arrived from Paris in the early hours of the morning and 918 were gassed before sunset. The same story with victims taken from the length and breadth of Europe was repeated daily on an ever-increasing scale for almost uninterruptedly for three years.

Following the removal of the bodies from the crematoria, everything of value was stripped from them, including the gold fillings from the teeth, and was shipped to the Reichsbank in Berlin where it was paid into an SS account opened in the bogus name of 'Max Heiliger'.

Right: The gas chamber, with its door on the right, and the crematorium at Mauthausen concentration camp where thousands died.

Soap was made of the fats drained from the bodies processed in the enormous crematoria, fertilizer concocted from human bones while hair was kept for stuffing mattresses or for making cloth.

In addition to gassing, people were also shot, usually with a bullet to the back of the neck, received fatal injections or were shot and thrown on a fire while still alive.

When the trainloads of people arrived at Auschwitz, their fate was decided at the flick of an eye. Blinking at the sudden daylight after hours or days penned up in an insanitary boxcar, the fittest that emerged were filed in one direction to work the rest of their useful days as slaves to the Reich. Included in this work was the everyday policing of the camp and the gruesome task of carrying and disposing of bodies. This was carried out by a group called Sonderkommando who enjoyed certain privileges including better rations and quarters. Yet every four months the Sonderkom-

mando were liquidated on the basis that they knew too much of how Auschwitz worked.

Those herded into shacks and sent out to work began their day at 3am when there was a cruel roll call. Each had to stand for four hours in the cold and dark while camp's sadistic criminal 'officials' and then the SS guards counted and re-counted their

---

◆ EYE WITNESS ◆

Commandant Rudolf Hoess, a veteran of concentration camps, investigated the most efficient way in which to carry out his grim task.

❝After the war in his affidavit to a war crimes trial, he explained: 'I was ordered to establish extermination facilities at Auschwitz in June 1941. At that time there were already three other extermination camps in the Government General: Belzec, Treblinka and Wolzek.

I visited Treblinka to find out how they carried out their extermination. The Camp Commandant told me that he had liquidated 80,000 in the course of one half year. He was principally concerned with liquidating all the Jews from the Warsaw ghetto. He used monoxide gas and I did not think that his methods were very efficient.

So at Auschwitz I used Zyklon-B which was a crystallized prussic acid dropped into the death chamber. It took from three to fifteen minutes to kill the people in the chamber, according to climatic conditions.

We knew when the people were dead because their screaming stopped. We usually waited about half an hour before we opened the doors and removed the bodies.❞

◆ EYE WITNESS ◆

For her 13th birthday, Anne Frank received a diary in which she recorded the silly and sentimental, the childish and the charming aspects of her life. And it was no ordinary life. For Anne was the daughter of Jews living in occupied Holland in 1942. Soon the charade of wearing yellow stars to indicate their Jewishness, segregation and harassment was not enough for the Germans. They began transporting Jews to far off concentration camps.

❝Rather than risk the unknown, Anne went into hiding with her parents and her sister Margot. Within days they were joined by the Van Daans, who had a 15-year-old son called Peter, and then a dentist called Dussel. Dutch friends kept the hideaway near the centre of Amsterdam a secret. But the Germans finally discovered the secret rooms shut off at the back of her father's former business and her cat-and-mouse game with the Germans was abruptly over.

On 4 August 1944 Anne was sent to Bergen-Belsen concentration camp where she died of typhus in March 1945, three months before her 16th birthday. Her diary was discovered after the family's arrest by a cleaner and given to her Dutch friends. They were able to hand it back to her father Otto Frank when he returned at the end of the war. In her last entry into the diary, made on Tuesday 1 August 1944, Anne echoes many other teenagers with her thoughts and her dreams.

'I never utter my real feelings about anything and that's how I've acquired the reputation of being boy-crazy, a flirt, know-all, reader of love stories. The cheerful Anne laughs about it, gives cheeky answers, shrugs her shoulders indifferently, behaves as if she doesn't care, but, oh dearie me, the quiet Anne's reactions are just the opposite. If I'm to be quite honest, then I must admit that it does hurt me, that I try terribly hard to change myself but that I'm always fighting against a more powerful enemy.❞

Below: **Nazi crematoria were built to cope with vast numbers of bodies. Those at Auschwitz worked ceaselessly to cope with the victims.**

until it was finally collected by wheelbarrow for disposal. Given the physical degeneration in their condition during a long journey with little water and no food, many failed to endure the working life for long.

On the walls of the camps were posters which read 'Cleanliness brings freedom'

The rest who arrived by train went another direction, to their doom. This group were informed by loudspeaker that they were going for a shower and delousing before being reunited with their loved ones. Curiously, the camp staff appeared to revel in a charade which never once gave away the fact that people were about to be killed. Every effort was made to convince people of the legitimacy of the 'delousing' including posters which read 'Cleanliness brings freedom'.

■ CHILD KILLINGS ■

This was probably because any signs of panic or dissension from the victims would have seriously disrupted the production-line efficiency of the operation, including the orderly collection of clothes and valuables. Children were always exterminated because they were of little value to the Reich. Their mothers frequently faced the same fate on the basis that loving mums who knew their children had been killed made poor workers.

In a long wooden hut they were forced to strip, their heads were shaved and then they were marched into giant shower rooms. But instead of water, these humiliated, boney figures were gassed to death.

numbers. Absurdly, anyone who died in the night was equally required to attend the roll call. It was up to two inmates to support the naked corpse

Rudolph Hoess explained the finer points: 'Still another improvement we made over Treblinka was that at Treblinka the victims almost always knew that they were to be exterminated while at Auschwitz camp we

The gas chambers at Auschwitz regularly slaughtered between 6,000 and 12,000 a day

endeavoured to fool the victims into thinking that they were to go through a delousing process.

'We were required to carry out these exterminations in secrecy but... the foul and nauseating stench from the continuous burning of bodies permeated the entire area and all of the people living in the surrounding communities knew that exterminations were going on at Auschwitz.'

Although the gas chambers at Auschwitz housed 2,000 people at a time and they regularly slaughtered between 6,000 and 12,000 people a

day, the camp was unable to cope with the demand it was put under during 1944 when the killings were at their peak. By now Jews in the Yugoslavian states, Greece, Hungary, Rumania and France were deluging into the east. As German successes dwindled in the field, the hierarchy became more focused on its stated aim of killing Jews in which they were achieving greater success. Thanks to the personal attentions of Adolf Eichmann, trains ferrying the victims to Auschwitz and other death camps were given priority above those carrying troops needed for national defence. Until the bitter end, the authorities refused to liberate the inmates of Auschwitz, choosing instead to kill them or march those who were still

Above: Hitler's elite, the Waffen-SS, burgeoned during the war and was responsible for scores of killings.

Below: Emaciated corpses piled up at Buchenwald. The sight shocked and sickened the liberating Allied soldiers.

able-bodied to further camps deeper inside the Reich.

■ WAFFEN SS ■

In charge of the extermination programme for the most part were members of the Gestapo or the rapidly expanding Waffen SS. At the start of the war, this elite band numbered just three divisions. By its end, there were 35 containing more than half a million men. They were pitched by Hitler as a tough state police force against the army and as a reward for their efforts they were promised powers and increased status after the end of hostilities.

The power and prestige of the Waffen SS units didn't appeal to

Germans alone. Many foreigners were enlisted into its ranks and happily carried out the most gruesome and grotesque of its chores. Of the 900,000 men who passed

The most feared of the 900,000 men in the Waffen SS were the Ukrainians

through the Waffen SS, less than half were Reich Germans. A further 300,000 were racial Germans from outside the boundaries of the Reich, 50,000 were from other Germanic races while 150,000 were foreigners. The most feared of the SS guards were the Ukrainians.

■ FREE AT LAST ■

Their master, SS Reichsführer Heinrich Himmler, urged them to show no restraint. He told them in October 1943: 'One basic principle must be the absolute rule for the SS men; we must be honest, decent, loyal and comradely to members of our own blood and nobody else. What happens to a Russian and a Czech does not interest me in the slightest. What the nations can offer in the way of good blood of our type we will take, if necessary, by kidnapping their children and raising them here with us.'

Such was their enthusiasm that up to 90 per cent of incoming prisoners went immediately to their deaths, depriving the Reich of the slave labour it needed to replenish its armaments and food supplies. This became a source of some dissastisfaction among the Nazi hierarchy.

Battle-hardened soldiers who arrived to liberate Auschwitz and other extermination camps were sickened at what they found. Those who remained alive were little more than skin and bone, their enormous sunken eyes glazed, their heads

Below: **Freedom for the children of Auschwitz. This picture was taken just hours after the camp was liberated.**

Above: **The funeral procession for victims of the Nazis at Auschwitz held in January 1945 stretched as far as the eye could see.**

shaven, capable of little movement on their own account.

Conditions by then were abominable. There was widespread disease as well as infestations of lice and other bugs. Those who witnessed the terrible scenes, together with the gas ovens and the overworked crematoria, all spoke of the odour of death emanating from the camps. To be passing nearby and remain ignorant of the killings there was surely impossible, they questioned.

At last, the Allies were convinced beyond doubt of the scale of the killings. Although detailed figures across the board were not kept, it seems upwards of five million died. Some claim that fully one third of the Jewish population in Europe was murdered in the Holocaust. The decision not to bomb Auschwitz and smash the operation now seemed to have been made in error.

One man who suspected the truth all along, the most ardent of anti-Nazis,

HOLOCAUST

Although six million is the most quoted figure for the death toll of Jews during the Holocaust, it remains impossible to apply an exact figure. There could have been fewer – or far more – killed as Hitler and his henchmen implemented 'the Final Solution'.

There were only six extermination camps, the largest being Auschwitz, but killings were carried out at most of the concentration camps, too. Rudolph Hoess, commandant at Auschwitz until December 1943, admitted after the war that at least two and a half million people were executed during his time at the camp and a further half million died from hunger and disease. This comprised not only Jews, but Russians, gypsies, homosexuals, dissidents and the disabled. However, the most terrible measures taken against the Jews came after his tenure was finished.

One man who suspected the truth all along was the most ardent of anti-Nazis, Winston Churchill

was Winston Churchill. As early as July 1944 he wrote to Anthony Eden to say: 'There is no doubt that this is probably the greatest and most horrible single crime ever committed in the whole history of the world.'

DOCTORS OF DEATH

For centuries people have been fascinated by twins. Two identities from the same womb who may even be the spitting image of one another were worshipped by some ancient races, feared by others.

To the rabid Fascists of Nazi Germany twins were a short cut to peopling the Third Reich with blond-haired, blue-eyed super specimens of the master race. This noble breed of Aryans so adored by Hitler would have the run of Europe at the expense of the Czechs, Poles, Slavs and Jews.

Women in Germany were already being encouraged to produce as many children as possible. If only every good German woman could produce multiple sets of twins with the requisite physical qualities, that problem of populating the expanding empire would be cut at a stroke.

In order to achieve a larger incidence of twins, there was the need to do detailed medical research. The man who came forward to lead this investigation was Dr Josef Mengele. The place to do it was the notorious death camp, Auschwitz.

The investigation was led by Dr Josef Mengele at the notorious death camp Auschwitz

Here, Mengele worked long and hard to establish the special characteristics of twins. Any that were transported to the camp were set aside for his special attention.

First came the rigorous medical check-ups on them while they lived. Each was examined together and separately in the quest to break new ground. Then Mengele played his

Left: A prisoner in a pressure chamber is the subject of a painful experiment.
Right: No pity was shown to children.

trump card. Until now, it was rare that twins ever died together. So medical probing into their inner likenesses was severely curtailed.

Mengele, with the aid of his pistol or a fatal injection of chloroform to the heart, could personally dispatch twins to their maker within moments of each other – although frequently he got one of his faithful entourage to do the dirty deed. The still-warm bodies of the ill-fated twins would be the subject of postmortems to reveal whether or not the similarities of twins was more than just skin deep.

Internal organs removed in the dissection thought to be of particular interest were pickled in alcohol and sent to the Anthropological Institute at Berlin-Dahlem for further study. His aim was to clone the perfect Ayran and he would stop at nothing to fulfill this warped dream.

■ HUMAN GUINEA PIG ■

Using live humans, he would attempt to change hair and eye colours. It is said he once returned a gurgling tot to the arms of his anxious prisoner mother with a bloodied red cavity where an eye used to be. He was blatantly unconcerned that many of his patients died, were crippled or blinded during his experiments.

■ DOCTOR OF DEATH ■

Mengele was without any doubt dedicated to his work. The eldest son of a Catholic German industrialist, he went to the University of Munich where he secured a doctorate in philosophy and proceeded to medical school at the University of Frankfurt. At both places of study it appears he was infected with virulent anti-Semitism which was rife in Germany at the time.

A former member of the discredited SA, Mengele joined the Nazi Party in May 1937 and embraced the SS a year later. Injured on the Eastern front in 1942, he recovered from his wounds, received the Iron Cross for his actions against the Red Army and then volunteered to be camp doctor at Auschwitz despite a marked lack of experience in practical doctoring.

Although short in stature, he was suave, sophisticated in conversation and graceful in movement. Associates at Auschwitz, even inmates, remember him still with a certain awe and occasionally even adoration. Ironically, while he laboured to perfect the blond-haired, blue-eyed image of true Ayrans, he was himself dark and could pass as a Mediterranean.

Speculation about how Mengele got out of Germany at the end of the war is rife. Some claim he was

> **Speculation is rife about how Mengele got out of Germany at the end of the war**

smuggled out by a Jewish mistress and was kept in hiding in various European cities until he could safely be spirited away to Argentinian shores. Others maintain that he was captured by the Allies but slipped through their fingers in the chaos of newly-won peace.

Below: **To halt the population, Nazi doctors carried out painful sterlisiation operations on Jewish and Slavic women.**

Still, he certainly made it to Argentina and felt so secure in his new home that he used his real name to apply for an Argentinian passport in 1956. He also won permits to visit Germany and Switzerland. An extradition bid failed in 1959 on a technicality, by which time Mengele was concerned in a pharmaceutical company in Buenos Aires.

■ DEATH IN BRAZIL ■

He left Argentina for Paraguay in 1960, apparently to work on a cattle cloning project for which he was eminently qualified, thanks to his time at Auschwitz. From there he travelled to Brazil where it is almost certain that he drowned in 1979. His death was cloaked in secrecy for six years. In the early Eighties, Dr Simon

---

> ## *It is almost certain that Dr Josef Mengele drowned in an accident in Brazil in 1979*

Wiesenthal had drawn up a list of 10 prominent Nazis whom he wished to see brought to justice. At the time he said: 'If I could get all ten, it would be an achievement. But if I could get only Josef Mengele, I think my soul would be at peace.'

Wiesenthal, among thousands who yearned to see Mengele brought into a courtroom to face his crimes, was cheated by the apparent fluke death of the 'Angel of Death'.

In addition to his forays into medical experiments, Mengele was also guilty of vicious beatings. Afterwards, he would meticulously clean the blood from his hands using perfumed soap.

His research into the incidence of twins was not the end of the

---

ALDERNEY

Alongside the names of Dachau and Belsen in the annals of horror ranks Alderney, one of the Channel Islands which became the site of three harsh work camps for slave labour and a fourth, fully fledged concentration camp called Sylt.

All four camps, in particular Sylt, became living hell for hundreds of prisoners, particularly Russians, who were sent there to be literally worked to death for the Third Reich.

In charge was the Todt Organisation, tasked with building the defences for Hitler's Fortress Europe. Food was short, the working days long and the beatings meted out by the Germans in control were cruel beyond belief.

One Russian recalled how a fellow countryman died in one of the work camps. 'In Alderney camp, I saw a Russian beaten for half an hour until he bled to death. Willi, a cook, did it. The Russian had taken some potato peelings.'

One Todt officer beat at least one Russian prisoner to death for picking up discarded cabbage leaves.

Officially, the death toll on Alderney is 530 although the real figure is thought to be much higher. Alderney stands out not only because it is on British soil but because the atrocities associated with the Third Reich are normally thought to have been committed by the SS while in this case it was the Todt Organisation building the Atlantic Wall which was responsible. The British government has decreed that records linked to the events on the Channel Islands will be kept under wraps until 2045, probably to save the face of islanders who collaborated.

---

grotesque activities which took place in the name of medical advances at Auschwitz and other camps throughout the Reich.

Bacterial cultures were grown in live humans afflicting them with the ravages of terrible disease no matter what the pain and suffering that went with it. 'Volunteers' were injected with all manner of vile germs to see what effect they would have.

Surgical operations were carried out by SS doctors without anaesthetics in their crazed attempts to establish the precise effects.

A 'cause celebre' of the manic medic was to sterilise women from the 'sub-human' races around Europe to prevent them procreating further. One technique was to subject each woman to an X-ray for minutes on end to wither the reproductive organs. Poisonous injections were

Right: **Tests at high-altitude on pyjama-clad prisoners revealed new information to German scientists about the effects of decompression on human beings.**

also administered into the womb, their effects being carefully monitored as the 'guinea pig' female writhed in agony.

In one of the most callous experiments, Jewish people were lined up to be shot so German scientists could assess how many bodies a bullet

Left: Dr Sigmund Rascher used inmates at Dachau concentration camp for immersion experiments like these, deep in chilling ice water.

In the past, the government has claimed the bones belonged to victims of the Allied bombing raids. Marks on them suggest otherwise but all attempts to analyse the bones have been blocked.

At the head of Japan's grotesque probes beyond the bounds of medical science was Lt-General Shiro Ishii. He oversaw experiments in which prisoners were infected with bubonic

Lt-Gen Ishii oversaw experiments in which prisoners were infected with bubonic plague

could travel through before finally coming to rest.

News of the medical research carried out by the Nazis caused worldwide distress and distaste when details emerged following the war. Yet that stark fact didn't stop medics making full use of the research material gathered by the Nazis amid such appalling anguish and pain.

For more than 40 years British university lecturers showed X-rays taken by the Nazis of their mad work to students. The remains of death camp victims have also been used for teaching purposes.

■ TEACHING AIDS ■

One Cambridge University doctor defended the controversial use of such heartbreaking material in the years following the war by saying: 'It was excellent teaching material. It was used here for over 30 years and served a valuable purpose. There was

obviously a degree of revulsion felt but at least the suffering of those involved was of benefit.'

The X-ray film was in use as recently as 1987. Continued observation of the findings of SS doctors has caused outrage among holocaust survivors who have urged doctors to now give the remains in question a decent burial.

Medical experiments also took place in Japan, an issue which has for years been a source of embarrassment and denials by the government.

Circulating today in Japan are severed skulls and thigh bones. The skull bones contain drill holes, some of them square, indicating brain surgery has taken place.

The bones were discovered in 1989 buried in the grounds of an army medical college where medical experiments are thought to have been carried out following the outbreak of the Sino-Japanese War in 1931.

plague and other fatal diseases and then disembowelled to see the effects on their inner organs. It was his practice to perform autopsies while the 'patients' were still alive. Ultimately, his aim was to perfect a biological weapon which would win Japan's war.

■ COLD EXPERIMENTS ■

Another of his quests was to find a cure for frostbite. Prisoners had their hands dipped in iced water and were then forced outside into freezing winter weather until the hand was thoroughly affected.

The most notorious venue was Unit 731 in occupied China where some 3,000 were killed.

After the war, staff used on the trials admitted the knowledge they gained during these experiments was used after the war. Some felt they had been cheated out of due credit for their endeavours.

A Japanese professor who spoke to these scientists after the war reported: '[They] felt they were victims because they felt they had spent a golden time in fruitful research but the work at 731 would not be recognised by ordinary scientists.' He found only one man who expressed any guilt about what had happened.

He used predominantly Chinese, Korean and Russian guinea pigs but some British and Americans are also thought to have been involved.

Below: **The 'Anatomy Institute of the Academy of Medical Sciences' in Danzig received this human skin.**

SMOKING

Vegetarian, teetotaller and non-smoker, Hitler was keen to use his propaganda machine to spread the word about clean living and good health. When links between smoking a lung cancer were detected by German scientists in the Twenties, he became one of the first anti-smoking campaigners in the world.

Magazines and newspapers contained warnings about the dangers of smoking. Women were forbidden to buy cigarettes in cafes, smoking was restricted among soldiers and banned in scores of public places. It was illegal to use tobacco in advertising to advocate manly qualities and those who abstained were awarded shining qualities of good Aryan citizens.

Despite his iron grip on the propaganda system, his move to cut smoking failed. The number of smokers rose in Fascist Germany in much the same way as it did in other European countries. The shortcomings of preventative medicine in a totalitarian regime where everyone is subject to the message has cast doubt among some doctors on its value in democratic states today.

ATROCITIES

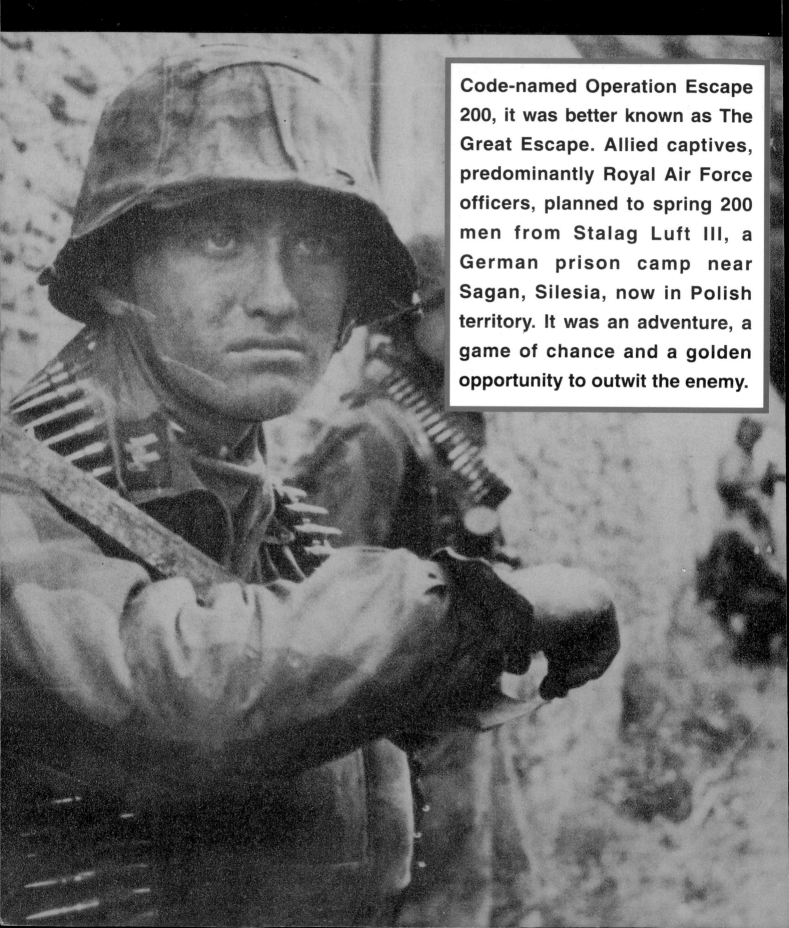

Code-named Operation Escape 200, it was better known as The Great Escape. Allied captives, predominantly Royal Air Force officers, planned to spring 200 men from Stalag Luft III, a German prison camp near Sagan, Silesia, now in Polish territory. It was an adventure, a game of chance and a golden opportunity to outwit the enemy.

But the men who slaved to pull off the most memorable prison breakout ever were to be sorely disappointed. On the night of the escape, 24 March 1944, a conspiracy of events allowed just 76 men to flee the barbed wire and watchtowers of the Stalag. And of those, only three made it to freedom, two Norwegians and a Dutchman.

Worst of all, 50 RAF servicemen chosen at random were shot by the Gestapo as a reprisal for the daring plot, to satisfy Hitler's fury. The Nazis committed an atrocity which the men of the Royal Air Force would never forgive and forget.

Stalag Luft III was built in 1941 on the orders of Hermann Göring, head of the Luftwaffe, to house the increasing numbers of Allied airmen shot down in raids over Germany.

It was a far cry from the concentration camps for which Hitler and his henchmen became famous. Although 12 men were forced to share a room, some days around the clock, they were allowed to play games like rugby and football and enjoyed reasonable rations. The prisoners of war totalling 5,000 were even allowed to build their own theatre where they staged productions twice weekly.

It was an indication of the sneaking regard in which Göring held the courageous airmen – as was the treatment dished out to them if they escaped. Until 1944, when the tide of war had turned against Germany, British airmen had to endure only a verbal lashing and a spell in solitary

Left: By 1944, Waffen-SS troops were battle-hardened desperate men.
Right: Stalag Luft III, the camp from which RAF officers planned a daring breakout.

confinement if they were recaptured. They were treated to applause and cheers when they emerged to rejoin their comrades.

■ ESCAPE COMMITTEE ■

Stalag Luft III was constructed on sand. It wasn't long before enterprising airmen housed in the officers' compound desperate to escape to Britain and resume the battle against Hitler had dug a maze of different tunnels from inside the complex. The escape committee run by Senior British Officer, Wing Commander Harry 'Wings' Day, a veteran of the Great War was active if something of a shambles.

Only when South African Roger Bushell, an experienced escapee, took charge did the plans for The Great Escape take shape. He believed the best way to harry the Germans was to have scores of their internees turned loose at one time. To do it, he hit upon the idea of having three tunnels only for escaping purposes, nicknamed Tom, Dick and Harry. Work started in the summer of 1943 but was dramatically halted when the existence of Tom was discovered in October. It wasn't until January 1944 that work resumed. This time the

intention was to complete Harry as quickly as possible.

Its entrance in Hut 104 was disguised beneath a heating stove. Digging with usually nothing more than empty tins, a team of two men squeezed into a tiny shaft scooping away the sandy earth and propping up the extending tunnel with wooden supports taken from the prison bunk beds. Engineers among the prisoners designed and made a trolley running on wooden rails large enough to

> *The entrance to the tunnel in Hut 104 was disguised beneath a heating stove*

carry a man on which the diggers and their sand were eventually ferried. At first the operation was lit by fat-burning lamps. Later however, a supply of electricity was filched from the camp itself by means of some stolen cable. There was also an air pump made of a kit bag and piping constructed of old food tins which provided fresh oxygen to the tunnel while digging was in progress.

Beyond the designing and digging, there were teams of prisoners involved in scattering the dug-out sand. One technique was to fill two sausage-like containers with sand to wear down each trouser leg, releasing it slowly during a trudge around the campsite. The sand bags were the ingenious idea of another escape organiser, Captain Peter Fanshawe, taken prisoner during the Norwegian

There were teams of prisoners involved in scattering dug-out sand during exercise

campaign. Nicknamed 'Hornblower' by his comrades, he was dispatched to another camp shortly before the breakout and so, to his immense disappointment, was unable to take part. Following liberation, he was later put in command of the sloop

Amethyst during the Korean War and died shortly before the commemoration of the 50th anniversary of the Great Escape in 1994, aged 82.

Those who made friends with camp guards elicited further tools and even cameras for forging the documents that would be needed outside the camp. Yet another group set to work making service suits look like civilians' garb using dye concocted of boot polish or ink.

■ 200 TO ESCAPE ■

More than 500 officers worked frantically on the project – although not everyone in the camp chose to get involved. Many thought the end of the war was imminent and considered that it would be foolhardy to risk lives at this belated stage. They had a point. The notion that the men were escaping to freedom was quite wrong. They were escaping from the camp into German territory from where it would be a long and dangerous haul home.

Above: RAF men held in Stalag Luft III enjoyed many privileges, thanks to the esteem of Göring.

Nevertheless, when the 330 ft tunnel was completed by 14 March there was no shortage of volunteers to go through it. Bushell selected the first 25 himself. The rest were drawn out of a hat. Astonishingly, guards noticed nothing as the 200 men converged silently on hut 104 before dusk when the doors were locked. Three men went down the tunnel to complete the last two feet of digging. With horror, when they finally pierced the crust of snowy, frozen ground above them, they discovered the tunnel fell 30ft short of the forest which would give them essential cover. It was in clear sight of the watchtowers and their guards. Quickly, the determined bunch devised a rope alarm system, in which a man in the forest would signal the all-clear to the next in line to escape by giving two tugs.

Below ground, things were not going well. The electric lights rigged up to aid the men in the tunnel cut out due to an air raid on Berlin. The troops of men sweeping through on the trolley caused landfalls which had

Disaster struck. A German soldier happened on the tunnel exit and raised the alarm

to be repaired. In the end, it was decided only 80 men would escape that night before the tunnel had to be sealed. Then disaster struck. A German soldier accidentally happened on the tunnel exit and raised the alarm.

Those in the tunnel had to beat a hasty retreat, gorging their rations and burning their papers and money before being discovered. Seventy-six

men who had made it to freedom had to scatter at speed. While they were mostly British, the number included some Canadians, Australians, New Zealanders, Poles, Czechs and Norwegians as well as one Lithuanian and one Greek. Although there was help and support given by Americans in the construction of the tunnels, all were moved to other camps before the date of the escape.

In the national alert that followed, most of the escapees were picked up almost immediately. With appalling weather conditions, anyone who remained on the loose soon suffered the effects of exposure. Only three made it to freedom, including Norwegian Jens Muller. He described being on the run in the Third Reich as 'just as exciting as the film [The Great Escape] but not in that wild cowboy fashion.'

Fifty officers were chosen by the local Gestapo for execution. With the

exception of Bushell, the selection appears to have been made randomly. Bushell, the barrister and bon viveur, had been warned that if he broke out again he was a prime target for the Gestapo who were irritated by his escape artistry. His sadly ill-advised response was merely to say: 'I am not going to be caught.'

■ **SHOT IN THE BACK** ■

In groups of twos and threes, they were driven into a forest and shot in the back of the head after being invited to leave the car they were travelling in for a 'pinkelpause' or toilet break. Their bodies were cremated and the ashes taken back as an example to the men left in Stalag Luft III. There, news of the merciless killings was greeted with disbelief.

A poster went up in the camp stating: 'The escape from prison camps is no longer a sport!' It went on: 'Urgent warning is given against making future escapes! In plain English, stay in the camp where you will be safe! Breaking out of it is now

Above: Equipment needed by tunnel builders who burrowed their way through sandy soil beneath barbed wire fences.
Left: A trolley used to move sand then men sits in the entrance of Harry, the escape tunnel.

◆ EYE WITNESS ◆

Alf Toombs was a German prisoner of war for five years after he survived the Normandy barn massacre of British troops shortly before Dunkirk.

'For the first two and a half years the treatment was really bad. After that we got Red Cross parcels. If it hadn't have been for them, many of us would not be alive today.

All we got was a cup of coffee in the morning. For lunch there was a loaf of brown bread between five of us. We had to take it in turns to have the small end of the loaf. We worked until 6pm when we were given soup, usually potato. Once we had conds' heads which was disgusting. The cooks were German and they didn't give them much to do.

The Poles were very good to us. Women took bits of bread and food to us while we worked. But when we got back we were searched so we had to be careful.'

a damned dangerous act. The chances of preserving your life are almost nil! All... guards have been given the strictest orders to shoot on sight all suspected persons.'

Below: **A diagram of the escape tunnel and its route out of the Stalag Luft III prison camp.**

■ SENSELESS MURDER

For many, it merely hardened the resolve to escape. Of the survivors of The Great Escape, at least two tunneled out of the next prison camp they were sent to and as punishment for that spent a soul-destroying five months in solitary confinement until the end of the war.

The feat of the men was immortalised on film in 'The Great Escape' made in 1963 with stars James Garner, Steve McQueen, Richard Attenborough, Donald Pleasance and James Coburn. A warm if glorified account of the breakout, it differed from fact because there were no Americans in the escape itself.

The feat of the men was immortalised in the film 'The Great Escape'

However, throughout the Second World War there was no shortage of senseless killings like these which offended against all the common laws of humanity.

British servicemen once again bore the brunt in an appalling slaughter which took place as the Germans powered into Europe during the spring of 1940. After an unexpected period of calm following the declaration of war, British troops sent to France to bolster defences suddenly found themselves embroiled in a fast-moving conflict. Their only hope of escape was to reach Dunkirk from where a massive evacuation would take them to England.

It was those soldiers prepared to sacrifice their own chance of escaping to mount a rearguard action who were caught up in the bloodshed.

■ DUNKIRK ■

Men of the 2nd Royal Warwicks dug in at Wormhoudt, 12 miles south-east of Dunkirk, to confound the enemy. Little did they realise that they would encounter the 2nd Battalion of the crack SS-Liebstandarte, Hitler's favoured troops.

The British soldiers put up a brave resistance, claiming clutches of casualties including the commanding

British soldiers have testified that prisoners were shot in cold blood by the Germans

officer of the army group in opposition, Schutzeck. Many German soldiers were already stoked up to fury by the continuing backlash from the British troops. When word of their commander's head injuries spread, the SS men became inflamed. In place of the injured commander came Wilhelm Mohnke.

British soldiers have since testified that prisoners of war, including those who were injured, were shot in cold-blood by the Germans as they advanced on the retreating enemy.

By 28 May, much of the organised resistance by the British had been knocked out, with only pockets of

Below: A poignant photographic memorial to 25 of the men shot after 'The Great Escape'. All these men were taken in twos and threes to a forest and shot in the back of the head.

26. Langford, P.W.
27. Leigh, T.B.
28. Long, J.L.
29. Mc Garr, C.A.
30. Mc Gill, G.E.
31. Marcinkus, R.
32. Milford, H.J.
33. Mondschein, J.T.
34. Pawluk, K.
35. Picard, H.A.
36. Pohe, P.P.
37. Scheidhauer, B.W.
38. Skantzikas, L.
39. Swain, C.D.
40. Stevens, R.
41. Stewart, R.C.
42. Stower, J.G.
43. Street, D.O.
44. Tobolski, P.
45. Valenta, E.
46. Walenn, G.W.
47. Wernham, J.C.
48. Wiley, G.W.
49. Williams, J.E.
50. Williams, J.F.

ARMY JAIL

Army jails, named 'glasshouses' because the first military prison at Aldershot had a glass roof, were notoriously barbaric.

They were the destination of those evading military service by faking illness, men who overstayed their leave or were guilty of behaviour which was otherwise interpreted as 'malingering'. During the war a string of jails was established across Britain and across the world in the wake of the British advance.

During the week, inmates had to get up at 6am for a day of strenuous physical activity, deprived of all comforts including razors, knives, forks and plates and performing every task 'at the double'. Talking was often banned for hours on end, as was smoking. At weekends, men were often locked up for hours at a time. There were frequent accusations of beatings from sadistic prison guards although this was denied by the army.

Punishments for misdemeanours inside the jail included three days on bread and water and the withdrawal of bedding so that men were forced to sleep on bed springs.

men remaining to stem the tide of Germans. At Wormhoudt a posse of prisoners about 50-strong had been taken, not only from the 2nd Warwicks but also the Cheshires and the Royal Artillery.

Ominously, they were forced to hand over their dog-tags, personal papers and other identification before being marched through the town to the Germans' Battalion Battle Headquarters. As they trudged on, they spotted with horror the bodies of British soldiers by three burnt-out trucks. The corpses themselves were smouldering. One man saw 20 men lined up and shot by the Germans beside a town's building.

Mohnke confronted the officer in charge of the British men and told him 'take no prisoners'

A further 50 prisoners including men from the 8th Battalion of the Worcestershire Regiment and the 20th Anti-Tank Regiment joined their ranks at the HQ where Wilhelm Mohnke was now in charge. It is now believed that a raging Mohnke left the HQ, confronted the officer in charge of the British men and told him: 'Take no prisoners'.

The meaning of the order filtered through to a few of the British men,

Left: **Wilhelm Mohnke, the war crimes suspect, meets with his commanding officer Sepp Dietrich.**

who were scarcely able to comprehend what grim fate awaited them.

Now a new guard of higher ranking SS men marched with them over fields and in double time. The panting prisoners who fell by the wayside were beaten or bayonetted. Their destination was a wooden barn with a straw roof, about the size of a garage, mucky and airless.

Herded into the barn, four men found their way out through a back door and escaped. Still, there remained about 100 men inside under the eagle eye of the SS men gathered around the main entrance. As one British captain complained about the deplorable conditions the men were forced to endure, there came a taste of what was to come. The irate guard, weary of the Britisher's complaint, suddenly hurled a grenade into the crowd of men.

■ IN COLD BLOOD ■

Two men took their cue and tried to escape in the mayhem. One of them, the vocal captain, was shot dead soon afterwards as he tried to hide in a pond. A private with him was injured and left for dead.

Back at the barn, more grenades were thrown, killing and maiming the men as they exploded. The carnage stopped as suddenly as it had begun when the senior SS men decided on a different approach. They demanded five volunteers to step outside. After a brief hesitation, five brave men stepped forward.

They were marched outside, forced to turn their backs to a five-strong firing squad and shot in cold blood. A further five men marched off to meet the same grisly end. Just as the firing squad pulled the triggers, they turned around to look their executioners square in the eye.

Now the men in the barn were not only frightened but belligerent as well.

Right: US troops advance towards Malmedy, Belgium where 30 vehicles were ambushed and 140 men massacred.

As rain deluged down, the SS men stepped inside the barn and began shooting their prisoners by the score. Those who survived were pinned beneath the bodies of their dead comrades. Some died holding photographs of their loved ones, others reciting the Lord's Prayer. Bodies were piled high around the walls of the flimsy shack in which about 90 people had died. Survivors amounted to perhaps 20, some of whom were so badly wounded they would die of their injuries before receiving help.

> ## Some died holding photographs of their loved ones; others recited the Lord's Prayer

The SS men pulled out, content with the success of their operation. There was no help at hand. Some of the men, in groups or separately, tried to escape. They were to a man all picked up by the Germans although one managed to stay on the run for five months. Their luck had changed, however, and they were captured by patrols of the regular German army who treated them decently and accorded them their rights. When the appalling tale of their plight emerged, many German soldiers expressed their disgust.

The injured who were too ill to move were finally rescued by members of an Austrian Red Cross team. One badly wounded man, Richard Parry, recalled the moment of rescue. 'The one thing which stands out is that their handling of me was ever-so gentle. There were six or seven of us taken from the barn wounded but alive, thank God. I remember the great feeling of relief which came over me as I was placed in the ambulance. Inside the vehicle, I fell asleep.'

It wasn't the last wartime massacre to bear the mark of Wilhelm Mohnke. Four years later disarmed members of the Canadian invasion forces at his mercy were to be killed at his command.

On 8 June 1944, the Battle of Normandy was centred around Caen with Canadian forces making repeated attempts to take the city's environs. Striking back was the 2nd Battalion of the 26th Panzer Grenadier Regiment, Mohnke's regiment, who managed to take about 40 prisoners. The prisoners were marched towards the German lines, pushed into a field and then shot by their guards who were brandishing machine guns. Only five escaped by making a run for it.

The same SS group are believed to have murdered six more Canadians who were attending a first aid post. Their bodies were discovered when the area was finally taken by the Allies – they had suffered various wounds to the body and fatal gun shot injuries to the head.

There were other scattered examples of military terrorism in those frenzied days following the invasion in which Mohnke's men are implicated. Then Mohnke himself becomes a leading player in the killing of three more Canadians.

■ WILHELM MOHNKE ■

As Regimental Commander, he stalked out to interrogate the three prisoners who had been captured laying mines and taken to his headquarters at Forme du Bosq. Bellowing and snorting, Mohnke quizzed the men through an interpreter for some 20 minutes. At the end of the interrogation the prisoners were searched and stripped of all their identification.

Abruptly, the questioning ended and the men were marched across a meadow to a bomb crater. As they approached it, they were shot in the back at close range by an SS man – while Mohnke stood and watched.

Left: Bodies of men, women and children await formal identification before burial after the massacre at Malmedy, Belgium.

Mohnke was not alone in overseeing bloody murder following D-Day. Kurt Meyer, who commanded the 25th Panzer Grenadiers, dispatched his prisoners in much the same manner. His headquarters were in the Abbaye Ardenne, near Caen, where 11 Canadian prisoners were killed on 7 June 1944, seven were murdered on 8 June and two more died on 17 June.

According to witnesses, the Canadians killed on 8 June were fully aware of what was about to happen. From a place of interrogation in a stable, each man was summoned to his death by name. He shook hands with his comrades and bade them farewell before walking up the steps to the garden – where a German guard was waiting to put a bullet in the back of his head.

Others who died at the Abbaye were battered to death or cut down in a hail of bullets.

This was not the end of the story, either. Mohnke handed down an order given by Hitler himself, that

during the Battle of the Bulge – Germany's last ditch effort against the Allies – soldiers were to fight with zeal and commitment and to do what it took to achieve victory.

Taken with regard to Mohnke's men and their unenviable past record, the results were not altogether surprising. There was spasmodic violence in the treatment

Christmas 1944 was scarred by one of the worst German excesses of the war

of prisoners of war, this time from the American forces. Yet the German campaign at Christmas 1944 was scarred by one of the worst excesses of the war.

It occurred when an American convoy of 30 vehicles and about 140 men was ambushed at the town of

Malmedy on 17 December. Overwhelmed by Germans, a substantial number of Americans surrendered.

After being searched, the men were lined up in eight rows in a nearby field with their hands held above their heads. There were some 120 men in the field when two armoured vehicles pulled out of the German columns to take aim at the unarmed prisoners. A pistol shot claimed the first victim. Then the machine guns on the vehicles burst into life, killing many before they could even raise their voices in protest.

The bodies collapsed in a heap, some dead already, others dying and still more feigning death in the hope they would escape. Blood oozed from the bodies on to the frosted ground, soaking those still alive who could feel the life ebb from their comrades.

■ EYES BAYONETTED ■

Their agony was far from finished, however. For when the armoured cars moved on, others passing by opened up with a rattle of gunfire at the human debris in the field.

Men began strolling among the bodies, kicking them over and shooting where they saw signs of life. All the time they were laughing hysterically. In common with the other massacres carried out by Mohnke's SS-Liebstandarte men, the perpetrators of the killings were wild-eyed and cackling as if they had been drinking or taking drugs.

Some victims were battered to death. Others had their eyes bayonetted while they were still breathing.

When the coast was clear, the living rose from the dead. About 20 survived. But fortune was not on their side because they were spotted staggering to a nearby cafe by the German rear guards. The Germans set the building ablaze – and fired on the Americans as they dashed out to escape the flames.

Amazingly, 43 Americans survived the Malmedy massacre while an estimated 86 perished. And the rampaging Germans continued to shoot US soldiers and Belgian civilians as they tried to break through to Antwerp and the Belgian coast.

Colonel Jochen Peiper was in charge of the unit which had so savagely murdered that day.

After the war a military tribunal heard from German Corporal Ernst Kohler about the scope of the operation. 'We were told to remember the women and children of Germany killed in Allied air attacks and to take no prisoners nor to show mercy to Belgian civilians.'

Peiper was sentenced to hang among others deemed responsible for the bloodshed. The case, however, caused disquiet because there was evidence that confessions were beaten out of some of the SS prisoners by vengeful American officers and men.

■ TRIGGER-HAPPY ■

And a question mark hung over the fairness of the trial in view of the lack of action taken against US soldiers who committed a similar atrocity in shooting unarmed prisoners of war as they made they way up Italy. Indeed, there is ample evidence to suggest that Allied soldiers were criminally triggerhappy following D-day. The spoils of victory apparently stretched to immunity from prosecution. Peiper was finally sentenced to 35 years in jail and was released after 11 years.

Mohnke, the man who linked the massacres of Wormhoudt in 1940 and those of Canadian soldiers in 1944, was also alleged to have handed specific orders requiring a barbarous response to prisoners down to Peiper before his thrust through Malmedy.

He fell into Russian hands at the end of the war and served 10 years in a Soviet jail. Afterwards, he returned to Germany and lived in Hamburg. He has never been brought to court to face charges on account of the deaths of the Allied prisoners.

Authors Ian Sayer and Douglas Botting compiled a detailed dossier about Mohnke called 'Hitler's Last General'. It outlines the disgraceful

---

The disappearance of 15,000 Poles in Russia remained a mystery for 50 years

---

massacres linked with Mohnke, finding proof against the general in the words of men who were there. They maintain: 'It shows beyond all reasonable doubt that a prima facie case exists against Wilhelm Mohnke on a number of counts; and it urges that the American, Canadian, British and Belgian governments should take action now or prevail upon the West German authorities to pursue the case with the utmost vigour in order that justice might take its proper course before it is too late.'

The disappearance of some 15,000 Polish officers in Russia after the division of their homeland remained a mystery for almost 50 years until secret files revealed the grim truth. The men had been liquidated on Stalin's order by his secret police, the NKVD. Their unmarked resting place was Katyn Wood.

Right: **Jochen Peiper photographed in 1943. He was to serve 11 years in prison for his part in the Malmedy massacre.**

Each man was killed by a single shot in the nape of the neck. It took from 3 April to 13 May to transport the men from three different camps and complete the grisly task.

■ KATYN WOOD ■

Their bodies fell into sandy pits alongside those of their companions. It wasn't until 1943 that the mass graves were uncovered by German soldiers. The shocking story appeared to have all the hallmarks of a German propaganda coup. Instantly, Stalin's regime counterclaimed that Nazis were responsible.

In 1990 the truth was revealed when a box containing NKVD files was handed by the Russians to Poland. It detailed the actions of the violent men who ran the secret police, the forerunner of the KGB, and revealed they themselves had fallen victim to Stalin's ruthlessness and were later killed. While the shroud of mystery had at last been lifted, nothing could erase the grief of the families whose young men were killed so meaninglessly.

■ LIDICE ■

Atrocities in wartime were not confined to fighting men. Civilians in the occupied territories saw many unspeakable horrors, like the ill-fated residents of Lidice. The village outside Prague may have had its fair share of those keen to see the Nazis thrown out of their land and a return to independence. Every village in

Below: At a war crimes trial in 1946, a Malmedy survivor identifies the man who fired the first shot of the massacre.

◆ EYE WITNESS ◆

Chester Wilmot reported the words of an anonymous Frenchman on the BBC in April 1945 which revealed another German atrocity carried out against slave labourers travelling by train away from the Allies.

❝ On Sunday evening the train stopped in the yard at Celle while the engine filled up with water and coal. Our carriages were left standing between an ammunition train and a petrol train and we hadn't been there long when some Allied bombers came over. We heard them coming and we tried to get out of the train, but as we jumped down on to the tracks the SS guard opened fire on us with machine guns. Then the bombs began to fall and they hit the train. The ammunition and petrol began to explode. Many must have been killed. But those who survived tried to get away from the fire and explosions. Some of us reached shelter but most of the rest were shot down by the SS guards. After it was all over, there were only 200 left out of the 4,500 and we 200 were rounded up by the SS and herded into a stable – a filthy stable, and there we lay on straw that barely covered the manure underneath. Many of us were wounded or burnt but they left us there for four days without medical attention, food or water. We were rescued only when the British came. ❞

Czechoslavakia, taken by Hitler by force in 1938, had the same. It was no more of a thorn in the side of the German rulers than any other.

Yet on 10 June 1942 it was surrounded by German security police prepared to carry out a massacre. All

Lidice was surrounded by German security police prepared to carry out a massacre

the men and boys of Lidice and a neighbouring village Lezaky, amounting to 199, were shot dead. Their wives were shipped off to Ravensbruck conentration camp and 90 children were dispatched to other camps around the Reich. The entire village was then burned to the ground. Its name was even erased from German maps. In addition, there were the usual round-ups in reprisal, bring-

The atrocity was carried out as a reprisal for the assassination of Reinhard Heydrich

ing the total dead to some 2,000. The village of Lidice was paying dearly for the death of one German. Reinhard Heydrich, one of the arch exponents of the Final Solution, died on 4 June from injuries he received when his car was blown up.

■ BUTCHER ■

Heydrich, the Governor of Bohemia, was a particularly loathsome Nazi who had well earned his nickname of 'the Butcher of Moravia'. From the velocity of the revenge thought up by Himmler, one might have thought the killers were from Lidice or were in hiding there.

In fact, the assassins were two members of the Free Czech movement, Joseph Gabcik and Jan Kubis, native Czechs who joined the French Foreign Legion and the 1st Czech Brigade in Britain. They had trained for their mission in Britain, were in the pay of the British army

Right: **Weeping Polish wives and mothers flock to identify the bodies of their loved ones cut down in Katyn Wood by Stalin's secret police.**

and were parachuted onto their home territory from an RAF plane.

After tossing a bomb in Heydrich's car on 27 May, they sought sanctuary in a church but were eventually killed following a gun battle. The name of Lidice was found in the papers of a third Free Czech agent, unrelated to the pair who carried out the killing. The razing of Lidice was nothing more than a crude kick-back

by the Germans to repay the death of one of their own.

■ ORADOUR ■

One of the best remembered civilian slaughters of the war took place at Oradour-sur-Glane, near Limoges, in south-west France. One summer's afternoon in June 1944 the streets of this quiet village ran red with the blood of its inhabitants.

◆ EYE WITNESS ◆

Stanislaw Mikolajczyk, successor to Sikorski as leader of the Polish government in exile, recalled how a Soviet bureaucrat explained the Katyn Wood massacre. It happened following rumours that the Polish officers would join the Red Army.

❝ Senior commanders were aware of such talk but had nothing specific to go on. The staff officer was sent to get Stalin's clarification. The staff officer saw Stalin and briefly explained the problem. Stalin listened patiently. When the staff officer finished, Stalin supplied him with a written order. Such orders were common, often requested by subordinates as a matter of self-protection. In this case, said the informant, Josef Stalin took a sheet of his personal stationery and wrote only one dreadful word on it: 'Liquidate'. The staff officer returned the one-word order to his superiors but they were uncertain what it meant. Did Stalin mean to liquidate the camps (housing the officers) or to liquidate the men? He might have meant that the men should be released, sent to other prisons or to work in the Gulag system. He might also have meant that the men should be shot or otherwise eliminated. No one knew for sure what the order meant but no one wanted to risk Stalin's ire by asking him to clarify it. To delay a decision was also risky and could invite retribution. The army took the safe way out and turned the whole matter over to the NKVD. For the NKVD, there was no ambiguity in Stalin's order. It could only mean one thing: that the Poles were to be executed immediately. ❞

Every one of the village's 254 buildings was reduced to rubble as the population looked on aghast. More than 200 men were locked into a barn and cut down in a hail of bullets. Women and children were herded into the church and the doors were locked behind them. Then explosives rained down into the building, all thoughts of its traditional use as a sanctuary forgotten by the bloodthirsty killers.

If the 450 women and children were not dead from suffocation through the choking smoke, they

Below: **It is thought that NKVD men murdered these Polish officers at Katyn Wood rather than query an ambiguous order from Josef Stalin.**

were killed by grenades thrown through the blasted windows. To ensure the massacre was done thoroughly, however, the doors were finally opened and bullets from a machine gun were pumped inside. Anyone who tried to run or was too sick or old to leave their home was mercilessly shot.

Today Oradour looks exactly the same as it did at the moment when the murdering German troops pulled out. Although the smell of fear, death and spent explosives has long since faded, the walls of the wrecked church are still scorched and the doctor's car remains in the street in the same spot it was when he was pulled from its seat and taken away for execution. Visitors come to pay homage to those 642 innocent people who died and wonder at the barbarity of those responsible.

Indeed, the reason behind this most brutal of repressions has perplexed and intrigued observers of

Above: **The funeral of Reinhard Heydrich. His death led to the razing of the Czech village of Lidice.**

Today Oradour looks exactly the same as it did when the murdering German troops left

---

subsequent generations. For years it was believed the action was carried out as a reprisal following the deaths of three German soldiers at the hands of the French resistance.

However, another explanation has come to light which better explains the severity of the massacre.

A truck allegedly containing plundered loot intended to line the pockets of three SS commanders was attacked by the resistance on its way to being hidden in the Loire valley. Only

one German soldier who fled with his clothes aflame escaped the ambush. And the return of fire killed five out of six of the French attackers. The remaining member of the Maquis could hardly believe his eyes when he cautiously probed the back of the truck and discovered it packed with gold.

Known only as 'Raoul', the wide-eyed peasant hurriedly buried the boxes of treasure at the roadside before himself fleeing. When the three German officers heard about the ambush and the subsequent loss of their booty, they were furious. Recent intelligence pinpointed Oradour as a centre of the resistance. General Heinz Lammerding and his cohort Major Otto Dickmann decided here would be a good place to start their search for the missing gold. In addition, the third member of their conspiracy Helmut Kampfe had co-

incidentally been taken prisoner by the resistance. His prospects for survival were not good.

Consequently, Lammerding sent troops from the Waffen SS under the command of hardline Nazi Captain Kahn into Oradour to extract from its residents the whereabouts of the gold. When they professed ignorance, Kahn simply shot them.

■ SHOCKING TALE ■

The shocking tale of what happened at Oradour-sur-Glane only emerged much later when an entrepreneur called Robin Mackess met the mysterious and still unidentified Raoul long after the war during some dubious business transactions. Mackess was unable to prove conclusively the validity of Raoul's story when he was arrested for customs irregularities and jailed for 21 months. But in his book 'Oradour – Massacre and Aftermath' he outlines his amazing theories for the appalling events that took place.

DEATH RAILWAY

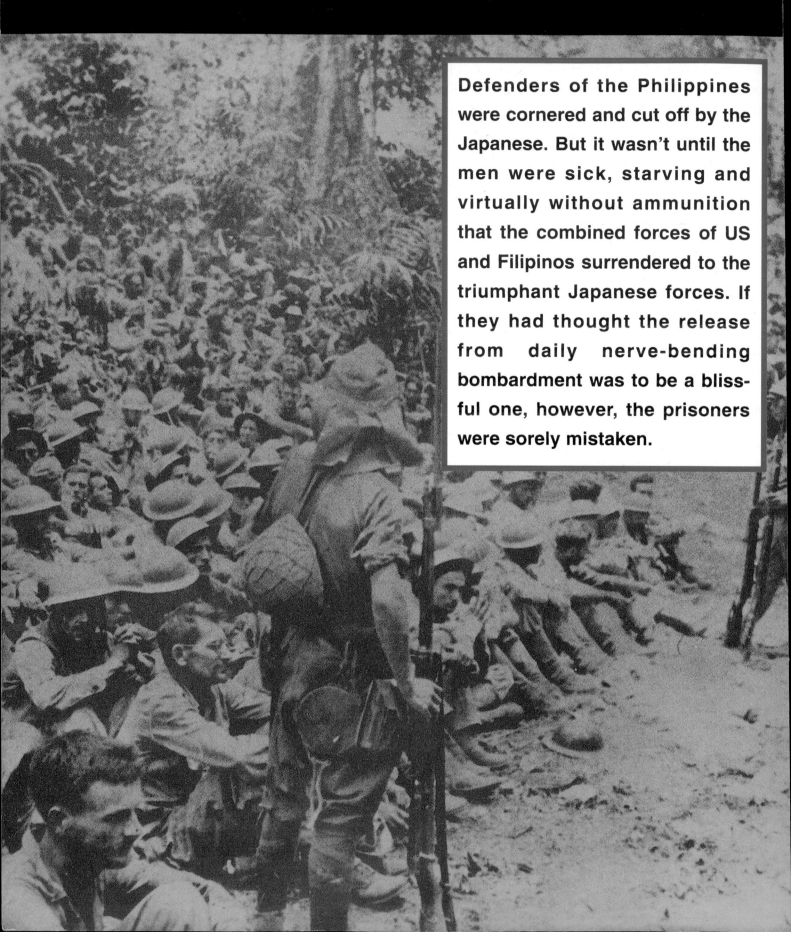

Defenders of the Philippines were cornered and cut off by the Japanese. But it wasn't until the men were sick, starving and virtually without ammunition that the combined forces of US and Filipinos surrendered to the triumphant Japanese forces. If they had thought the release from daily nerve-bending bombardment was to be a blissful one, however, the prisoners were sorely mistaken.

Immediately, the captured forces of 12,000 Americans and 63,000 Filipinos were compelled to embark on a 60-mile trek to a prison camp. Heat, hunger, thirst and barbaric treatment from the Japanese guard soon won the gruelling expedition a new title, that of 'Death March'.

Up to 10,000 died as they made their way along the jungle track, victims who were already dangerously weak from the deprivations of fighting on the island peninsula for so long.

Afterwards, men told how they were pushed past cool streams and plentiful wells even though they were parched. Sadistic guards would club men who stumbled. Little or no food was handed out to men who became faint with desperate hunger. Many who fell by the wayside were summarily shot.

US Air Corps pilot William Dyess was among the prisoners. His account of the march, published in 1944, gave an insight into the sufferings endured.

■ STARVATION ■

'I heard a cry, followed by thudding blows at one side of the paddy. An American soldier so tortured by thirst that he could not sleep had asked a Jap guard for water. The Jap fell on him with his fists then slugged him into insensibility with a rifle butt...

'...Troop-laden trucks sped past us. A grimacing Jap leaned far out, holding his rifle by the barrel. As the truck roared by he knocked an American soldier senseless with the gun's stock. From now on we kept out of reach if we could...'

Following a day without food, the prisoners came to a camp where they found bubbling cauldrons of rice and hot sausages.

'They ordered us out of the patio and lined us up in a field across the road. As we left, grinning Japs held up steaming ladles of sausages and rice. The officer followed us to the field then began stamping up and down, spouting denunciations and abuse. When he calmed enough to be understood we heard this:

> **'When you came here you were told you would eat and be let to sleep. Now that is changed'**

'"When you came here you were told you would eat and be let to sleep. Now that is changed. We have found pistols concealed among three American officers. In punishment for these offences you will not be given food. You will march to Orani [five miles to the north] before you sleep."

■ MENTAL TORTURE ■

'The accusation was a lie. If a pistol had been found, the owner would have been shot, beaten to death or beheaded on the spot. Besides, we knew that the searchers hadn't overlooked even a toothbrush, to say nothing of a pistol. The Japs simply were adding mental torture to the physical.'

Not all the men on the march received the same treatment. Some arrived in poor physical shape at the other end following their exertions but were nevertheless unaware that brutalities had taken place en route.

Left and below: Two scenes from 'The Death March' from Bataan which claimed the lives of 10,000 men.

Above: **Mean Japanese guards staged a picture of a lavish prison camp Christmas dinner before removing the food from the hungry men.**

Some men even rode in trucks. For those still able to summon up the energy, there was ample opportunity for escape. Yet the death toll was a shocking one.

■ CAMP O'DONNELL ■

Those that did arrive at the destination – Camp O'Donnell – had further nightmares to counter. Four out of ten men inside the primitive camp died of disease, starvation or cruel treatment during the first three months of their stay.

There is evidence that the Death March won its inglorious name thanks to the actions of a few barbaric guards, that the orders from Lt General Homma, now in charge of the Philippines, were to treat the prisoners humanely, to supply food, water and medicines along the way.

Yet the cruelty and viciousness of the guards were symptomatic of the treatment dished out to US, Australian, Canadian, British, New Zealand and Dutch prisoners of war all over the Japanese empire.

The range of obscene abuses which were time and again revealed to prisoners stemmed from their culture which viewed fighting men who surrendered as dishonourable. For them, truly brave men would die in battle rather than lay down their arms to the enemy. Consequently, few Japanese soldiers were ever taken prisoner and those that were often tried to commit suicide.

Japan was a signatory of the Hague Convention of 1907 which decreed that prisoners of war must be treated humanely. Alas, the convention went on to rule that prisoners should be treated similarly to the men in the army of the state which

> **The Japanese were brutal even to their own men, and prisoners got even worse treatment**

held them. The military regime in Japan was brutal even to its own men. Captains frequently lashed out at sergeants who in turn would bash rank and file soldiers. There was to be little respite for the unfortunate men who fell into the clutches of the forces of the Rising Sun.

Red Cross officials were hindered and hampered in their attempts to observe what was happening in the Japanese-run prisoner of war camps. Despite enormous efforts, they were blocked by a deluge of red tape. When Red Cross officials did gain entry to camps, they were closely

One Red Cross delegate was executed after being charged with conspiracy against the Japanese

chaperoned, their access to prisoners severely restricted and their questions stonewalled. One Red Cross delegate was himself executed after being charged with conspiracy against the Japanese government. Few, if any, parcels of aid were received by the men in the camps.

Below: **Though General Homma, the victor in the Philippines, was thought 'too soft' by Japanese High Command, he was still condemned by a war crimes trial.**

◆ **EYE WITNESS** ◆

Ken Gray, of the Australian 8th Division, was one of the few to survive an epidemic of cholera when he was a 22-year-old Japanese prisoner of war in the Far East.

❛ I finished up in a camp called Sonquari. The number of deaths that occurred in that camp during the height of the cholera far outweighed deaths that occurred in others. There were no medical supplies. On one day alone 38 men died.

I saw a doctor on one occasion weep over the body of a dead Allied soldier, saying he could have saved the man with a sixpenny packet of Epsom Salts.

One of my mates was about the first to die from cholera. Within 36 hours he had gone from a man weighing perhaps 10 stones to five stones. The normal body fluids ran out of him from the bowels and the mouth. His body just shrivelled up. Unless cholera is arrested in three to four hours, that is the end.

I was delirious for seven days. Apparently I was given a saline solution in a home-made injection kit which saved me.

The survivors were not strong men, they were lucky men. Those far more robust than I went down like ninepins. I feel the public today cannot possibly comprehend how shocking conditions were. ❜

■ **TORTURE** ■

The worst treatment was meted out to Allied airmen who were kept blindfolded and bound until they were tortured, usually until they died.

It has left the names of Japanese prisons including Rangoon Central Gaol in Burma, Changi and Selerang Barracks in Singapore, Padang on Sumatra, Kuching in Borneo, Karenko in Formosa and Mukden in Manchuria haunting the annals of wartime horror. Perhaps the most appalling memories among survivors are those evoked by the building of the Burma-Siam railway.

Above: Changi jail, 'home' for thousands of British and Australian servicemen following the fall of Singapore.

Japan was looking for a means of transporting supplies to its posts in southern Burma other than the sea route which was subject to attack by the Allies. Only when this route was complete could the Japanese consider extending their imperial tentacles into India.

On 14 May 1942 a 3,000 strong force left the confines of Changi prison to begin work on the massive project. Before the main building force left Changi, however, the camp commander Major General Fukuye insisted that all prisoners sign the following statement. It read: 'I, the

Japan was looking for a means of transporting supplies to its posts in southern Burma

undersigned, hereby solemnly swear on my honour that I will not under any circumstances attempt escape.'

British troops under the authority of Lt Colonel E. B. Holmes and Australians under Lt Colonel 'Black-jack' Galleghan flatly refused to make the undertaking.

Outraged, Fukuye ordered the men from Changi into Selarang Barracks, cut their meagre rations to a third and allowed the 15,000 men to get water from just two taps. It meant endless hours of queuing in the heat of the day. The overcrowded conditions were a sure indicator that disease epidemics would follow.

The Japanese commander was finally convinced to make his request for prisoners to sign an outright order. Leaders of the prisoners decided this meant the men could sign the document but were not obliged by it.

There was little to inspire the men to escape. Deep in Japanese territory, they could not rely on local assistance nor, with their Western appearance, could they disappear into a crowd. The penalty for escape bids was death.

Four men who had slipped away from an island working party were brought to Changi in order that senior Allied commanders could witness the executions. Two of the men were British, two Australians. The older of the two Australians pleaded for the life of his young accomplice, maintaining he had only been obeying orders. It was to no avail.

■ FIRING SQUAD ■

All four came before a firing squad manned by Sikhs who had joined the Japanese. Their aim was awry and round upon round had to be let off before the bullets found their targets. The courageous older Australian, Corporal R. Breavington – who had refused to be blindfolded – finally bellowed: 'For God's sake, shoot me through the head and kill me.' It was a deeply scarring experience for those forced to watch.

Four more Australians who later attempted to escape from Burma were killed in the same grotesque way. The brigadier who witnessed their executions wrote in his diary: 'They spoke cheerio and good luck messages to one another and never showed any sign of fear. A truly courageous end.'

The courageous Australian bellowed: 'For God's sake shoot me through the head'

The nightmare of those sent to build the railway began almost immediately. Travelling to the site was deeply unpleasant. For example, the men who first left Changi were crammed into the hold of two rusty tubs for 12 days during which time the only food given to them was rice. Dysentery was rife and rats had the monopoly on the floor space and the health of the men plummeted.

■ SLAVE LABOUR ■

Still, when they arrived they were put to work as slaves of the Nippon empire. The Japanese, eager to complete the ambitious task and armed with strict schedules and quotas, brought in more and more prisoners to speed up the rate of progress. Suddenly, life in the harsh prison camps seemed positively bearable set against the appalling conditions which faced men in the camps along the railway. Each new batch of men was horrified at the sight of those who had been working there for weeks or months before.

JAPAN

When Japan attacked Pearl Harbor, there were about 126,000 people of Japanese ancestry living in the US, about 93,000 of whom were resident in California.

Those born in America were called Nisei while those born abroad were known as Issei. Roosevelt authorised the removal of 112,000 Japanese Americans to so-called relocation centres which, with armed guards, barrack huts and barbed wire, were little more than prison camps. The first people to be released from them did not return to freedom until 1944 by which time most had lost homes and jobs. Later, Justice Frank Murphy called it: 'One of the most sweeping and complete deprivations of constitutional rights in the history of this nation in the absence of martial law'.

Malaria, dysentery, infestations, biting bugs and all manner of other jungle afflictions plagued the working men. Eventually, when monsoon rains had turned camps into mires, the dreaded cholera spread, shrinking men's bodies through painful dehydration.

As their clothing deteriorated, men were reduced to wearing only underpants or home-made loin cloths, battered hats and often no footwear at all. At night there were few mosquito nets available, exposing the men to all the dangers of the tropics. Often, they had little more than a blanket or rice sack with which to cover themselves.

As previously, the lack of proper nutrition brought its own miseries for the men who had to battle with problems brought about by vitamin and calorie deficiencies. Every day, the toil made huge demands on the

Below: **Two bridges built over the River Kwai with the sweat and blood of Allied prisoners of war.**

THE JAPANESE IN BURMA

The Japanese invasion of Burma began in mid-December 1941 in the south of the country. General Iida's Southern Army seized the region's airfields and began bombing Rangoon. On 20 January 1942, the main ground assault began from the direction of Raheng. The Allies struggled to hold back the tide but on 8 March Rangoon fell. The British and Empire forces, reinforced by Chinese troops, then carried out a fighting withdrawal to India.

men's bodies which grew ever more emaciated and unfit for work.

Work began at both ends of the railway and the parties were to join up in the middle. It entailed clearing vast tracts of jungle, felling giant trees and constructing cuttings. The tools they had were primitive and all the clearance of rocks and stones had to be done by hand. Men worked by day and night, when their labours were lit by bamboo fires. Even the elephants brought in to assist in the heavy work lost their health.

There were stories of extreme mental torture as well as physical hardship. Sometimes the guards threw rocks and boulders at the men working below. Others forced individual prisoners to push mighty

Men worked by day and night in the light of bamboo fires; even the elephants fell ill

rocks up a steep gradient. It would take every ounce of the victim's strength to stop the rock from crushing him and others below. Those who perished by plunging down the forested ravines or being crushed by rock falls were considered by their comrades to be the lucky ones.

In total, more than 60,000 Allied prisoners were used on the project alongside 270,000 forced labourers from China, Malaya, Thailand, Burma and India. These conscripted civilians enjoyed even fewer comforts than the prisoners with no medical facilities at hand and less concept of hygiene and discipline.

It was undoubtedly the commitment and enterprise of the medical men which saved many Allied lives. One such hero was Lt Colonel

Right: Printed leaflet dropped by B-29s on 28 August 1945 into POW camps in Japan, Taiwan, Sumatra and Malaya. The drop killed three and seriously injured two.

Edward 'Weary' Dunlop. His dedication to the survival of his fellow men never wavered nor did his courage in the face of the tyrannical Japanese. The plucky Australian wrote in his secret diary: 'I pledged myself to face them unflinchingly.'

■ WHIRLING SWORD ■

Dunlop was in Java before he and his men were moved to work on the railway. During his time in captivity he leapt between a Japanese soldier charging with a bayonet and one of his crippled patients; stood almost unblinking while an enraged Japanese commander whirled a sword around his head; defied Japanese orders to force patients into work and carried one of his men like a baby across to a sadistic commander, pronouncing: 'This man can't walk, Nippon.'

He kept a radio set, an offence punishable by death in Japanese eyes.

> *Dunlop was chained to a tree trunk; four men fixed their bayonets and prepared to charge*

In the absence of the necessary evidence, an officer screamed at him: 'We know all about you and your set. You will be executed but first you will talk.'

When he refused to co-operate, Dunlop was chained to a tree trunk and four men with bayonets fixed prepared with the customary screeches and yells to charge.

'Have you a message for relatives? I will convey,' barked the officer.

'Conveyed by a thug like you? No, thanks,' said Dunlop. Only after several hours was he cut loose.

Dunlop devised a system to treat men dying of cholera. The steam from water boiled in petrol cans was funnelled through a lorry feed pipe and mixed with rock salt. The saline solution was then stored, filtered through cotton wool, fed into bamboo pipes and into a syringe. It helped to save countless Australian lives.

Afterwards, Dunlop, who died in 1993, said: 'I can say that the Australians outworked and outsuffered any nationality on that accursed river [Kwai]. I hardly ever saw a man refuse to go out in another's place or a man's spirit break until the time came to turn his face to the wall.'

Work was for the most part completed by September 1943 when the two ends met near Three Pagodas

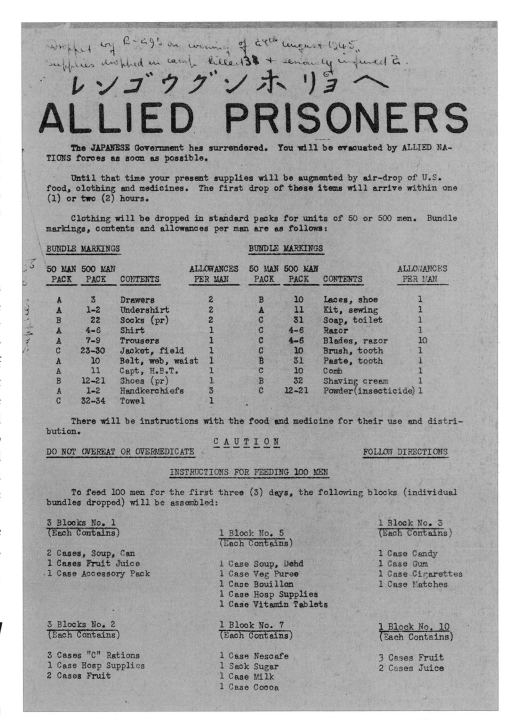

レンゴウグンホリョヘ

ALLIED PRISONERS

The JAPANESE Government has surrendered. You will be evacuated by ALLIED NATIONS forces as soon as possible.

Until that time your present supplies will be augmented by air-drop of U.S. food, clothing and medicines. The first drop of these items will arrive within one (1) or two (2) hours.

Clothing will be dropped in standard packs for units of 50 or 500 men. Bundle markings, contents and allowances per man are as follows:

BUNDLE MARKINGS

50 MAN PACK	500 MAN PACK	CONTENTS	ALLOWANCES PER MAN
A	3	Drawers	2
A	1-2	Undershirt	2
B	22	Socks (pr)	2
A	4-6	Shirt	1
A	7-9	Trousers	1
C	23-30	Jacket, field	1
A	10	Belt, web, waist	1
A	11	Capt, H.B.T.	1
B	12-21	Shoes (pr)	1
A	1-2	Handkerchiefs	3
C	32-34	Towel	1

BUNDLE MARKINGS

50 MAN PACK	500 MAN PACK	CONTENTS	ALLOWANCES PER MAN
B	10	Laces, shoe	1
A	11	Kit, sewing	1
C	31	Soap, toilet	1
C	4-6	Razor	1
C	4-6	Blades, razor	10
C	10	Brush, tooth	1
B	31	Paste, tooth	1
C	10	Comb	1
B	32	Shaving cream	1
C	12-21	Powder(insecticide)	1

There will be instructions with the food and medicine for their use and distribution.

CAUTION

DO NOT OVEREAT OR OVERMEDICATE   FOLLOW DIRECTIONS

INSTRUCTIONS FOR FEEDING 100 MEN

To feed 100 men for the first three (3) days, the following blocks (individual bundles dropped) will be assembled:

3 Blocks No. 1
(Each Contains)

2 Cases, Soup, Can
1 Cases Fruit Juice
1 Case Accessory Pack

3 Blocks No. 2
(Each Contains)

3 Cases "C" Rations
1 Case Hosp Supplies
2 Cases Fruit

1 Block No. 5
(Each Contains)

1 Case Soup, Dehd
1 Case Veg Puree
1 Case Bouillon
1 Case Hosp Supplies
1 Case Vitamin Tablets

1 Block No. 7
(Each Contains)

1 Case Nescafe
1 Sack Sugar
1 Case Milk
1 Case Cocoa

1 Block No. 3
(Each Contains)

1 Case Candy
1 Case Gum
1 Case Cigarettes
1 Case Matches

1 Block No. 10
(Each Contains)

3 Cases Fruit
2 Cases Juice

Pass. The railway was peppered with graves of men who died as they worked. An estimated 12,000 British, American, Australian and Dutch men died. In addition, 70,000 of the Asian labourers perished.

■ DIET OF RATS ■

Life had not improved much in the camps during this period. Officers were tortured in order that the Japanese might elicit military information. Hospitals were periodically cleared so that the ailing patients could join work parties. Food was

reduced to snails, rats and snakes as the tide of war turned against Japan and supplies were sunk at sea.

Scores of prisoners were shot, stabbed or died from exhaustion during the forced marches

In Borneo there were a series of forced marches inflicted on the captive Allies as the liberating forces

Above: In the Japanese prisoner of war camps, men had to queue in the heat of the sun to collect their meagre rations. This is the officers' mess at Kanburi.

closed in. This claimed the lives of scores of prisoners who were shot, stabbed or died from exhaustion en route. Prisoners installed after just such a march at the Ranau camp were subsequently massacred in August 1945 before the arrival of Australian forces. Only six Australians who escaped on the march or from Ranau itself survived.

It wasn't only captured troops who suffered at the hands of the Japanese. There were an assortment of Dutch women who had been residents of the invaded Dutch East Indies, Australian nurses and British women snared in Singapore and an assortment of Western children and other refugees. They, too, were victims of forced marches, food shortages and disease.

The Japanese showed their disregard for the fairer sex when 22 nurses were washed up on an island beach after their boat was sunk off Singapore. All the surviving ship's crew were bayonetted and the nurses were herded into the sea where a machine gun was turned on them. Just one survived.

In 1994, Prince Mikasa, brother of the Emperor Hirohito and a cavalry officer in China in 1943 and 1944 admitted Japanese responsibility for war crimes. Besides talking of atrocities committed on the battlefield, he also spoke of an incident in 1931. That year a team of investigators from the League of Nations led by

the Earl of Lytton had visited Japan to analyse who was to blame for the start of the Sino-Japanese conflict. There was apparently an attempt to poison them. The Prince claimed that 'fruit laced with cholera germs' had been administered to the high-ranking officials in their food although none of them died.

The bitterness felt towards Japanese camp guards by those who came home is still very much in evidence on four continents, even today.

The bitterness felt towards Japanese camp guards is still very much in evidence, even today

Left: When they were released, PoWs were shadows of their former selves. Years of deprivation took their toll on previously strong, healthy men.

JUSTICE AT NUREMBERG

World War I was billed as the 'war to end all wars'. It wasn't. And warfare came of age when the World War II broke out just 21 years after the end of the Great War. It was politically more complex and shocking than its predecessor, its effects far more wide-ranging and its aftermath wholly different.

For the victors there was the dilemma of how to lay the foundation for tomorrow's world and build a lasting peace. More immediately, in their custody were some of the architects of Hitler's Third Reich. What would be their fate now?

Some believed that with Hitler, Himmler and Goebbels dead (all three committed suicide) the arch villains were already dispatched. There were a series of other trials taking place simultaneously in Germany dealing with those at the dirty coal face of the concentration camps. Their obscene activities amounted to murder of the worst degree for which suitable charges and penalties already existed.

Many felt the high-profile men held, including diplomats and banking chiefs, could essentially be absolved. There was at least a

Left: The Palace of Justice at Nuremberg housed the most momentous trial of the century. *Below:* Tojo, the Japanese Prime Minister, was brought to justice in 1948.

question mark over whether or not these men truly had blood on their hands. In addition, it would be wrong to punish a military man – soldier, sailor or airman – for doing his job during times of war.

Others thought the only good Nazi was a dead one and that those held by the Allies should be shot, the sooner the better. With so many lives lost and families in mourning, it was wrong to allow these types to posture and pedal their propaganda ever again.

■ TRIALS OF NAZIS ■

Yet there was a different school of thought, equally enthusiastic about wiping the slate clean, which won the day. The captured Nazi leaders should face a trial and answer for their crimes. The Americans particularly among the Allies felt the application of the rule of law was fair and correct and would define once and for all who was guilty by association. Here was the opportunity of laying the blame for the disaster that befell Europe in the early Forties on the heads of those responsible and freeing the German people as a whole of guilt. The trials held at the end of

World War I were nominal, inconclusive affairs which barely reflected the carnage that had gone before. This time it was going to be different.

Once the British, French and Russian allies had been persuaded, there were a host of difficulties to unravel which would make the difference. Firstly, no statute books held charges which befitted the appalling crimes carried out in the name of Nazism. There was the clear danger that if the prosecutions were bodged, the world's best-known killers could end up getting away with murder.

The legal brains of the victorious countries got to work in creating charges which reflected the crimes which had taken place, identifying and closing possible loopholes at the same time as creating a scrupulously even playing field, fair to all sides. All this had to be done swiftly. Everyone

> **There were four main charges at Nuremberg, including Crimes Against Humanity**

was keen to get the business of retribution out of the way in order to look ahead.

Afterwards, there were accusations that the charges had been worded to fit the crimes and so offended the principle of justice. Yet as early as November 1945 the groundwork was laid for the most sensational trial of the century, Nuremberg, an astonishing feat by any standard.

There were to be four main charges which broadly covered a variety of individual acts. They were Crimes Against Peace, which covered the planning and waging of aggressive war; War Crimes, including the execution of prisoners of war; Crimes

Left: The judges at the Nuremberg trials *(left to right)* Britain's Mr Justice (Norman) Birkett and Lord Justice Lawrence, US Attorney General Francis Biddle and Judge John J. Parker.

responsibility. The Americans sought prosecutions on the conspiracy count in addition to probing the criminal organisations like the SS. The British proceeded with the charge of Crimes Against the Peace. The Russians and

---

The trials created the precedent that acts of war were the individual's responsibility

---

Against Humanity, dealing with the the genocide of Jews and other minorities; and finally the Common Plan or Conspiracy.

The final charge was defined as follows: 'All the defendants, with divers other persons, during a period of years preceding 8 May 1945, participated as leaders, organisers, instigators or accomplices in the formulation or execution of a common plan or conspiracy to commit, or which involved the commission of, Crimes Against the Peace, War Crimes and Crimes Against Humanity... and are individually responsible for their own acts and for all acts committed by any persons in the execution of such plan or conspiracy.'

An important precedent was being created, that acts of war were the responsibilty of the individual not just the state.

Each of the four countries on the winning side had their realms of the French dealt with the remaining two charges for Eastern and Western powers respectively.

Due to the complexity of the conflict, it remained an irony that Russia was prosecuting Germany for war crimes when it was also involved in waging aggressive wars against Poland and Finland.

■ WHY NUREMBERG? ■

The army of occupation in Germany was almost rivalled in size by that of lawyers, interpreters, researchers, clerks, prison guards, journalists and other observers linked to the Nuremberg Trial. Hearing the case were two judges from each of the main Allied countries, any four of whom would sit together at one time.

From America came Francis Biddle and John Parker, the British judges were Sir Geoffrey Lawrence and Norman Birkett. Professor Henri Donnedieu de Vabres and Robert Falco represented France while Russia sent Major-General I. Nikitchenko and Lieutenant-Colonel A. F. Volchkov. Prosecuting was

---

◆ EYE WITNESS ◆

Seaghan Maynes was a journalist working for Reuters who attended the Nuremberg trials. In 'Eyewitness at Nuremberg', a book by Hillary Gaskin, he recalls his impressions.

'The trial to me was a showpiece. It wasn't a juridical process; it was a revenge trial. This is my opinion and I think it was shared by a lot of other correspondents. It doesn't say that they shouldn't have been held because the purpose was to show crime followed by punishment, as an example to the other. But the legal process was very suspect. They made a charge to fit a crime after the crime had been committed. In that atmosphere, as distinct from now, I can see good reasons for having the trial because public opinion all over the world had been convinced that an example must be made. But take the case against Schacht. If Germany had occupied Britain, would our Minister of Transport, or somebody, be on trial for his life? Should Ribbentrop, the German foreign minister, have been executed? He was a diplomat; he didn't take part in any killing. I had niggling doubts about these things at the time. "What did he do to deserve death? After all his country was at war." In hindsight, I can say that the winner calls the shots and fixes the charges and the vanquished haven't as much of a chance as they should have. I wouldn't have missed it but I wouldn't want to see it again.'

◆ EYE WITNESS ◆

Following the armistice, John Gorman, VC, a 22-year-old captain in the Irish Guards, was put in charge of a German prison camp housing 500 men suspected of war crimes.

❝ The camp was at Sieburg, near the Dutch border. The majority of men were Germans but there were some French, Belgian and Dutch collaborators who had been denounced in their local communities. They were accused of various crimes including slaughter and other atrocities.

I had six officers to help me. We were superimposed on a structure which already existed with an administrator, who was not thought to be a criminal, and his team of warders.

Our job was to run the prison as humanely as possible and to produce these people for trial before the war crimes commissions. We did what we could and organised football matches, sport and encouraged them to help in the prison garden.

I was given a platoon of Belgian soldiers to help me who had previously been members of the resistance. They didn't like the inmates at all. I was away for a weekend in Brussels when I received a frantic telephone call from the officer in charge. The Belgians had decided they couldn't stand the prisoners having the freedom to look out of the window. Every time one of them had the temerity to show his face, the Belgians tried to shoot him.

I rushed back, thinking I would find a pile of corpses. Fortunately, the Belgians were bad shots. All we had was a badly pock-marked wall. They didn't hit any of them.

As for the British officers there, we prided ourselves on our discipline. We ran the prison on orthodox lines. We certainly didn't want them to say we were doing to them what they had been doing to others.

For their part, the prisoners were very servile and obsequious. They would have kissed our boots if they thought it would do them any good. The bully, when bullied, becomes a coward. They were not nice people.

It was very difficult finding enough to eat. Everybody was hungry. The Dutch had been eating their bulbs, the seedcorn of their future, to keep themselves alive.

We had to order the German authorities in the local town to produce food for the prison. The inmates had diet of soup, rice and occasionally meat.

One man died while I was there. He was terribly thin and a doctor told us he was severely undernourished. That gave the idea that something was amiss.

I used to patrol the prison at all times of day and night. Early one morning I happened on the German prison administrator leaving the kitchen with a large suitcase. When I ordered him to open it, I found it was fulll of meat. He was stealing meat from the prison kitchens to sell on the black market and had made a fortune. It was most underhand when you consider that the majority of the prisoners were his fellow countrymen. He went straight into a spare cell. ❞

Justice Robert Jackson from the United States, Sir Hartley Shawcross from Britain, Francois de Menthon of France and General Roman Rudenko of Russia.

The location of the trial was not a random choice. Few could forget the impressive and sinister rallies held by Hitler and his Nazi followers at Nuremberg before and after the outbreak of hostilities. And it was there in in 1935 that a special session of the Reichstag unanimously approved the Nuremberg Laws, depriving Jews of German citizenship and associated rights.

◼ PALACE OF JUSTICE ◼

The session went on to agree further anti-Jewish legislation which prevented marriages between Germans and Jews and forbade the employment of German servants by Jews. Nuremberg represented the fiery heartland of the Nazi doctrine and it would be here that the evil light would be extinguished.

Symbolically, the notorious city, in the American zone of occupation, was by now in ruins, the victim of the saturation bombing so potently used by the Royal Air Force in the last few years of the conflict.

The courtroom of its Palace Of Justice was now to house the momentous – and frequently monotonous – proceedings that were designed to

Right: **US soldiers mounted a heavy-weight guard outside the Palace of Justice during the trial.**

Above: **Flamboyant Göring refused to be cowed. Here he is quizzed by journalists shortly after being captured.**

turn the page on one of the worst periods of Europe's history.

In the dock were 20 by-now infamous characters from Hitler's hierarchy. Hermann Wilhelm Göring had been a long time cohort of Hitler and was best known as Commander in Chief of the German air force. In addition, he was a general in the feared SS and the Reich Hunting and Forest Master.

Next to him sat the enigmatic Rudolf Hess, a co-author of 'Mein Kampf', the book by Hitler explaining his dubious philosophies. A question mark remained over his sanity following his mysterious flight to Britain in 1941, apparently to seek

a peace settlement with King George VI. He had been held by the British since then, latterly in an asylum.

Joachim von Ribbentrop was next in the line-up. A Nazi party member since 1932, he rose quickly to become Hitler's adviser on foreign affairs. His devotion was rewarded with the post

It was no coincidence that the trials were held at Nuremberg, the site of the great Nazi rallies

of ambassador to London between 1936 and 1938 and finally with the plum job of foreign minister.

World War I spy Alfred Rosenberg took part in the abortive 1923 putsch

when Hitler tried to seize power in Germany. The anti-semitic Reich Minister for the Occupied Eastern Territories wrote 'Mythos des 20 Jahrhunderts', a tome reflecting the Fatherland's distasteful philosophies under Hitler.

Lawyer Hans Frank had been Bavarian Minister of Justice and was in 1939 made Governor General of occupied Poland. Ernst Kaltenbrunner, born in Austria, coupled his own legal talents with those of commanding key SS units. Wilhelm Frick was also legally trained and strongly associated with the SS. When the war ended, he was Reich Protector.

Former schoolmaster Julius Streicher was a well-known anti-Semite who had been editor of the Fascist newspaper Der Sturmer and honorary leader of the thuggish SA force.

Wilhelm Keitel was a Field Marshal and held the title Chief of Oberkommando der Wehrmacht. His loyalty to Hitler was never in question.

Dr Walther Funk, paymaster of the Reich machine in his post as President of the Reichsbank, sat beside another economist Hjalmar Schacht, latterly out of favour with the Führer.

Ex-teacher Julius Streicher had been editor of the anti-semitic newspaper Der Sturmer

The second row of defendants began with Karl Dönitz, the U-boat supremo who had become Commander in Chief of the Kriegsmarine and, on Hitler's death, Chancellor to the ruins of Germany.

Beside Dönitz sat longtime Hitler Youth leader Baldur von Schirach, who wrote songs and verses which inspired the country's youth to lay down their lives without question.

Fritz Sauckel was an eminent Reich Defence Commissioner assigned to the organisation of slave labour who sat in the shadow of charismatic Albert Speer, the man responsible for arming Germany's forces.

Diplomat Franz von Papen was seated beside Alfred Jodl, Chief of Staff in the High Command of the Wehrmacht, who in turn was next to Constantin von Neurath, an eminent member of the Reichstag and SS General.

■ MARTIN BORMANN ■

Dr Arthur Seyss-Inquart was an SS general, Reich minister without portfolio and President of the German Academy. Erich Raeder, the former Commander in Chief of the German navy, was next to him and beside him sat Hans Fritzsche, a leading light in the propaganda machine. Tried in his absence was Martin Bormann, Hitler's personal secretary who went missing in the chaos of the Reich's last days. Only in 1973 was it established that, despite various post-war sightings of him, he had probably committed suicide in May 1945.

The defendants were charged with all or a combination of the charges. The trial opened on 12 November 1945. Making the opening speech was Justice Robert Jackson, the American attorney:

'The privilege of opening the first trial in history for crimes against the peace of the world imposes a grave responsiblity. The wrongs which we seek to condemn and punish have been so calculated, so malignant and so devastating, that civilisation cannot tolerate their being ignored because it cannot survive their being repeated.

'That four great nations, flushed with victory and stung with injury, stay the hand of vengeance and voluntarily submit their captive enemies to the judgement of the law is one of the most significant tributes that power ever has paid to reason...

'In the prisoners' dock sit twenty broken men... their personal capacity for evil is forever past. Merely as individuals their fate is of little consequence to the world. What makes this inquest significant is that these prisoners represent sinister influences that will lurk in the world long after their bodies have returned to dust.

Above: Top Nazis on trial *(front row, left to right)* Göring, Hess, Ribbentrop, Keitel, Rosenberg. *Back row (left to right):* Dönitz, Raeder, Shirach, Sauckel, Jodl.

Martin Bormann went missing at the end of the war but was tried in absentia

We will show them to be living symbols of racial hatreds, of terrorism and violence and of the arrogance and cruelty of power.'

It was for the prosecution to prove that the primarily frail, vacant and occasionally quivering men lined up in the dock should be held responsible

Jackson's examination of Göring drew crowds into the courtroom expecting to see this swaggering man scythed to pieces. In fact, gloating Göring turned the tables and batted off questioning from the American prosecutor with ease. Jackson, hindered in no small part by inaccurate translations of evidence against

Guilty of racial hatreds, terrorism, violence and the arrogance and cruelty of power

Above: **Lt Thomas F. Lambert, Jr presents the case for the US prosecution against the absent Martin Bormann, who was sentenced to death but never caught.**

for the calamities of wartime Europe. One of the first problems facing the prosecution was that posed by Hitler's one-time deputy, Rudolf Hess.

Hess was showing the signs of a disturbed character – and had been since his escapade to Britain back in 1941. Was it right for a man in this state to stand trial? The decision to press charges against him came in December 1945 when he admitted that he faked amnesia to fool British interrogators and Hess chose to conduct his own defence. Many privately felt that he was nevertheless a man devoid of many of his senses.

■ HERMANN GÖRING ■

For different reasons Hermann Göring caused the Allied prosecutors a major headache, too. Göring was a somewhat glamorous and charismatic figure, the last commander of

Right: **Hermann Göring conducted his own defence at Nuremberg and made mincemeat of US prosecutor Jackson.**

the Richthofen Fighter Squadron of World War I known for his unscrupulous and amoral behaviour. He relished the luxuries of life including good wines and flashy cars and had acquired a magnificent collection of art during his tenure, pilfered from the cultural capitals of Europe. Even in the courtroom, he could not contain his lustful gaze which appraised young women on the staff. More than that, he was witty, razor sharp and intelligent as Justice Jackson discovered to his cost.

Göring, had to appeal to the court to control the defendant and finally retired flustered and frustrated. It was left to the cool-headed Briton Sir David Maxwell-Fyfe who was assisting with prosecution to compromise the German.

Despite his straitened circumstances, Göring was always ready with a quip for the interpreters, an insult for witnesses or a putdown for his fellow defendants as they tried to wriggle out of some damning evidence as it was presented against them. He remained a dominating force roundly unapologetic for his beliefs.

For the most part, the other defendants sat listening raptly to the evidence, occasionally aloof but for the most part displaying little or no emotion. Hess would read from a book of fairy tales by the Brothers' Grimm. Those with sufficient English occasionally corrected or aided the interpreters. Others simply sank into a murky silence. Stripped of their braid and regalia, they were grey-faced men who knew they faced a bleak future.

The prosecution relied heavily on documentary evidence – and there was plenty of it

Kaltenbrunner suffered a stroke early in the proceedings but recovered sufficiently to appear in the dock again later on. Streicher suffered a heart attack in January 1946 but later returned to the stand.

Finally, tension gave way to tedium as each day passed. The

prosecutors relied heavily on documentary evidence – and there was plenty of it. With characteristic Germanic efficiency, the Nazi regime had noted many of its activities down for its own future reference. Even in the grimmest of the concentration camps details of the exterminations were put into writing. The worst of the massacres were often filmed and now provided excellent evidence. Although there were many German witnesses to the Holocaust, it was felt their testimony could be unreliable because they might try either to ingratiate themselves with the victors or else to settle old scores with the defendants in the dock.

■ DEATH SENTENCE ■

The trial ended on the last day of August 1946 and the International Military Tribunal, as it was also known, began delivering its judgement a month later.

A dozen of the men on trial were sentenced to death. Hess received a life sentence, six more were also jailed and three were acquitted.

On 16 October 1946 the gallows were prepared in the prison gymnasium at Nuremberg. In a final

flourish, Göring cheated the executioner by taking a cyanide pill smuggled in to him, perhaps by his Swedish wife Karin.

Julius Streicher screeched 'Heil Hitler' before the trap door opened beneath him

First to the rope at 1.11am was Hitler's Foreign Minister Ribbentrop. As the black hood was placed over his head, he called out: 'I wish peace to the world'.

Next to the gallows was Field Marshal Wilhelm Keitel. His final words were: 'More than two million German soldiers went to their death for their fatherland. I follow now my sons – all for Germany.'

Filing up the steps after him were Kaltenbrunner, Rosenbrug, Frank (a recent convert to Roman Catholicism), Frick, Streicher (who screeched 'Heil Hitler' before the trap door opened beneath him), Sauckel, Jodl and Seyss-Inquart. Martin Bormann was sentenced to death in absentia.

Right: The Japanese war crimes trial went on for three years after the end of the war and lacked the drama of Nuremberg.

Funk and Raeder were jailed for life, Doenitz for 10 years, Speer for 20 years, Neurath for 15 years and Schirach for 20 years. Fritzsche, Schacht and von Papen were acquitted.

It was far from the end of the story. The Subsequent Proceedings dealt with a further 182 Nazis from the doctors who set up experiments in the concentration camps to industrialists, government ministers, military men and SS officials.

Twenty-six were sentenced to death while the rest received various prison sentences, forfeited property or were acquitted. The last of the Subsequent Proceedings ended in October 1948.

When Japanese Emperor Hirohito came before General Douglas MacArthur on the surrender of Japan in September 1945, he told him: 'I come to you to offer myself to the judgement of the powers you represent as the one who bears sole responsibility for every political and military decision made and action taken by my people in the conduct of the war.'

Yet despite his frankness, he was not charged as a war criminal. It wasn't until December 1948 that General Tojo, one of Japan's prime ministers during the war, was hanged along with six others. He had tried but failed to kill himself even though a Japanese doctor refused to treat his wounds.

■ ATROCITIES ■

The accused were convicted of 'crimes against peace and responsibility for atrocities'. The sentence was carried out by the American Army at Sugamo Prison in Tokyo. A further 16 men were jailed for life their roles in the war.

Among those executed for war crimes was Lt General Homma, the Japanese commander victorious in

---

◆ EYE WITNESS ◆

Hugh Trebble, a clerk with the Royal Air Force, was taken prisoner by the Japanese on Java after fleeing Singapore.

'I was taken prisoner at the beginning of March. We were rounded up in Dutch Air Force hangars at Tasek Malaja and dispersed all over the island. I was sent to Surabaya, the principle port on the north coast to help repair bomb damage – by scraping burnt sugar coating the jetties into the sea. We dug air raid shelters – which was against the Geneva Convention – and then began planting castor oil plants.

A party of about 30 was taken to a walled garden. Our guard was a Korean, built like a barn door. He was a Christian. He produced an English bible, selected me to read it and I started with verse one, chapter one of Genesis. While the others worked I sat beside him reading the bible, interpreting what I could for him.

Soon after we were lined up in a playing field with a manned Japanese machine gun post in each corner while they decided whether to shoot us or not.

The Japanese were very ready with their fists and their rifle butts.

I contracted malaria and eventually dysentery in two forms. I was finally sent for treatment at a hospital staffed by Dutch medics. After I recovered I was sent by boat to Singapore then on to Sumatra to build a railway. We managed to wreck three full-sized steam locomotives in the process!

We had to work 16 hours a day, seven days a week. We had a bowl of rice in the morning and a bowl of rice at night and it was all we had to live on. At our base camp we used to bury about 16 men a day.

The Japanese were utterly ruthless and they were all the same. It was impossible to find anything good about them. The only mitigating circumstances were that they treated their own troops in the same way they treated us.

One of the native soldiers pushed a Japanese guard while he was being beaten with a rifle butt. He was tied up with wire, put in a bamboo cage with no roof and kept there for days. Every time a guard went past he would poke his rifle butt in to give him a thump. Eventually, the bloke died. There was nothing we could do about it. We would squirm every day when we had to file past him – but that kind of treatment was commonplace.

When we were building the railway, we were beaten with rails and spanners. The thing to do was to stay concious. If you fell over and blacked out you were beaten and could get badly injured. One of the guards was so short he would make you stand in a monsoon drain in order to beat you.

When I was released in 1945 I was 6 stones 7lb instead of my usual 12 and a half stones. I was blown up like a balloon and as yellow as a guinea fowl.'

Above: **A PoW of the Japanese displays the classic signs of malnutrition.**

the Philippines who was removed by his overlords for being too soft. He ordered his men to treat the Filipinos as friends and refused to distribute propaganda criticising US rule. It was General MacArthur, whose forces had been routed in the Philippines, who ordered the trial of Homma.

The trial of Lt Gen Homma was ordered by US General Douglas MacArthur

Below: **In the dock, those accused of carrying out war crimes on behalf of Japan listen intently to proceedings.**

HITLER'S BODY

After Hitler shot himself in his Berlin bunker alongside his wife Eva Braun who had taken poison, his body was taken out and burned by the few remaining faithful in his entourage.

Yet Russian dictator Stalin was convinced that his arch enemy had somehow cheated death by using a double and staging the suicide. When the bodies were recovered by a Russian soldier in the rubble outside the bunker, it seems Stalin's crack troops from Smersh, a trusted security team, took over. The charred bodies of Hitler and Braun underwent not one but two post mortems as Stalin quested to know for certain whether they were the genuine articles.

After that, the fate of the bodies and their final resting place is subject to controversy. Some ex-Russian soldiers have claimed that Hitler and Braun, together with the Goebbels family, are buried at Magdeburg in a garage. A few historians are convinced the body is buried in the grounds of a Moscow prison. Others believe it to have been destroyed following Stalin's death.

Even if it was turned to dust, at least a few remnants remain. In 1993 a Russian journalist claimed she had held some of the the skull of Hitler in her hand after she discovered parts of it in the Moscow state archives. The two sections were believed to have been discovered in Berlin following the removal of the bodies. It is also thought that Hitler's jaw bone and that of Eva Braun are kept in Moscow where they were taken for identification purposes.

NAZIS ON THE RUN

For years it was known that scores of Nazis slipped out of the Third Reich and sought asylum in far off countries, particularly those of South America.

To smuggle themselves out of danger, they used the services of the sinister and infamous ODESSA – the Organisation of Former Members of the SS – which provided the necessary cash and papers. Sometimes they donned the robes of priests to avoid detection. There are even cases of submarines bringing fugitives to the coast of South America.

Much of the finance came from treasures looted up and down Europe and from the victims they had murdered, converted through Swiss bank accounts.

From their bolt holes Hitler's henchmen were able to escape retribution for the horrible war crimes they had perpetrated. For the most part their host governments refused to hand them over to either the Allied governments wishing to proceed with a trial or the Jewish groups in search of justice.

Josef Schwammberger, commandant of the concentration camp at Przemysl fled to Argentina along with the notorious Adolf Eichmann

Eichmann and Mengele fled to Argentina where they were sheltered by President Peron

and 'doctor of death' Josef Mengele. Less well-known figures took shelter in Argentina with the apparent complicity of its President Juan Domingo Peron. They included Ludolph Von Alvensleben, adjutant to Himmler, who escaped Germany in 1946 and died in Cordoba in 1972. Gestapo chief Heinrich Muller was sighted in the Fifties, also in

Cordoba, and could still be alive there today. Rudolf Mildner, held responsible for numerous Jewish deaths at Auschwitz, may also be living in peace there.

SS commander Walter Kutschmann, who entered Argentina dressed as a Carmelite priest, became director of sales of a German-owned light bulb company. He died in 1986 before efforts to extradite him came to fruition. Lung cancer claimed the life of Walter Rauff in 1984, an SS officer who also went into hiding in South America, running a meat-freezing plant in Chile under his own name.

■ REFUGE IN SYRIA ■

Alois Brunner, designer of the mobile gas chambers and the man responsible for the death of many Greek Jews, found the protection he needed among the Arabs in Damascus.

Some were finally brought to trial after protracted arguments. Others died in their hideaways. The fight continues for still more to be brought before the courts, despite their extremely advanced years.

But only recently did the Nazi hunters begin to realise the scale of their task. Files released from Argentina show that more than 1,000 suspected war criminals and Nazi collaborators fled there after the war. Previous estimates put the number at less than 100.

The news stunned the Jewish groups which had long been pressuring the Argentinian government to come clean on its shadowy involvement with Nazis. Until the recent attempt by Argentina to rid itself of Nazis and the unsavoury image accompanying them, just two were

Right: Martin Bormann. Did he commit suicide in 1945 or escape to South America? *Left*: Ernst Kaltenbrunner, chief of security police, sentenced to death.

extradited, Nazi doctor and lawyer Gerhardt Bhone in 1966 and Josef Schwammberger in 1988.

In the files was further evidence that Martin Bormann survived the collapse of the Reich and was among those who slipped into South America, possibly carrying a stateless

Bormann escaped to South America on a stateless passport in the name of Goldstein

251

ALESSANDRA MUSSOLINI

The name of Mussolini has survived in Italian politics through his grandaughter Alessandra. In 1992 she was elected to the Italian Parliament under the banner of the neo-fascist party, the MSI.

Alessandra, married to a financier, has had a chequered history. Before entering politics, she was a nude pin-up, an actress, a TV chat-show host and a graduate in medicine. Her aunt is actress Sophia Loren.

Her policies are often at odds with those of the party which is anti-divorce and anti-abortion, for the death penalty and in favour of sending immigrants to their country of birth. For her part, Alessandra supports increased independence for women, including state payments for housewives. Not surprisingly, the voluptuous blonde is employed mostly by her party in travelling around the country as an emissary to drum up new votes.

person's passport in the name of Eliezer Goldstein. Sightings of him reported in 1947 and 1948 were never conclusively proved and the Argentinian government of the day refused to co-operate in a search for him. Other historical detectives are convinced he died in the Berlin

Below: Adolf Eichmann was kidnapped from his new hideaway home in Argentina by the Israelis to stand trial in Tel Aviv for his role in the Nazi atrocities.

Right: **Dr Josef Mengele – the so-called 'doctor of death' – escaped from Germany after the war and fled to South America, where he lived for many years.**

bunker with his beloved Hitler or soon afterwards.

Adolf Eichmann slipped through the fingers of the Allies even though he was arrested in May 1945. Eichmann was one of the architects of the Final Solution who devoted himself to transporting large numbers of Jews to death camps as quickly as possible. Dressed as a Luftwaffe pilot, Eichmann was not recognised and managed to slip away from his preoccupied interrogators.

It wasn't until 1957 that the men who dedicated themselves to hunting down stray Nazis received a confirmed sighting of the man they were so keen to interview.

A man named Nikolaus Klement bore a striking resemblance to the wanted Eichmann

A former internee from Dachau who had emigrated to Argentina following the war became suspicious of a man by the name of Nikolaus Klement. Not only did Klement bear a striking resemblance to Eichmann but his son had been heard making offensive anti-Jewish remarks.

The Argentinian government was not convinced. It took all the persuasive powers of the Israeli agents to get permission even for surveillance. When it finally came, they took snaps of the suspect entering and leaving the family home at 4261 Chacabuco Street, Olivos, Buenos Aires. Blurred and indistinct, it was impossible for camp survivors back in Europe to use

them to identify him positively as Adolf Eichmann.

It wasn't until Klement was seen carrying a bunch of flowers on 21 March 1960 that the Israelis were convinced they had got their man. It was the same date that Eichmann celebrated his wedding anniversary.

■ EICHMANN TRIAL ■

The slick Israeli operators went into action at once. On 11 May they pounced on Eichmann as he got off a bus, bundled him into a car and spirited him off to a safe house. When he was stripped, bodily scars and a giveaway SS tattoo confirmed their suspicions.

To smuggle him out of Argentina, he was drugged with his captors posing as the caring relatives of a helpless car crash victim. With ease they boarded the El-Al jet which took them to Tel Aviv. Eichmann was to face the justice he richly deserved.

His trial began on 12 December 1961 and he faced 15 charges emanating from his activities in Nazi Germany. In his defence, Eichmann claimed he tried to promote Jewish emigration and bore no responsiblity for the 'Final Solution'.

Yet voices of the past returned to condemn him, including that of a trusted lieutenant Dieter Wisliceny, executed soon after the war in

REMAGEN

American troops were delighted when they found the Remagen Bridge across the Rhine intact and finally crossed in their droves. However, just 10 days after the first soldiers edged their way across under enemy fire, the vital link crumbled forcing 400 men in the US 1st Army, who were on it at the time, to scramble to safety.

Czechoslovakia for his part in war crimes. He revealed to the Allies the extent of Eichmann's evil by recounting a comment made by him as the end of the war beckoned.

'He told me in 1944 that he did not care what happened if Germany lost the war. He said he would leap into his grave laughing because the feeling that he had five million Jews on his conscience only filled his heart with gladness.'

Eichmann was hanged shortly before midnight on 31 May 1962 at Ramleh Prison near Tel Aviv.

Argentina was also the destination for hundreds of Jews after the war.

After the war many Jews went to Argentina, and they often went there on the same ships as Nazis

---

They even travelled alongside Nazis to the promised land of Argentina, whose Jewish population thrived every bit as much as the Fascist one.

Jose Jakubowicz, a Jew who had been held in Dachau and Auschwitz, arrived in Argentina in 1948 aged 23.

'We sailed from Le Havre and at the table in the evening we were eight. A Jewish woman and myself and six Nazis. You must remember there were not only German Nazis on board but Hungarian, Romanian and Croat Nazis too.

'One day, one of the Nazis said to another at the table: "I hear you killed 5,000 Jews during the war. It is a pity that you did not kill them all."

'At that point we asked to be moved to another table.'

Another runaway who was also eventually returned to answer for his crimes was Klaus Barbie, a notorious Gestapo chief in Vichy France. Barbie earned his nickname as 'the butcher of Lyons' due to his harrowing exploits both with local Jews and members of the French resistance.

■ BUTCHER OF LYONS ■

It was Barbie who discovered a refuge for Jewish children high in a mountain village near the Swiss border. Instead of turning a blind eye in common with other German commanders, Barbie had the house raided and the children as well as their minders sent off to Auschwitz. Not a single one survived. On his orders, young men were shot in the street while scores more men and women were rounded up and machine-gunned in cellars.

His headquarters in the Ecole Sante Militaire were kitted out with chains, spiked coshes and whips and resembled a medieval-style torture chamber. He relished watching prisoners being dunked alternately in boiling hot then freezing cold baths. He experimented with the effectiveness of acid injections, amateur electric shock treatment and burning by blow torch.

One of his most famous victims was Jean Moulin, the courageous leader of the French resistance who was so fiercely beaten by Barbie that he died soon afterwards from his injuries. Moulin had refused to utter a word despite the barbaric excesses of his tormentor.

Barbie's sadism reached such extremities that he would oversee the most agonising tortures – with a naked woman seated on his knee.

He too disappeared at the end of the war, fleeing to Frankfurt where he lived covertly for some years until in 1951 he and his family emigrated to La Paz, Bolivia.

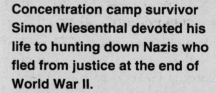

◆ EYE WITNESS ◆

Concentration camp survivor Simon Wiesenthal devoted his life to hunting down Nazis who fled from justice at the end of World War II.

❝ When I was liberated from the last camp I felt that as a man from the intelligentsia my duty was bigger than the duty of the others to find those responsible for the atrocities.

I was very naive. I thought it would be completed in a few years. Yet the moment I started, I could not finish. I feel it is a moral duty that is never ending. 'I am satisfied that I have done it because I was the only one who stood up and asked people not to forget and said 'tell all this to your children'. If this does not happen history will repeat itself. ❞

During the early Eighties, Bolivia was no longer a safe spot following the resolution by a new President to clear his country of Nazis. France had maintained its case for extradition. On 4 February 1983 Barbie was finally arrested and sent back to France. During his trial France was gripped by revelations about the extent of French collaboration with the Nazis and Allied complicity with his freedom.

Heinrich Muller, head of the Gestapo, has proved a mysterious case. Although his hand was never on the trigger, he was undoubtedly the man responsible for thousands of Jewish deaths, killings that were carried out on the orders of the Nazi. Despite every attempt made by Simon Wiesenthal and other eminent Nazi hunters, the trail on Muller went cold too quickly after the war.

■ IVAN THE TERRIBLE ■

Others that vanished after the war include Friedrich Wartzog, commander of the Polish Lemberg-Janowska camp, where guards used prisoners for target practice; Dr Aribert Heim, director of Mauthausen concentration camp in Austria where prisoners of war were among the thousands who died; and Richard Gluecks, Inspector General of all concentration camps.

Yet the passing years pose increasing problems for Nazi hunters. This was richly illustrated in the case of John Demjanjuk, a Ukrainian-born car worker in America thought to be a cruel concentration camp guard nicknamed 'Ivan the Terrible'.

Demjanjuk was sentenced to death then acquitted because of doubts about his identity

Demjanjuk was extradited from the States where he emigrated following the war to face charges in Israel. Despite his advancing years, he was sentenced to death. However, he was subsequently acquitted because of doubts over his identity. The case crystallises the dilemma for those still

seeking justice following the atrocities of the Nazis. The testimony of witnesses appears ever more doubtful as the years go by while public sympathy for frail old men in the dock of a hostile court increases.

British authorities considering the prosecution of at least 10 alleged Nazi war criminals have been delayed as they search for irrefutable evidence against the suspects to eliminate all possible confusion.

Simon Wiesenthal, who has devoted his life to hunting Nazis, is

well aware of the difficulties: 'When you have a man aged over 80 in the dock, the whole sympathy of the audience is for him. Let this old man die in peace, they say. They don't realise that through his crimes, he has lost the right to die in peace.'

Wiesenthal admits that as time goes by he is looking for a smaller

Below: Nazi-hunter Simon Wiesenthal has scoured the world for escaped Nazis because he believes they have forfeited their right to a peaceful retirement.

and smaller number of criminals who played lesser roles in the Nazi Holocaust. 'Most of those people who gave the orders are not alive today. They committed suicide or were living in old age homes under a false name until their deaths.'

One of the last remaining key figures in the Nazi hierarchy who

Brunner lived in Syria. He even gave interviews from there boasting that 150,000 Jews were killed on his orders. The Syrian government continually claimed it was unable to trace him even though he was believed to have a police guard around his house. Rumours have reached the Wiesenthal Centre in

Vienna that his death occurred in 1992 or early 1993.

Wiesenthal explains that the hunt for Nazis was irreparably damaged by the Cold War.

'During 12 years of the Cold War between 1948 and 1960, nothing happened. Both sides were more interested in harassing each other than the

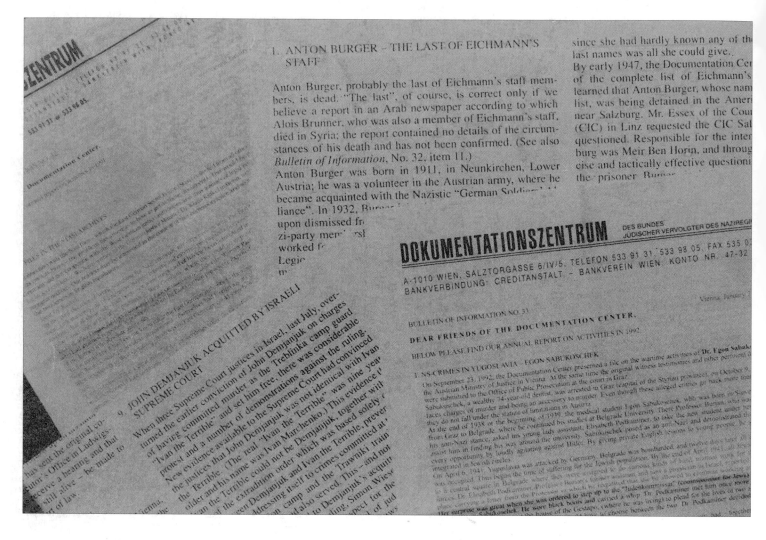

Above: **Some of the documents produced by Simon Wiesenthal and his workers from their Vienna headquarters. Each wanted man has been closely tracked.**

had still to be accounted for was tracked down recently. Anton Burger, a leading member of Eichmann's staff, was found to have died in 1993 in Germany. He had adopted the common German surname of Bauer. 'Even though we knew the false name he used, every telephone directory had many pages of the same name,' sighs Weisenthal.

He is intrigued to know if Alois Brunner, has now died. For years

Simon Wiesenthal is deeply troubled by the neo-Nazi groups that exist today

war criminals. The only winners of the Cold War were the Nazis.'

Simon Wiesenthal's mission to bring fugitive Nazi war criminals to justice still goes on. The fact that neo-Nazi groups are tolerated today by nations that ought to know better troubles him greatly. He cannot understand why governments allow them to exist: 'This is a slap in the face for all the people who survived,' he says with deep feeling.